Defining and Selecting Key Competencies

Defining and Selecting Key Competencies

Edited by
Dominique Simone Rychen
Laura Hersh Salganik

Hogrefe & Huber Publishers
Seattle · Toronto · Bern · Göttingen

Library of Congress Cataloging-in-Publication Data

Defining and selecting key competencies /
Dominique S. Rychen, Laura H. Salganik, editors.
  p. cm.
Includes bibliographical references.
ISBN 0-88937-248-9

1. Life skills. I. Rychen, Dominique Simone. II. Salganik, Laura Hersh

HQ2037.D44   2001   646.7—dc21   2001024626

National Library of Canada Cataloguing in Publication Data

Main entry under title:
Defining and selecting key competencies

Includes bibliographical references.
ISBN 0-88937-248-9

1. Core competencies. 2. Psychology, Industrial. I. Rychen, Dominique S. II. Salganik,
Laura H. III. Organisation for Economic Co-operation and Development.

HF5548.8.D43   2001   158.7   C2001-930375-0

USA: P.O. Box 2487, Kirkland, WA 98083-2487
                      Phone (425) 820-1500, Fax (425) 823-8324
CANADA: 12 Bruce Park Avenue, Toronto, Ontario M4P 2S3
                      Phone (416) 482-6339
SWITZERLAND: Länggass-Strasse 76, CH-3000 Bern 9
                      Phone (031) 300-4500, Fax (031) 300-4590
GERMANY: Rohnsweg 25, D-37085 Göttingen
                      Phone (0551) 49609-0, Fax (0551) 49609-88

Printed in Germany
ISBN 0-88937-248-9

Foreword

In the face of social and economic change, education is undergoing far-reaching modernization, with the focus shifting from input-oriented policies to outcome-oriented ones. This inevitably places questions about the objectives of education on center stage. Tomorrow's curriculum has become a favorite subject of politicians' speeches and the core of everyday efforts geared to education reform. Furthermore, the question of assessing and measuring the output of educational processes triggers keen interest all over the globe.

Though literacy has been measured throughout OECD countries, and indeed, the world, we are still far from assessing a comprehensive set of competencies, particularly key competencies. One of the main reasons for this is that there is no general agreement as to precisely what competencies are, and furthermore, which are the ones that warrant being systematically tested. Thus, it is important for an overarching framework to be developed so that key competencies can be defined and selected based on transparent conceptual guidelines and according to accepted premises. The project *Definition and Selection of Competencies: Theoretical and Conceptual Foundations* (DeSeCo), under the auspices of the OECD, is led by the Swiss Federal Statistical Office in collaboration with the United States Department of Education, National Center for Education Statistics. Its goal is to conduct research that will help foster the development of the needed conceptual framework.

The contributions published in this volume represent the result of the scholarly work conducted during the first phase of the DeSeCo Project. They may appear rather heterogeneous initially, but a close reading reveals many shared preoccupations and suggestions regarding the task of defining and selecting key competencies most relevant to OECD countries. The discussions also shed light on a variety of related issues, such as what it means to lead a successful and responsible life; what the potential consequences of defining a set of more or less universal key competencies are on society; what assumptions underlie the definition of such a set of competencies; and most importantly perhaps, what does the concept of competence actually entail.

This book is an important step toward the DeSeCo Project's goals to strengthen the theoretical foundations for defining and selecting key competencies as well as to lay down guidelines for future development work for the assessment of key competencies in an international context. It does this by sounding out perspectives on competencies from different academic disciplines, as well as from various areas of policy and practice.

Because this book is comprised of essays written by different authors, from different backgrounds, it will appeal to a varied readership, including policy-makers, educators, economists, and politicians. We believe that it provides much food for thought and will enrich the debate about the topic of key competencies.

Finally, we would like to take this opportunity to thank the editors, Dominique Simone Rychen and Laura Hersh Salganik, for their efforts in pursuing this project and for bringing together these essays, which provide a valuable start toward defining and selecting key competencies.

Heinz Gilomen
Director
Society and Education Statistics
Swiss Federal Statistical Office

John P. Martin
Director
Education, Employment, Labour and Social Affairs
Organisation for Economic Co-operation and Development

Eugene Owen
Director
International Activities Program
National Center for Education Statistics, U.S. Department of Education

Contents

Acknowledgments

We would like to thank first and foremost Heinz Gilomen, of the Swiss Federal Statistical Office (SFSO), who as chair of the DeSeCo Steering Group is responsible for the project and contributed time and ideas toward the development of this book. Our thanks go to the SFSO and Carlo Malaguerra, its Director General, and to the OECD and John Martin, Director, and Tom Alexander, former Director of its Directorate for Education, Employment, Labour, and Social Affairs, for taking on the DeSeCo Project. We are also grateful to Eugene Owen, Director of the International Activities Program of the U. S. National Center for Education Statistics, for his ongoing commitment.

We would like to express our thanks to each of the authors in this volume and to the many others who have generously contributed ideas and support to the DeSeCo Project since its inception in 1997, in particular, Marilyn Binkley, Norberto Bottani, Helmut Fend, Walo Hutmacher, Barry McGaw, Scott Murray, Jules Peschar, George Psacharopoulos, Andreas Schleicher, Judith Torney-Purta, Albert Tujinman, and Leonardo José Vanella.

Our thanks go to all the individuals who assisted with the preparation of this book. We are grateful to Catherine Khordoc, who provided invaluable editorial support throughout the process, John Konstant, who assisted us with the research, and Céline Bourquin, of the Swiss Federal Statistical Office, who was responsible for the layout of the volume. We also thank Jennifer A. Anderson and Thomas Nachazel, of the Education Statistics Services Institute of the American Institutes for Research, for helping us to prepare the final manuscript.

Finally, we fondly remember our colleague Franz E. Weinert, who passed away on March 7, 2001, before the release of this book. His contribution to the DeSeCo Project is a seminal one, and we will miss having him as a colleague as we continue our work.

Biographical Notes

Carlo Callieri is the former Vice-Chairman of Confindustria in Rome and sits on the boards of several Italian firms. He published *Il lavoro possibile* with Bruno Trentin in 1997, and in the same year, *I lavoratori della conoscenza*. He has been involved in various aspects of business management with firms such as Fiat and the Gruppo Rizzoli, publisher of *Corriere della Sera*. He has also worked as a consultant for the Ministry of Labor in Italy dealing with issues relating to the cost of labor and wage negotiations.

Monique Canto-Sperber is Director of Research at the Center for National Research in Paris. She is the author of many essays on ancient philosophy and moral and political philosophy, including *La philosophie morale britannique* (1994), *Dictionnaire d'éthique et de philosophie morale* (Ed.) (1996, 3rd ed. 2001), *Philosophie grecque* (Ed.) (1997), *L'inquiétude morale et la vie humaine* (2001). She is currently focusing her research on the topic of common good within liberal traditions.

John Carson is assistant professor of history at the University of Michigan. His work focuses on the history of the human sciences, especially in the United States and Europe. His publications include "Minding Matter/Mattering Mind: Knowledge and the Subject in Nineteenth-Century Psychology," in *Studies in the History and Philosophy of the Biological and Biomedical Sciences* (1999) and "Army Alpha, Army Brass, and the Search for Army Intelligence," in *Isis* (1993). He is currently working on a book tentatively titled *Making Intelligence Matter: Cultural Constructions of Human Difference, 1750–1940*.

Jacques Delors was the French Minister for Economy and Finance from 1981 to 1983 and for Economy, Finance and Budget in 1983. From 1984 to 1985, he was the President of the Commission of the European Communities (now European Commission). He acted as Chairman of the UNESCO International Commission on Education for the Twenty-first Century from 1992 to 1996, and of its report, *Learning: The Treasure Within*. Since then, he has been President of the Research Group *Notre Europe*. He is the author of numerous publications on European economic and social matters and is the recipient of a number of international awards and honorary doctorates from more than twenty universities.

Alexandra Draxler has been working for UNESCO as an education specialist since 1971. From 1992 to 1996, she was Secretary of the International Commission on Education for the Twenty-first Century, and since that time, she has been Director of the Task Force on Education for the Twenty-first Century. She is also responsible within UNESCO for the development of the use of information and communications technologies in education.

Jean-Pierre Dupuy is professor of social and political philosophy at the Ecole Polytechnique in Paris as well as visiting professor at Stanford University. He is also Director of Research at the C.N.R.S. (Centre National de Recherche Scientifique) in Philosophy as well as the Director of C.R.E.A. (Centre de Recherche en Epistémologie Appliquée), the philosophical research group of the Ecole Polytechnique, which he founded in 1982. His most recent publications include *The Mechanization of the Mind – On the Origins of Cognitive Science*, published in 2000 by Princeton University Press, and *Self-Deception and Paradoxes of Rationality*, published by Stanford University in 1998.

Jean-Patrick Farrugia was formerly with *Mouvement des Entreprises de France* (MEDEF), a French employers' association. He was involved with the division responsible for education and training.

Heinz Gilomen is the Director of Society and Education Statistics at the Swiss Federal Statistical Office and a member of its board of directors. He is responsible for statistics relating to education and science as well as for social reporting and social indicators. He is the National Coordinator for the OECD Education Indicators Programme in Switzerland and the lead person for the OECD project *Definition and Selection of Competencies: Theoretical and Conceptual Foundations* (DeSeCo).

Jack Goody is a Fellow of St. John's College at Cambridge University, and until his retirement, was professor of social anthropology at Cambridge. He worked for two years as a Further Education Officer in Hertfordshire and as an anthropologist in West Africa, North India, and Southern China. He has been especially interested in the consequences of literacy and has worked with the psychologist Michael Cote on social aspects of learning to read (see *The Domestication of the Savage Mind*, 1977, and *The Interface Between the Written and the Oral*, 1987). In Europe, he has written on the family, on inheritance, and on the supposed uniqueness of that continent with respect to modernization (*The East in the West*, 1996).

Bob Harris is Senior Consultant to the General Secretary of Education International in Geneva, and chairs the Working Group on Education, Training and Employment of TUAC (the Trade Union Advisory Committee to the OECD). In 1993, he was one of the founders of Education International, and served as Executive Director for Intergovernmental Relations and member of the Executive Board of Education International from 1993 to 1995. He has served as President of the Conference of Non-Governmental Organizations at the United Nations (1995–1998) and at UNESCO (1985–88). He was editor of *Teaching About Contemporary World Problems*, UNESCO, 1986.

Helen Haste is professor of psychology at the University of Bath, England. Her main research interests are in values and citizenship, gender, and in cultural metaphors and symbols, including the interface of science and culture. She is the author of *The Sexual Metaphor*, published in 1994 by Harvard University Press, and numerous scientific and popular articles.

Robert Kegan is the first William and Miriam Meehan Professor of Adult Learning and Professional Development at the Harvard University Graduate School of Education. Chairman of the Learning and Teaching Area, and Educational Chair of the Institute for Management and Leadership in Education, he is also Co-Director of a joint program undertaken by Harvard Medical School and the Harvard Graduate School of Education to bring principles of adult learning to the reform of medical education, and Co-Director of a Gates Foundation-funded program to assist the change efforts of school leaders. He has published several books, the most recent one, co-authored with Lisa Laskow Lahey, being *How the Way We Talk Can Change the Way We Work: Seven Languages for Transformation*.

Frank Levy is the Daniel Rose Professor of Urban Economics at M.I.T.'s Department of Urban Studies and Planning. He has written extensively on both trends in living standards and on education and the economy. His 1987 book, *Dollars and Dreams*, was updated in 1999 under the title *The New Dollars and Dreams*. With his colleague, Richard J. Murnane of the Harvard School of Education, Levy is the author of *Teaching the New Basic Skills*, published in 1996 by the Free Press. He is currently working with Murnane on a book entitled *What's Left for People to Do?* that describes how the computerization of work makes some human skills more important than others.

Richard J. Murnane is the Thompson Professor of Education and Society at Harvard University's Graduate School of Education. An economist who specializes in education issues, he has written extensively about how changes in the economy affect the education sector. Murnane's books include *The Impact of School Resources on the Learning of Inner City Children* (1975), *Who Will Teach: Policies That Matter* (1991), and, with his colleague, Frank Levy of MIT, *Teaching the New Basic Skills* (1996). Murnane is currently working with Levy on the book mentioned above, *What's Left for People to Do?*

Philippe Perrenoud is professor of sociology at the University of Geneva, focusing on the areas of curriculum research, pedagogical practices and teaching institutions. Through his work on inequalities and failure within education, he has become interested in topics such as the job of being a student, teacher training, policy-making in education and training, and the functioning of schools. He has published many scholarly articles and books, including *Enseigner: agir dans l'urgence, décider dans l'incertitude. Sa-*

voirs et compétences dans un métier complexe (1996, reedited in 1999); *Construire des compétences dès l'école,* (1997, in 2000 was in its third edition), and *Dix nouvelles compétences pour enseigner. Invitation au voyage* (1999).

Cecilia Ridgeway is professor of sociology at Stanford University in California. Her research focuses on status and social hierarchies among individuals and the role of perceived competence in shaping social hierarchies. She also studies gender inequality. She is particularly interested in the role that social hierarchies in everyday social relations play in the larger processes of stratification and inequality in a society. She has published several articles in scholarly journals such as the *American Journal of Sociology* and the *American Sociological Review*. She is also the author of *Gender, Interaction, and Inequality* (Springer-Verlag, 1992) and the current editor of *Social Psychology Quarterly*.

Laurell Ritchie has worked in the labor movement for 30 years. In 1994, she became a National Representative with the Canadian Auto Workers (CAW), Canada's largest private sector union representing 240,000 workers, principally in the automotive and transportation sectors, but also in a variety of other sectors, from textiles to hotels. She works in CAW's Work Organization and Training Department where her responsibilities include sectoral training councils, adjustment and training programs for laid-off workers, and basic skills and literacy programs in the workplace. She was the workers' delegate for Canada to the 1997 *ILO Tripartite Technical Meeting on New Technologies and Working Conditions in the Hotel, Catering & Tourism Sector* in Geneva.

Dominique Simone Rychen is the Program Manager of the OECD project *Definition and Selection of Competencies: Theoretical and Conceptual Foundations* (DeSeCo). She has been responsible for the coordination of the various activities, the organization of the first international symposium, and the reporting of the interim findings to the OECD. Previously, she has worked on indicator development related to continuing education, labor market, workplace, and informal learning in particular, and co-authored two publications related to continuing education.

Laura Hersh Salganik is the Deputy Director of the Education Statistics Services Institute of the American Institutes for Research. Her areas of specialty include education indicators and international comparisons of education systems, and she has participated in numerous activities in the OECD Education Indicators Programme (INES) during the past ten years. She has been collaborating with the DeSeCo Project for the past three years. She is a co-author of *Education Indicators: An International Perspective*, published by the U. S. National Center for Education Statistics.

Uri Peter Trier is professor of psychology at the University of Neuchâtel (Switzerland). He was Director of the National Research Program *The Effectiveness of Swiss Educational Systems* (1993–1999), Chairman of the Pedagogical Commission of the Swiss Conference of Ministers of Education (1972–1986), and Director of the Department for Educational Research and Development of Zurich (1971–1992). His main interests are the development of schools and educational systems, cognition and learning, and psychoanalysis.

Franz E. Weinert was Director Emeritus of the Max Planck Institute for Psychological Research in Munich. From 1968 to 1981, he was professor and Director of the Psychological Institute at the University of Heidelberg. He served as President of the German Psychological Association, Vice-President of the German Science Foundation, and Vice-President of the Max Planck Society. He was engaged in research on cognitive development (changes and stabilities of individual differences) and on the relationships between learning and instruction. He received honorary doctorates from the Free University of Berlin and the University of Würzburg.

Introduction

Dominique Simone Rychen

Overview

Societies all over the world are facing rapid social and technological changes. While increasing uniformity through economic and cultural globalization is one facet of today's world, another is increasing social diversity. This representation of a changing world, however, does not preclude the idea of continuity and persistence of certain established practices and beliefs or of other forces that resist structural change.

Large-scale value changes, instability of norms, substantial global inequality of opportunities, social exclusions, poverty in all its forms, and environmental threats are some of the most salient challenges we all are facing at the beginning of the 21st century. It is in this context of an interdependent, complex, and conflictive world that education is becoming increasingly crucial as an investment and an important asset for both individuals and societies. Sustainable economic development, social welfare, cohesion, and justice as well as personal well-being, are closely bound to knowledge, skills, competencies, and learning. For instance, understanding public policy issues, participating in the democratic process and its institutions, and realizing human rights all assume a well-educated and knowledgeable citizenry. We propose to consider the benefits of education and lifelong learning in light of these contemporary societal challenges. Yet diverse and sometimes contradictory demands expressed in the social, economic, political, and educational fields place issues regarding the objectives of education and the strategies to achieve educational goals on center stage of national debates on broad educational reform.

In line with a growing concern from governments and the general public about the adequacy and quality of education and training, and the actual return on public educational expenditure, there has been, since the mid-1980s, an increased policy interest in comparable outcome indicators in the education field. In fact, assessing the quality of education outcomes, estimating economic and social returns on learning, and identifying key determinants to a successful life and full participation in society are ongoing discussion topics that stimulate keen interest around the world. Several empirical studies and projects have been launched in response, some of which are under the direction of or in collaboration with the Organisation for Economic Co-operation and Development[1] (OECD) (Salganik, Chapter 1).

---

[1] The Organisation for Economic Co-operation and Development (OECD) is an organization of 30 countries that share the principles of the market economy, pluralist democracy, and respect for human rights. It provides governments a setting in which to discuss, develop, and perfect economic and social policy. Member countries compare experiences, seek answers to common problems, and work to coordinate domestic and international policies.

The OECD is committed to providing policy-makers with education indicators relevant to human development and political and economic governance that are not only reliable and internationally comparable, but also grounded in theoretical foundations. While the development of the empirical components of these efforts is well advanced, the OECD constituency has recognized the need for an overarching theory-based framework for defining and selecting relevant human competencies. Beyond reading, writing, and computing, what competencies and skills are relevant for an individual to lead a successful and responsible life and for society to face the challenges of the present and future? What are the normative, theoretical, and conceptual foundations for defining and selecting a limited set of key competencies?

These questions constitute a starting point for an international and interdisciplinary endeavor conducted since the end of 1997 under the auspices of the OECD and led by the Swiss Federal Statistical Office (SFSO). This study, entitled *Definition and Selection of Competencies: Theoretical and Conceptual Foundations* (hereafter referred to as the DeSeCo Project, or simply, DeSeCo),[2] was launched to provide theoretical and conceptual inputs and eventually a solid foundation for building a consensus about a set of key competencies to be assessed at the international level.

While many remain unanswered, the following questions exemplify some of the issues that have guided the work within DeSeCo and the reflections of contributors to this volume:

- Can a set of competencies of prime importance for a successful life and effective participation in different fields of life – including economic, political, social, and family domains, public and private interpersonal relations, and individual personal development – be identified?

- If so, what is the nature of these competencies and what distinguishes them as key competencies? How can they be described and theoretically justified? What are the components of these competencies? Is the premise of a limited number of key competencies justified?

- Do key competencies operate independently, or should they be viewed as an interdependent set or constellation of competencies?

- To what extent are key competencies immutable with reference to social, economic, and cultural conditions? To what extent are they generally valid from country to country or region to region?

- To what extent is it possible to identify key competencies independent of age, gender, status, professional activity, etc? Are certain competencies particularly important in the various phases of life, and if so, which ones? Do we need the same key competencies when we are young, join the workforce, establish a family, advance in our professional or political careers, and retire?

The present volume consists of essays prepared by a number of renowned scholars from various disciplines (psychology, sociology, anthropology, economics, philosophy, and history). Other experts, including leading representatives from the public and private sectors (business, labor, education, and policy spheres) contributed their

---

[2] www.deseco.admin.ch

knowledge and experience through commentaries on the scholars' work. Each contribution gives a particular insight into the general topic of defining and selecting key competencies.

The first three chapters provide background information. In chapter 1, Laura Salganik discusses past and ongoing empirical studies of skills and competencies developed in an international context. In chapter 2, John Carson delineates the social history of measuring IQ in order to draw attention to some of the pitfalls of defining standards. In chapter 3, Franz E. Weinert reviews a number of theoretical approaches to the concepts of competence, including metacompetence and key competence. The five chapters that follow are discipline-oriented essays from scholars commissioned to identify theoretically grounded sets of key competencies: Monique Canto-Sperber and Jean-Pierre Dupuy approach the topic from a philosophical viewpoint (Chapter 4). Helen Haste proposes key competencies taking a social-psychological stance (Chapter 5), while Philippe Perrenoud addresses the topic from a sociological viewpoint (Chapter 6). The economists Frank Levy and Richard Murnane rely on an empirical approach to tackle the question of which competencies are needed in the labor market (Chapter 7). Jack Goody discusses the topic from an anthropological standpoint (Chapter 8). The remaining two chapters (9 and 10) mainly represent comments on the scholars' work. The ideas developed in the five discipline-oriented essays are discussed in chapter 9 by psychologist Robert Kegan and sociologist Cecilia Ridgeway. Selected viewpoints and reactions from policy and practice are compiled in chapter 10: Jacques Delors and Alexandra Draxler, Bob Harris, Jean-Patrick Farrugia, Carlo Callieri, Laurell Ritchie, and Uri Peter Trier provide insight from their respective professional contexts.

An issue regarding terminology must be addressed before continuing. The terms *compétence* in French and *Kompetenz* in German can be rendered into English by two words: *competence* and *competency*. Examining the usage of *competence* and *competency* in the literature does not reveal any hard and fast rules, and English dictionaries do not further elucidate how these words are distinctive. However, the editors of this volume believe that there are nuances or connotations associated with each term that are useful when discussing the topic. Therefore, *competence* is used to refer to a) the concept (e.g., the competence-performance model) and its theorization, and b) a level of ability of a specific skill or competency (e.g., a person's competence in reading or mathematics). *Competency* is used when referring to a particular demand that a person may or may not be able to meet (e.g., the competency to join and function in groups). In the plural, only the term *competencies* is used in this book.

This introduction first provides a picture of the main features, relevance, and rationale for the ongoing DeSeCo Project. Then, what follows is a discussion of some of the challenges and issues at stake in identifying key competencies in light of the various essays and comments.

Laying Out the Foundations for DeSeCo

A Theory-Oriented Study

In the last ten years, several empirically oriented international studies in the domain of skills and competencies have been conducted, though at irregular intervals and mostly in selected areas of the school curriculum (Salganik, Chapter 1). When its education indicator program was initiated, the OECD adopted a pragmatic approach towards outcome-related data on education systems, mainly drawing from assessment studies conducted by the International Association for the Evaluation of Educational Achievement (IEA), an association of research institutions, universities, and ministries of education. The comparison of school quality, effectiveness, and efficiency in and between national education systems focused on school curricula in major subjects such as reading, mathematics, and science.

In recent years, OECD countries have engaged in more systematic, long-term data-collection strategies. Recognizing that curricular-based and subject-related competencies do not capture the full range of education outcomes, the OECD has opted to broaden the coverage of human competencies on the basis of conceptual and theoretical foundations. The DeSeCo Project has been set up to

- advance the theoretical foundations for defining and selecting relevant human competencies
- provide a conceptual basis that is both rooted in theory and interpretable in policy terms for the continued development of international assessments of key competencies in the long term
- provide a reference point for the interpretation of empirical results about outcomes of education

Through an interdisciplinary approach, DeSeCo is attempting to elaborate meaningful categories and criteria for developing a common, theory-grounded, overarching framework for the construction of key competencies. Thus, the study seeks not so much to address the issues by proceeding with an inductive method, starting from factual situations, but rather by starting at a more general level, laying out some conceptual and theoretical considerations. This theoretical approach, which receives broad support and interest within and beyond the OECD, does not preclude empirical considerations. In fact, the key to future success in this field depends on theoretical and empirical work, as well as on the explicit links that are established between the two approaches.

A Multidisciplinary Approach

DeSeCo has been set up as a policy-driven, research-oriented project, which originated in a governmental context in response to policy needs. Thus, defining and selecting key competencies calls for a multifaceted approach. The topic of human competencies is not the exclusive domain of traditional educational research. It is situated at the forefront of research across the social sciences, as it addresses issues fundamental to human behavior and society's institutions with regard to the challenges of contemporary social problems and broad complex demands from different sectors. Defining and selecting human competencies affects both the individual – in his or her role as a worker (employer or employee), citizen, family member, and group member – and society as a whole. It concerns issues such as the acquisition of mental prerequisites, the use of competency with regard to the role and position of the individual in the social hierarchy, the influence of socio-economic and cultural factors, and the nature of power relations.

Further, the notion of competence implies a broad learning context. Both the practice of labor recruitment and certain theories indicate the importance of skills, behavior, attitudes, and values that are acquired and developed outside the domain of formal education. Although schools will continue to play a crucial role, the workplace, mass media, family, voluntary associations, political, religious, and neighborhood organizations, and other cultural and recreational activities constitute other relevant settings where competencies are needed, enacted, and assessed, and where formal and informal learning takes place.

The premise of this study is, therefore, that the discussion of such issues benefits from multidisciplinary viewpoints and interdisciplinary collaboration. What can the perspective of an anthropologist, an economist, an historian, a philosopher, a psychologist, and a sociologist contribute to the construction of a set of competencies? Among the different proposed approaches, are there common features relevant from the standpoint of multiple perspectives? What conceptual or theoretical elements or models show promise for contributing to the development of a coherent frame of reference for defining and selecting key competencies? Also, to what extent are these theoretical and methodological models and concepts applicable in practice? This volume lays out a number of disciplinary perspectives and policy-oriented viewpoints. There remains the challenge of gaining more interdisciplinary insights based on these and other contributions and on further debate and exchange. Some preliminary ideas in this direction have been suggested to the Fourth General Assembly of the OECD Education Indicators Programme (INES)[3] and are referred to in this introduction.

Linking Research to Policy and Practice

Defining and selecting key competencies for a successful life is an attempt to explicitly value some competencies over others. With respect to the multitude of possible approaches to the subject as well as the diversity of societies and lifestyles, a certain skepticism towards the attempt to identify a limited number of key competencies valid across nations and regions is not unwarranted. Many authors expressed reservations and cautions about the undertaking. Indeed, defining and selecting key com-

---

[3] Rychen, D.S. & Salganik, L.H. (1999). Definition and selection of key competencies. In *The INES compendium: Contributions from the INES networks and working groups* (GA[2000]12). Paris: OECD.

petencies raises certain problems from the onset. First and foremost, no generally accepted definition of the concept of competence exists and there is no overarching unifying theory (Weinert, Chapter 3). Another problem concerns the decision-making process: most decisions regarding the organization of education are not strictly based on educational research. Rather, they are largely dependent on power relations, political and economic factors, as well as ethical choices. Furthermore, if abstract and general formulas of humanistic and ethical goals for education should reach a consensus in democratic societies, their implementation in specific socio-economic and cultural contexts may raise conflicts of interest in what is taught, how teaching takes place, or how educational institutions are organized. The acceptability of assessing competencies and the potential impact of assessments in different contexts presents other topics of debate (Carson, Chapter 2; Goody, Chapter 8). These are only a sample of some of the problems encountered in the process of defining and selecting key competencies.

The assumption of the DeSeCo Project is that multiple factors have varying impact on how key competencies are constructed, developed, transmitted, and assessed in relevant social fields. First, no frame of reference is neutral. One's underlying vision of the world, including conceptions of society and the individual and of what a successful life and a good society imply, affects the construction of key competencies. Second, the theoretical approaches and analytical tools used influence the way in which the topic is understood, how the problem is posed, and how it is approached. Third, factors such as culture, gender, age, and social status shape the forms that key competencies described at the abstract level take in a specific sociopolitical or biographical context. Finally, there is no direct linear relationship between theoretical models, research findings, development, and implementation and use of knowledge in particular settings concerning the individual, the group, or the organizational and large-system context. Defining and selecting a valuable and legitimate set of key competencies is ultimately the result of a political process in which researchers are partners among other constituents such as policy-makers and practitioners. To be sure, this holistic approach calls for a scientific discussion, albeit a broad and open-minded one, and, at the same time, one that implies political, ethical, and practical considerations.

Challenges and Issues at Stake

There is a range of issues at stake when defining and selecting key competencies. The authors of the discipline-oriented essays were asked to make explicit their underlying normative frame of reference, to focus on the conceptualization of competence, and to propose theory-based criteria for identifying key competencies. They found various ways to tackle these questions. Following is a brief discussion of some of these issues and how they were addressed by the scholars, as well as some of the convergences and initial lessons learned so far from this multidisciplinary approach.

Underlying Vision of Society: A Common Starting Point

Defining and selecting key competencies necessary for individuals to lead a successful and responsible life and for society to face the challenges of the present and near future raises many questions, such as: What type of society do we imagine and desire? Or, on the other hand, what is not desirable? What constitutes a successful life? What social and economic developments are we referring to? Are these discussions about transforming the existing social order or, rather, preserving it? Conceiving key competencies is inevitably influenced by what is valued in societies and by the goals set for human and socio-economic development. At the same time, depending on how key competencies are conceived, certain visions of society are strengthened or weakened. The challenge, therefore, is to define key competencies broadly, taking into account the plurality of values and life patterns.

The authors refer, more or less explicitly, to a democratic value system and human rights. Some of the basic assumptions are that a society cannot survive without setting standards and without defining "normality," thus giving priority to certain social practices and competencies while neglecting others (Perrenoud, Chapter 6); that there are some commonly agreed ideas and values from which one can derive competencies, at least descriptively, that cross cultural boundaries (Delors & Draxler, Chapter 10); and that there are sufficient commonalities among individuals and across societies to adopt a normative frame of reference for identifying key competencies relevant for contemporary democratic societies (Canto-Sperber & Dupuy, Chapter 4). As Ridgeway points out, the democratic commitment of the authors is illustrated by the focus on *learned* skills, rather than innate abilities, and on competencies essential for *all* (Chapter 9).

Successful life and democratic society are not objective facts or realities grounded in empirical and non-controversial evidence; rather, they are objects of value judgments. That said, a number of international texts and conventions related to human rights and human development constitute a solid basis for describing life and society as they should be. Thus, the principles postulated in major international human rights documents can serve as a starting point to describe key competencies (Delors & Draxler, Chapter 10). These principles convey a vision that includes democratic values; respect for the law and for the rights of others; the importance of school as an institution for imparting knowledge, skills, and competencies to the young; and learning as a lifelong endeavor.

Yet this kind of normative comprehension always remains prescriptive, and its translation into reality is subject to controversies and conflict. A gap continues to exist between what is ideally imagined and postulated in social discourse and the kind of actualities that are produced in a particular socio-economic context. It is therefore both a political and an ethical choice and challenge to construct and endorse key competencies in a manner that is consistent with the principles of human rights and human development, in particular, with the values of autonomy and liberty and, at the same time, with the ideals of equality and social justice.

Possible Definitional Criteria for the Term *Competence*

Without a preliminary clarification of the concept of competence, the whole endeavor is at risk. Generally speaking, any concept is a social construct. It is assumed to facilitate the understanding of reality while also constructing it. Concepts are conventions, explicit in scientific contexts, more often implicit in everyday use. In the social sciences and in everyday use, they often have vague and ambiguous meanings. Their meanings vary largely depending on the disciplinary perspective, ideological viewpoints, and underlying objectives associated with their use. The same is true for the concept of competence.

Weinert (Chapter 3) distinguishes several theory-based approaches to competence. He points out that in the social sciences there is no unitary use of the concepts of competence, key competence, or metacompetence. A broadly accepted and theoretically grounded definition and coherent unifying theory are lacking, although there have been many attempts to constrain and sharpen the concept of competence on phenomenological, definitional, and theoretical grounds. Furthermore, Weinert emphasizes that regardless of the extent to which scholars and practitioners agree on formal criteria for defining key competencies, considerable disagreement remains about which competencies should be classified as *key*. When defining and selecting key competencies, it makes a difference if one starts from a normative-philosophical or socially critical frame of reference, or if the definition and selection of competencies is based more on findings from observations of social practices and trends. Also at issue is the level of abstraction and generality with which key competencies are defined, the hypothetical structure underlying key competencies, and the extent to which psychological features can be modified through learning and how they can be acquired through planned instructional programs.

According to Weinert, none of the discipline-oriented contributions follow strict, formal, definitional constraints for the concepts of competence, key competence, or metacompetence. Thus, in all the present essays, the concept of competence is used in the relatively vague sense of being able to think, act, and learn. The authors take for granted that the identified competencies are theoretical constructs and hypothetical psychological processes that include clusters of cognitive, emotional, motivational, social, and behavioral components. And all the authors see competencies as being at least to some extent learnable. Thus, ongoing, lifelong learning processes are an indispensable condition for the acquisition of competencies. At the same time, a complex environment and the quality of interaction with others constitute important prerequisites for competency development (Canto-Sperber & Dupuy, Chapter 4).

Even while the formal requirements and criteria for defining competence, key competence, and metacompetence remain open to a large degree, it makes sense – at least for the DeSeCo Project – to go ahead with a workable, pragmatic, conceptual approach. First, the concept of competence should be used only to refer to necessary prerequisites available to an individual or a group for successfully meeting complex demands. These demands define the structure of competencies. Second, competencies generally imply complex action systems encompassing not only knowledge and skills, but also strategies and routines needed to apply knowledge and skills, as well as appropriate emotions and attitudes and the effective self-regulation of these competencies (Weinert, Chapter 3).

From a Multidisciplinary Approach to Interdisciplinary Insight

In contrast to Weinert's overview of concepts of competence, the main focus of the discipline-oriented essays is on the structure and content of competencies characterized as necessary, important, or desirable. In fact, the task put forward to Canto-Sperber and Dupuy, Haste, Perrenoud, Murnane and Levy, and Goody was to make explicit their normative premises, to delineate a set of key competencies, and to discuss theoretical models, concepts, and arguments underlying the proposed set of competencies. All but one author (Goody, Chapter 8) identified a set of critical competencies that are key to what they refer to as a successful life in contemporary democratic societies.

Multidisciplinary perspectives

Relying on an analytical approach, the philosophers Canto-Sperber and Dupuy draw on their expertise in the philosophy of mind and moral and social philosophy not only to address the question of key competencies, but also to consider what constitutes the "good life." It is in line with any major moral theory to include in the conception of the good life – understood as a regulative ideal – close relationships with others, an understanding of oneself and one's world, autonomous interaction with one's physical and social contexts, and a sense of accomplishment and enjoyment. The authors base their selection of key competencies on the premise that, beyond the variety of cultures and the diversity of ways of being human, certain constant features exist that are part of life in general. In keeping with this basic assumption, the authors are committed to two notions: first, some of the goods and values that make up the goodness of life are objective in the sense that they are not dependent on what one believes; and second, the good life requires a reflective perspective. On this basis, Canto-Sperber and Dupuy define key competencies at an abstract level that are partly independent of culture, context, and personal characteristics. Thus, the key competencies they have identified are not construed as particular skills, but rather, as dimensions of a multidimensional, abstract space in which particular skills, abilities, or capacities can be located. The five dimensions or key competencies identified as desired outcomes of education are competencies for coping with complexity, and perceptive, normative, cooperative, and narrative competencies (Chapter 4).

Haste emphasizes from her socio-psychological viewpoint the need to look at individuals in a cultural, social, and linguistic context. She bases her reflection on the assumption that humans are adaptive, social beings. In this view, the notion of competence implies effective interaction and agency in relation to the physical, social, and cultural world. According to Haste, effectiveness is not only related to technical performance, but to the interpretation of context and meaning. The author asserts that the definition of competencies is driven not only by the perceived demands, but also by differing psychological processes. She identifies three psychological models of the "competent human": the Puzzle Solver, the Story Teller, and the Tool User, and shows their implications for defining and selecting key competencies. She describes the competent individual as one who "is self-sufficient, able to focus attention and plan, with a future orientation, is adaptable to change, has a sense of responsibility, has a belief that one can have an effect, and is capable of commitment." The management of the tension between innovation and continuity constitutes an overarching metacompetency. Further, Haste identifies five competency domains that are essential in the immediate future and possibly universally relevant. These are: technological competency; the ability to deal with ambiguity and diversity; the ability to find and sustain community links; the management of motivation, emotion, and desire; and, finally, the sense of agency and responsibility (Chapter 5).

For Perrenoud, a sociologist, the central question to be addressed is what competencies are needed by everyone to cope in multiple social fields. He associates a successful life with not being abused, alienated, dominated, or exploited. Thus, the author focuses on competencies that empower the ordinary actors to live as well as possible, to defend their rights within society, and to preserve their autonomy without infringing on that of others. Grounding his discussion on the theory of *social fields* developed by Pierre Bourdieu, Perrenoud puts forward the hypothesis that in all relevant social fields, it is useful, if not essential, to possess the following competencies: to identify, evaluate, and defend one's resources, rights, limits, and needs; to form and conduct projects, individually or in a group, and to develop strategies; to analyze situations, relationships, and force fields systemically; to cooperate, to act in synergy, to participate in a collective, and to share leadership; to build and operate democratic-type organizations and systems of collective action; to manage and resolve conflict; to play with the rules, to use them, and elaborate on them; and to construct negotiated orders over and above cultural differences. Each competency necessitates an overall development of critical thinking and reflective practice that mirrors formal and informal knowledge and experiences accumulated throughout life. According to Perrenoud, these tactical and strategic competencies can be considered transversal in that they cut across all human activities because all human activity is embedded in social fields. Thus, comparative and further interdisciplinary analyses are needed to test the hypothesis that a small number of transversal competencies can be identified (Chapter 6).

Murnane and Levy, as well as Goody, differ from the other authors insofar as they use an empirical approach to the issue of competence. The observations that Levy and Murnane provide from an economic perspective come closest to the current framework of knowledge and skills applied at the OECD. The economists define success in terms of maximization of income. Recognizing the limitations of this definition, Levy and Murnane assume that productive work is a foundation for broader goals and argue that the competencies they identify as important to earning a living coincide with those required to live a responsible and fulfilling life in a democratic society. They use relevant economic theories and empirical results to address the question of the competencies workers need to succeed in the labor market. The human capital theory postulates that individuals treat education as an investment for which they incur costs (including foregone earnings) in order to increase future earnings above what they otherwise would have been. This theory, however, leaves open why employers should be willing to pay more for educated labor. The authors review two other theories – signaling theory and principal-agent theory – which attempt to fill parts of this gap. Together, these three theories form the basis for most empirical economic analyses of relevant labor market competencies. Levy and Murnane then refer to four empirical approaches to determining key competencies as evaluated by the market: studies of earnings inequality, wage function studies, ethnographic studies of the workplace, and studies of the hiring practices of high-wage firms. The authors show that despite the limitations of each of these methodologies, existing empirical studies combine to form a fairly coherent outline of labor market trends. The skills they propose as necessary for leading a successful life include basic reading and mathematics skills, communication skills, the ability to work in groups and to relate well to others, and a familiarity with computers (Chapter 7).

The anthropologist Goody rejects engaging in a decontextualized discussion of key competencies on the grounds that theory must always be considered in relation to practice. Recognizing that there may be some very general qualities required by modern life, Goody focuses on the intractability of specifying key competencies at a level that can span cultures, social contexts, and individuals and that would also be useful for developing methods of measurement. In his view, what a successful life means, and which key competencies are necessary to achieve it, depend largely on the respective society, individual lifestyles, and the specific relation to life and work. Goody emphasizes that competencies have to correspond to the many roles that individuals are called upon to fill throughout their lifetimes (Chapter 8).

Common ground

For the DeSeCo Project, the exploration of theoretical and conceptual models for constructing a set of key competencies relevant from multiple perspectives poses a central challenge. Beyond the heterogeneity of perspectives of the various approaches, is there a common denominator? Are there cross-disciplinary concepts and models useful for developing an overarching, politically relevant, theory-based framework for defining and selecting key competencies?

A number of common considerations and arguments transcend the heterogeneity of these discipline-oriented approaches, and the commentaries by Kegan and Ridgeway, in chapter 9, aptly bring some of them to light. Some of the elements seem promising in an interdisciplinary perspective for constructing key competencies and could possibly be elaborated further and eventually worked into a common frame of reference.

First, based on Weinert's review of concepts of competence, *key competencies* are considered as structured around meeting demands of a high degree of complexity and are comprised of cognitive as well as motivational, ethical, social, and behavioral components (Chapter 3). A second relevant element is the consideration of key competencies as *transversal* in the sense that they enable individuals or groups to participate effectively in all relevant social fields with their specific power and social relations, challenges and capital at stake (Perrenoud, Chapter 6). A third critical aspect concerns the question of the *mental complexity* involved. Key competencies call for a higher order of mental complexity. Coping with many demands of modern life implies not only abstract thinking and self-reflection, but also distancing oneself from one's own socializing process and even one's own values. This active and reflective approach is based on an evolutionary model of human development in which individuals can incorporate higher levels of complexity into their thinking and actions (Kegan, Chapter 9). Finally, although this is not specific to key competencies, it would also be useful to consider competencies as *being composed of multiple dimensions,* representing mental processes, such as "know-how," analytical, critical, and communication skills, as well as common sense (Canto-Sperber & Dupuy, Chapter 4).

If one focuses on the content of key competencies, it seems reasonable to posit that three broad categories encompass many of the features identified by the authors as necessary or desirable for an effective interaction with the environment: 1) to act autonomously and reflectively; 2) to use tools interactively; and 3) to join and function in socially heterogeneous groups.[4]

Acting autonomously means that individuals and groups can assert their own rights and interests, actively interact with their physical and social environments, form and conduct projects, and develop strategies to attain goals. The reflective exercise of autonomy requires awareness and an understanding of one's environment: how it functions and how one fits into it. Autonomous action, developed through knowledge and understanding of social dynamics, is needed to avoid being dominated and exploited. Many of these aspects are particularly well developed in Perrenoud's essay (Chapter 6).

Using tools implies not only having the tools and being able to use them effectively, but also understanding how they affect the way one interacts with the environment. In reference to the "Tool User" model proposed by Haste, "tool" is used in the broadest sense of the term. It encompasses instruments that are relevant to meeting many important everyday and professional demands of modern society. For example, being able to use tools does not strictly refer to having the technical skills required to use a computer and its software, but also to being aware of the new forms of interaction that can be established through the technology, and to be able to adapt accordingly.

The capacity to join and function effectively in socially heterogeneous groups is crucial in light of the demands and challenges of contemporary democratic societies. Ridgeway focuses much of her attention on this competency, which she considers universal (Chapter 9). Joining and functioning in socially heterogeneous groups consists of a number of components. An important one is perceiving and understanding the distinctive position of the other. Other components include negotiating conflicting interests in order to find mutually acceptable solutions, operating democratically in groups, constructing negotiated orders over and above cultural differences, and

---

[4] These categories have been proposed as generic key competencies in the DeSeCo Project at various occasions.

developing joint strategies, etc. These components require balancing commitment to the group and its norms with the capacity for autonomous action.

It is important to emphasize that the various sets of key competencies proposed in this volume, including the three broad categories, are multifaceted and complex, and do not represent inflexible guidelines in their applications. Yet these various constructs represent a starting point for further discussion, debate, and exploration. Studying and comparing concrete forms of key competencies as manifested in actions and choices of individuals and groups in different social fields (such as the personal, social, economic, and political life), at different stages in life, and in different national and cultural contexts is an indispensable next step in this research.

The Perspective of Practice and Policy

The theoretical framework that DeSeCo seeks to put in place is a prime objective, however, the theory cannot be developed in a vacuum, neglecting practical and political considerations. Policy-makers and main actors in the economic and social fields often follow their own rationale when defining and selecting competencies relevant to cope with the specific demands and challenges of a particular field or sector. Recognizing the potential benefit of a collaboration between the academic community and the practical world, and consistent with the basic assumption that this dialogue is an integral part of the process of defining and selecting key competencies, an exchange of ideas between scholars and leading experts working in various social fields was initiated. The scholarly contributions on key competencies were submitted to commentators for their evaluation and comments. This exchange of ideas, which will be pursued further, permits a more practical approach to defining and selecting key competencies, and allows the research findings to be critically addressed by policy-makers and those involved in fieldwork and practice. The commentaries compiled in chapter 10 provide important facets in the reflection on key competencies.

Delors and Draxler, former President and Director, respectively, of the Task Force on Education for the Twenty-first Century (UNESCO), point out the themes common to all of the essays and raise crucial questions concerning education from an international perspective. For example, the authors recognize the challenge to find an equilibrium among the normative, the universal, and the diversity of expressions of human behavior and actions. They reaffirm the necessity to invest resources in compulsory schooling in order to ensure that all individuals are able to read, write, communicate, and compute. In addition, compulsory schooling should focus much more, according to Delors and Draxler, on the development of group skills. Further, Delors and Draxler emphasize the importance of considering that if different competencies are needed at different times throughout life, then allowances must be made for individuals to acquire various competencies beyond compulsory schooling, whether it be by returning to formal educational institutions or through other means. Underlying their discussion is the understanding that although there may be many unanswered questions regarding the definition and selection of competencies, it is fundamental to ask them and to give them due consideration.

Harris, a consultant for Education International, provides a perspective from the field of education regarding the acquisition, measurement, and comparison of competencies. He indicates that even among educators, there is a diversity of views over the issues addressed by the scholars, although some general observations can be made. For example, he emphasizes that education cannot be limited to an economic function and that educators must prepare individuals for roles such as being citizens in a democracy. For Harris, the main dilemma in defining and selecting competencies lies in the limitations brought about by measuring curriculum-based competencies. But competencies required in life do not necessarily fit into categories that can effectively be measured. He suggests that qualitative and descriptive studies could be more revealing than quantitative research, which will essentially be subject to compromise in order to reach some common basis. In his discussion of measurability, Harris cites creativity and courage as examples of non-measurable, but nonetheless potential metacompentencies or generic competencies.

Farrugia, formerly with MEDEF, a French employers' association, represents the point of view of employers. This association is keenly aware of the importance of competencies. MEDEF is taking several initiatives to encourage employers and employees to develop competencies, as this will help firms gain and maintain their competitive edge. As markets become increasingly globalized and population growth declines, highly competent workers will become a rare commodity. Firms will have to invest in their principal asset: their employees. MEDEF is actively exploring new forms of social relationships between employers and employees and is focusing much attention on what it refers to as "competency management." In his commentary, Farrugia explains how competency management will have a positive effect on firms' ability to deal with the challenges of the 21st century and on employees' ability to take greater responsibility in their work, thereby ensuring their own employability.

Callieri, who also represents the view of business, is the former Vice-President of Confindustria, the main organization representing manufacturing and service firms in Italy. In his commentary, which is complementary to Farrugia's, he points out that the changes being brought about in industry due to digital technology are also affecting workers. Because of new technologies, the tasks required of workers at all levels are changing. It will become increasingly important for workers to use their creative and interpretive capabilities in their everyday assignments, thus changing not only the nature of their work, but also the traditional hierarchy between workers, as the distinctions between levels become more and more blurred. As such, the number of knowledge workers will continue to grow, and they will become important assets for their companies. In fact, companies with the strongest "knowledge resource" will come out ahead in global competition. It will therefore be important for firms to invest in their employees, promoting and encouraging lifelong education, in order to maintain their competitive advantages.

From the opposing perspective, Ritchie offers the viewpoint of the workers. As a National Representative for the Canadian Auto Workers Union, Ritchie approaches the reflection on competencies in a very different way from Farrugia and Callieri.

She examines each of the academic contributions, commenting on each individually, and concludes that none satisfactorily considers the labor perspective. In her discussion of the proposed competencies, Ritchie turns each one on its head in order to illustrate how a competency can be desirable in one context, but can also be a coercive tool used against workers in other contexts. She thus warns of the potential dangers in making certain competencies part of a job description and subject to evaluation. Ritchie also provides specific examples regarding workers' rights, and calls attention to societies such as the one in Canada, where employers and employees come from varied cultural backgrounds with different work ethics and traditions.

The chapter concludes with Trier's reflection on potential scenarios for the future and the implications for education. Trier, former Director of the National Research Program, *The Effectiveness of Swiss Educational Systems*, sketches six perspectives. First he notes the importance of political responsibility for the well-being of societies. Then, he discusses changes in the labor market, progress in genetic engineering, the meaning of non-salaried work, the increasing importance of knowledge and learning for social well-being, and the impact of new technology on learning. For Trier, lifelong learning and citizen participation are critical in order to maintain both a high standard of living and a social safety net in an increasingly complex world.

The following essays and comments mirror in many ways both divergent approaches and common ground. Thus, the volume presents a multifaceted sketch of issues related to defining and selecting key competencies in an open, still ongoing debate at national and international levels. It also illustrates the relevance of a multidisciplinary approach and the potential of a continuous dialogue between scholars and representatives from policy and practice.

Chapter 1

Competencies for Life: A Conceptual and Empirical Challenge

Laura Hersh Salganik

Introduction

Learning outcomes are an important element of any system of indicators of education or human resources. However, although a broad vision of the goals of education is shared by many, the smaller reality of available data has limited the production of indicators reflecting this view. In the early stages of the Organisation for Economic Co-operation and Development (OECD) Education Indicators Programme (INES), a set of "ideal" indicators included three groups of learning outcomes: academic achievement and cognitive skills, personal development (e.g., democratic values, and work-related skills and attitudes (e.g., higher order thinking skills, communication and interpersonal skills) (OECD, 1991). However, achievement in mathematics was the only measure in the first volume of *Education at a Glance* (OECD, 1992). At the time, there were no data available to calculate timely national-level indicators for other areas of academic achievement or for other learning outcomes.

Efforts to develop additional data and indicators of learning outcomes face a formidable challenge. Because the work typically begins with a broad or general construct, the first challenge is conceptualization: developing a more focused meaning for the idea that can guide future steps, collecting data and calculating indicators. Technical issues aside, identifying a concept that reflects a consensus among experts, policy analysts, and policy-makers (the eventual users of the indicators), and that is focused enough to be measured empirically, is a major task. As work progresses, empirical results inevitably lead to conceptual refinements. The path from identifying broad ideas about important learning outcomes to institutionalizing a set of internationally comparable indicators can be expected to be long and winding.

Recounting the development of indicators that are now solidly accepted in the United States – poverty, unemployment rate, standard household budget – De Neufville (1975) writes:

> The process takes a long time in part because it involves the exploration of basic values and assumptions and in part because the development of the concept is iterative with the development of the method of measurement. Developing a concept for a usable indicator is a process and not a one-time event. As we learn to define more precisely the phenomena that concern us, we must also learn to spec-

ify our concerns better, redefine problems and in turn alter the way we define concepts…What then does one do to find such a concept? Part of the answer is that it requires a lot of trial and error, which is why it takes so long. A process which produces a measure that stands the test of time and use tends to be an open one with participation by experts in statistics, potential users, analysts and even the general public (p. 122).

This chapter is about the development of internationally comparable indicators of learning outcomes, focusing on how the concepts behind them were defined.[1] This indicator development work, which grows out of a number of empirical studies, and the reflections of the OECD project *Definition and Selection of Competencies: Theoretical and Conceptual Foundations* (DeSeCo) are highly relevant to each other. Formulations and results from the empirical studies are a source of ideas for further refining the ideas put forth in the DeSeCo Project about what competencies are necessary for individuals to lead a successful and responsible life and for society to face the challenges of the present and the future. Likewise, the insights of DeSeCo provide new inputs for advancing the theoretical and conceptual foundations, the scope, and the policy relevance of the empirical efforts, and the indicators they generate.

For the purposes of this chapter, the studies have been divided into two groups, "first-generation studies," which resulted in publications by 1998, and "second-generation studies," which are ongoing and will provide new indicators during the next few years. After discussing each group of studies, the chapter will discuss the lessons learned, and conclude by suggesting some areas for future empirical and theoretical work in the development of indicators of learning outcomes.

First-Generation Studies

In the years immediately following the publication of *Education at a Glance* (OECD, 1992), three projects worked quickly to expand the range of indicators of learning outcomes. As a first step in the DeSeCo Project, the underlying rationale of these projects and the indicators they developed was examined. The findings of this study (Salganik, Rychen, Moser, & Konstant, 1999) are summarized in the following section.

Cross-Curricular Competencies

In the early nineties, a group of delegates of OECD member countries working on learning outcomes (Network A of the INES project) proposed a classification that distinguished two categories of outcomes indicators: *curricular-bounded knowledge and skills* based on school learning, and *non-curricular-bounded socio-cultural*

---

[1] The Third International Math and Science Study (TIMSS) is not considered here because the focus is on outcomes not structured around school subjects.

knowledge and skills, based on knowledge and skills needed to live an individually worthy and socially valuable life (Trier, 1992). At the time, several members – especially representatives of European countries – felt that substantial consideration should be given to further development of a conceptual base for student outcome indicators. From their perspective, presenting indicators of selected school subjects without a broader, underlying conceptualization of the larger domain of student outcomes would result in a misleading portrayal. The notion of a set of competencies as a *survival kit* including basic skills and life skills as an organizing framework emerged in early discussions. The ideas that competencies are learned within and outside of school, that competency development should be viewed in terms of preparation for life rather than achievement in school, and that ability to learn is a fundamental competency were also given consideration.

These discussions were put aside, however, when demonstrating that it is possible to produce indicators of cross-curricular competencies became a priority over continuing the theoretical and conceptual work. A decision was made to conduct a study of the feasibility of using existing instruments to develop such indicators. Based on the availability of instruments for testing, four domains were selected for inclusion in the Cross-Curricular Competencies (CCC) Feasibility Study, initiated in 1993. The domains were politics, economics, and civics; problem-solving; self-perception/self-concept; and communication. Although originally, there was a desire to test 18-year-olds after completing secondary education, the target population was lowered to 16 years for political, technical, and practical reasons. Nine countries participated in the study, and the results were published in *Prepared for Life* (OECD, 1997). In a majority of the countries, the overall results were judged of satisfactory quality for two out of the four domains: civics and self-concept. The study concluded that the problem-solving and communication areas needed further developmental work to meet scientific standards.

The overall goal of the CCC Feasibility Study was to see whether indicators not linked to school subjects could be developed. The answer was yes. Development in the area of self-concept was moved into the Programme for International Student Assessment (PISA), while additional work in problem-solving continued in Network A. Work on civics measures continued through the IEA Civic Education Study, a study done independently of the OECD but quite relevant to its work on competencies. Each of these will be discussed below in this chapter. Communication has been put on a longer-term track.

Adult Literacy

Unlike the CCC project, which conducted an exploratory study in new domains for cross-national assessment, the International Adult Literacy Survey (IALS) grew out of major assessments of adult literacy conducted in two countries: Canada's 1989 Survey of Literacy Skills Used in Daily Activities and the United States' 1990 National Adult Literacy Survey (NALS). The conceptualization and methodology for measuring literacy had been developed in the United States and used for the NALS.

In addition, the Canadian survey had already successfully demonstrated that a literacy survey could be successfully implemented in two languages. From that point, the extension of these surveys into the international arena reflected a confluence of interest among a number of key actors. The survey was conducted in 1994 in eight countries and resulted in *Literacy, Economy and Society* (OECD & Human Resources Canada, 1995).[2]

The definition of literacy adopted by IALS is "the ability to understand and employ printed information in daily activities at home, at work and in the community – to achieve one's goals, and to develop one's knowledge and potential" (OECD & Human Resources Canada, 1995, p. 14). Its theoretical foundation comes from work of Irwin Kirsch and Peter Mosenthal, which began in the early 1980s with the development of the Young Adult Literacy Survey in the United States (Kirsch & Jungeblut, 1986) and was refined for subsequent studies including the NALS (U.S. Department of Education, 1993). The idea that literacy involves understanding any printed or written information, not just prose that is typically associated with school reading, is key to the definition embodied in their work. In the IALS conceptualization, literacy involves the ability to complete tasks based on documents encountered in daily life and those involving arithmetic operations of the type encountered in everyday life when presented in written form, as well as comprehension of prose selections.

According to the view of literacy used in NALS and IALS, literacy can be subdivided into three domains: *prose literacy*, the knowledge and skills needed to understand and use information from texts including editorials, news stories, poems, and fiction; *document literacy*, the knowledge and skills required to locate and use information contained in various formats, including job applications, payroll forms, transportation schedules, maps, tables, and graphics; and *quantitative literacy,* the knowledge and skills required to apply arithmetic operations, either alone or sequentially, to numbers embedded in printed materials, such as balancing a checkbook, figuring out a tip, completing an order form, or determining the amount of interest on a loan from an advertisement (OECD & Human Resources Canada, 1995). IALS' conceptualization of literacy represents a significant departure from earlier ideas because it proposes a multi-dimensional continuum of skills ranging from none at all to high-level literacy skills rather than a single cut-off between literacy and illiteracy, and in its emphasis on skills for everyday life.

IALS also provided the first internationally comparable information for empirical tests of theories about the relationship between literacy skills and educational attainment (qualifications), and of the relationship between literacy skills and earnings, independent of educational attainment. Previously, educational attainment was the only measure available and had served as a proxy for actual skills in research relating worker characteristics to labor market outcomes.

---

[2] The second phase of the survey was conducted in four additional countries in 1995 and was used along with data from the first phase to produce *Literacy Skills for the Knowledge Society* (OECD & Human Resources Canada, 1997). *Literacy in the Information Age: Final Report of the International Adult Literacy Survey* (OECD & Statistics Canada, 2000), incorporated a third set of countries.

Human Capital

In 1996, the OECD Council of Ministers requested that the OECD prepare a report on human capital. The report was to develop indicators based on existing data, identify gaps in internationally comparable data, and discuss the cost of development of data collection for new measures of human capital. The request resulted in the publication of *Human Capital Investment: An International Comparison* (OECD, 1998).

Human Capital Investment: An International Comparison recognizes that the concept of human capital has been used in a number of different ways since its modern usage was initiated by economists in the 1960s (Becker, 1964), and adopts a definition of human capital as "the knowledge, skills, competences and other attributes embodied in individuals that are relevant to economic activity." (OECD 1998, p. 3). The report recognizes that social benefits of individual attributes extend beyond economic activity, but restricts human capital to "assets with the capacity to enhance or support productivity, innovation, and employability" (OECD 1998, p. 3).

Although *Human Capital Investment* includes indicators of human capital stock, investments, and economic returns to those investments, it takes a strong stand that most existing measures of human capital do not capture its full meaning. For example, traditional indicators based on the formal education system (enrollment, attainment, and costs) do not directly measure the capabilities of individuals. Nor do they reflect experiences in the range of environments outside of the formal education systems that contribute to accumulation of human capital in individuals. Indicators based on investments and wage differentials are even more indirect and based on larger assumptions. The report recommends that priority be given to developing direct measures of a range of individual attributes, with a viewpoint that these attributes are developed through institutions and experiences beyond primary, secondary, and tertiary education.

Second-Generation Studies

As the first-generation studies were completing their work, new activities to further the development of learning outcome indicators had already been initiated. This section discusses these activities, focusing on the conceptual work that was carried out in the course of designing the measurement instruments.

Knowledge and Skills of 15-Year-Olds

The Programme for International Student Assessment (PISA) grew out of the need to have regular comparable data for education indicators. The major focus of PISA is on reading literacy, mathematical literacy, and scientific literacy. Although each of these areas matches subjects in the school curriculum, PISA takes a view that is broader than the curriculum. Rather than covering material taken from school curricula, PISA "aim[s] at assessing the extent to which young people have acquired the wider knowledge and skills in these domains that they will need in adult life" (OECD, 1999, p. 9). The rationale for this approach is related to the notion of life-long learning, now widely used in policy discussions. Although specific knowledge may be important in school learning, application of knowledge in adult life depends on broader concepts and skills. In addition to reading, mathematics, and science, PISA plans to include at least one cross-curricular competency on each assessment and to incorporate information and communication technology (ICT). PISA data were first collected in 2000; results will be released in 2001. Current plans are to conduct PISA assessments every three years, with a rotating emphasis on reading, mathematics, and science literacy. The remainder of this discussion will describe the PISA conceptualizations of reading literacy, the main topic of the first assessment, and the cross-curricular competencies selected for the first two assessments: self-regulated learning and problem-solving. Work is also ongoing to develop frameworks for mathematics literacy and science literacy for future cycles of PISA (OECD, 2000).

Reading literacy

According to the PISA reading literacy framework, which presents the conceptual base used to guide the assessment, "reading literacy is understanding, using, and reflecting on written texts, in order to achieve one's goals, to develop one's knowledge and potential, and to participate in society" (OECD, 1999, p. 20). This definition is similar to the definition of reading literacy used for IALS in that it takes reading literacy beyond decoding and literal comprehension. However, it extends the conceptualization by implying that literacy involves using as well as understanding and by focusing on the active and initiating role of the reader. The words "reflecting on" emphasize the idea that readers are active participants in the reading process, thinking about the content in the context of their previous experiences and knowledge or about the structure or form of the text. In addition, the phrase "participate in society" in the PISA formulation is intended to imply that literacy allows people to contribute to society and to engage in cultural, economic, social, and political life. Participation may also include personal engagement through a critical stance toward society and personal empowerment. It replaces the more pragmatic "function in society," used in the IALS definition.

PISA also distinguishes several broad aspects of reading that go beyond basic decoding of texts. They are: forming a broad general understanding, retrieving information, developing an interpretation, reflecting on the content of a text (connecting information in the text to knowledge from other sources and in many situations to one's own point of view), and reflecting on the form of the text (standing apart from the text, considering it objectively, and evaluating its quality and appropriateness.)

Self-regulated learning

Based on the results of the CCC Feasibility Study, self-concept was selected as the cross-curricular competency for the first PISA assessment. The expert group developing the measure recommended that it be incorporated into the assessment as part of a wider competency: self-regulated learning. Also called "high-quality learning" and similar to the concept of "ability to learn" developed during earlier CCC discussions, self-regulated learning is the ability to organize and regulate one's own learning – both independently and in groups – and the ability to overcome difficulties in the learning process.

Self-regulated learning is conceptualized as having cognitive, motivational, and socio-cognitive aspects (Baumert, Fend, O'Neil, & Peschar, 1998). Cognitive components consist of prior knowledge, learning strategies and implicit theories of learning and ability. Components of motivation include motivational preferences (sources of motivation, e.g., intrinsic, extrinsic, career-related instrumentality, competition-related, compliance); goal orientations (e.g., task or ego); attitude toward life-long learning; self-related cognitions (agency beliefs including self-efficacy, general self-concept, and self-concept related to particular subjects or areas); and action control strategies (e.g., the investment of effort and persistence). The third aspect, socio-cognitive elements, includes preferences for different learning styles (e.g., independent, competitive, cooperative) and competencies related to cooperation and competition. Based on the results of a field test (Peschar, Veenstra, & Molenaar, 1999) using existing items and scales, the model was simplified to three basic elements:

- learning strategies (information processing, such as memorization and relating material to what is already known, and metacognative control strategies, such as making sure to remember important things and identifying concepts that are not understood)

- motivation (incorporating effort, persistence, and preferences for cooperative and competitive learning, as well as instrumental and interest-based motivation)

- self-concept

These elements are seen as related to subsequent learning in two ways: as factors influencing reading literacy and mathematics literacy in PISA and together with them, as factors influencing future learning. Participation in this component of PISA was optional, and 22 of the 32 countries participating in 2000 PISA used these scales.

Problem-solving

The second cross-curricular competency under development for PISA is problem-solving. According to the proposed conceptualization for problem-solving in PISA,

Problem-solving is the combination of many different cognitive and motivational processes that are orchestrated to achieve a certain goal that could not be reached by simply applying a well-known routine or algorithm. Problem-solving competence is the capability to do this kind of orchestration within a certain range of tasks and situations (Dossey, Csapo, de Jong, Klieme, & Vosniadou, 2000, p. 20). Consistent with earlier discussions about the need for preparation for life and for a broad context for learning, problem-solving is not limited to problems encountered through school curriculum.

Recognizing that academic and applied research emphasize different aspects of problem-solving, four broad components are proposed:

- *the problem* – the extent to which the problem is well-defined, the degree of specificity with respect to a particular area of content, the nature and relationship among the variables, the intensity (i.e., motivational attraction, degree to which the problem cannot be avoided), degree of realism, the nature of the solution (i.e., narrow or expansive), and the response mode (i.e., whether they require the solver to select or construct a solution)

- *the context* – specific situational requirements and disciplinary domains

- *the nature of the task* – including logical demands, requirements for communication, complexity of the issues, time constraints, need for additional resources, including both information tools and cultural tools, and social interaction

- *the problem-solver* – background, content, and procedural knowledge, including degree of knowledge and heuristic and algorithmic skills relevant to the problem, familiarity with the problem, and motivation

The problem-solving process takes place through the interaction among these components. The notion of analytical reasoning – including deduction, induction, and critical thinking – is central to this conceptualization of problem-solving.

Problem-solving is also incorporated into PISA assessments of reading literacy, mathematical literacy, and scientific literacy and as cross-curricular competency. For example, in reading, students are asked to interpret what they read and to identify the voice of the material. In mathematics, they are asked to solve problems by selecting a strategy, arriving at a solution, and reflecting on their work. In science, they are asked to identify knowledge relevant to a problem, and to draw and evaluate conclusions. The PISA assessment of cross-curricular problem-solving is proposed to include problems in contexts not seen in school but relevant to everyday life. It will provide a measure of students' ability to transfer problem-solving and reasoning to new settings and ask students to integrate their knowledge and understanding in new ways. Current plans call for cross-curricular problem-solving to be included in the PISA assessment of 2003.

Adult Life Skills

The Adult Literacy and Lifeskills Survey (ALL) expands the IALS to address a broader range of skills needed by adults for social and economic success. The ALL directly measures prose and document literacy (identical to the IALS), numeracy (replacing the IALS quantitative literacy), and analytical reasoning. In addition, it indirectly measures two other skill domains: teamwork, and information and communication technology (ICT) literacy.

ALL defines numeracy as "the knowledge and skills required to effectively manage the mathematical demands of diverse situations" (Gal, Tout, van Groenstijn, Schmitt, & Manley, 1999). Recognizing that ALL cannot assess all elements of such a broad definition, the framework specifies five key aspects of numerate behavior that will be assessed: Numerate behavior is observed when people *manage a situation or solve a problem in a real context*. It involves *responding* to *information about mathematical ideas* that may be *represented in a range of ways*; it requires the *activation of a range of enabling knowledge, behaviors, and processes*.

The final skill to be directly measured in ALL, *analytical reasoning*, addresses a form of problem-solving. Recognizing that there is little agreement on an exact definition of problem-solving, ALL concentrates on the component of reasoning represented by analytical reasoning in real world contexts. The assessment uses a "project approach" which focuses on cognitive competencies needed to solve tasks embedded in projects such as laying out a school garden. Projects are constructed in accordance with individual steps of the problem-solving process: defining the goal, analyzing the situation, planning the solution, executing the plan, and evaluating the result.

Indirect measures of teamwork and information and communication technology are also included in ALL. According to the ALL teamwork framework, the core team skills are communication, (which underlies the other three), interpersonal relations, group decision-making/planning, and adaptability/flexibility. Teamwork is dependent on core knowledge – knowing how and when to use the core team skills – as well as core attitudes, particularly belief in the importance of teamwork and collective orientation. Information and communication technology (ICT) is defined for ALL as the ability to make full use of existing, new, and emerging technology, in order to be successful both in professional and private life. The ALL background questionnaire will include items on knowledge of teamwork skills, attitudes about teamwork, general use of communication technology, computer use and skills, benefits of computer use, and receptivity to computer use among current non-users. Adult Literacy and Lifeskills Survey (1999) contains frameworks for each of the ALL assessments.

Item feasibility testing occurred during 1999; pilot testing will take place in 2001. The main testing is scheduled for 2002.

Overarching Framework for Understanding and Assessing Lifeskills

The *ALL Overarching Framework for Understanding and Assessing Lifeskills* (Binkley, Sternberg, Jones, & Nohara, 1999) is based on a review and integration of two areas of inquiry: efforts to identify broad categories of workplace skills and psychological theories of intelligence. It links these two perspectives with the goal of beginning to develop a means for consistent conceptualization of types of thinking across employability skills, thus allowing for more precise and useful descriptions of both the skills and the thinking abilities.

The framework begins by synthesizing skills from nine lists proposed over the past decade by major education- and labor-related organizations in Australia, Canada, the United States and the United Kingdom, and finds that behind the variations in terminology (e.g., employability skills, enabling skills, generic skills, core skills, key competencies, essential skills, and necessary skills), there is a consensus about what skills are important for success in the labor market. It proposes a set of skills and sub-areas to represent most of the skills identified in the nine projects: communication (speaking, listening, reading, and writing); mathematical; problem-solving; intrapersonal (motivation, metacognition); interpersonal (teamwork, leadership); and technology. Although the reports were generally formulated with a labor market orientation, they frequently state or imply that they are also relevant for life beyond the workplace.

In contrast to the work on identifying workplace skills which took place mainly in the 1980s and 1990s, efforts to describe and measure human intelligence dates back a hundred years. The ALL framework draws on two widely used theories. The first is the psychometric theory that proposes a hierarchy of abilities beginning with the most general, commonly referred to as *G*, and including more specific *crystallized* and *fluid* abilities, also called *Gc* and *Gf* (Carroll, 1993 and Horn, 1994). Crystallized abilities are represented by accumulated knowledge including the use of language; fluid abilities are those involving reasoning, including inductive and deductive reasoning and the ability to understand relationships, comprehend implications, and draw inferences. The second is the theory of successful intelligence (Sternberg, 1985, 1997a, 1997b), which stresses the importance of relevance for life success as a criterion for inclusion of a particular ability in the wider concept of intelligence. In this theory, there are three major and independent aspects of intelligence: analytical (used to analyze and evaluate); creative (used to create, invent, imagine, and hypothesize); and practical (used to apply knowledge and skills). The ALL overarching framework proposes a combination of the psychological approaches resulting in four core domains of intelligence: crystallized analytical abilities (recall of accumulated knowledge and previously-applied information processing skills); fluid analytical abilities (reasoning abilities); practical abilities (abilities to apply knowledge and skills in the context of the individual's daily life); and creative abilities (abilities to create, invent, imagine, hypothesize, and generally to cope with relative novelty).

Lastly, the framework proposes a matrix that combines the two approaches – tasks identified in employability skills models and types of thinking identified in psychological models. Theoretically, in each of the task categories, people can engage in the four types of thinking based on the psychological approaches. Specific tasks can be classified by the type of thinking that they involve. The framework is proposed as a starting point for developing a unifying direction for future assessment efforts. The authors note that since few of the employability skills efforts have included assessments, and most work on assessments of intelligence has focused on crystallized and fluid abilities, the approach represents a significant challenge.

Preparation for Citizenship

The goal of the Civic Education Study (CivEd) is to "identify and examine in a comparative framework the ways in which young people are prepared to undertake their role as citizens in democracies and societies aspiring to democracy" (Torney-Purta, Schwille, & Amadeo, 1999a, 1999b). The International Association for the Evaluation of Educational Achievement (IEA) initiated the study in 1993 in response to interest related to worldwide initiatives towards democratic reform and concern about social cohesion in many societies. It follows an earlier study of civic education conducted in 1971 (Torney, Oppenheim, & Farnen, 1975).

The IEA Civic Education Study addresses a domain of learning that is quite different from the other areas addressed by international assessments of children and school-aged youth. First, its content is addressed in multiple school subjects (e.g., civics, social studies, government, history, mother tongue, ethics) and reaches beyond classroom experiences to a wide array of areas of life in schools. Second, a great deal of civic education takes place outside of schools in the larger society. Last, although it is possible to develop a structure and elements of the domain that are common across countries, specific aspects of what young people should know and be able to do are quite country-specific. In recognition of these challenges – and of the conceptual development necessary for the success of the study – CivEd was designed as a two-phased effort.

Phase 1 consisted of case studies in participating countries and relied primarily on qualitative methodologies. Recognizing differences across countries in notions of topics such as citizenship, democratic government, and political participation, Phase 1 was a crucial element of the study's strategy for developing a common framework within which to develop comparisons across countries. An analysis of information provided by countries about expectations for 14- or 15-year-olds in areas under the umbrella of civic education and about definitions of central concepts, such as democracy and citizens' rights and responsibilities, identified three domains as most important for civic education: the meaning of democracy in the national context, a sense of identify with respect to one's own country and with other countries and supranational organizations, and social diversity and social cohesion.

The Phase 1 identification of the most important domains of civic education – democracy, national identity and international relations, and social cohesion and diversity – served as the foundation for developing items for the student assessment instruments used in Phase 2. Items related to five types of outcomes were developed: factual knowledge; skills in using civic-related knowledge; understanding of concepts such as democracy, citizenship, scope of government; attitudes regarding institutions and issues; and civic-related actions, practices, and dispositions toward actions. Only the first two types – knowledge and skills – have correct responses. The others are designed for international comparisons of profiles of students in different countries, to reveal how countries are similar and different, rather than to show whether the students knew the correct answers to the items. Data for Phase 2 were collected in 1999 from 14-year-olds in 28 countries, and the first results released in March 2001 (Torney-Purta, Lehmann, Oswald, & Schulz, 2001).

The primary theoretical concern of CivEd was to develop a framework for conceptualizing civic education that accounted for the complex environment in which it takes place. As part of the planning for the case studies, countries participated in a consensus process that resulted in the formulation of a Model for IEA Civic Education (Torney-Purta et al., 1999a), which is referred to as the "octagon model." The individual student, at the center of the model, is surrounded by public discourse about the goals, values, and practices relevant for civic education, which are transmitted by "carriers" including family, the school, peer group, neighbors, television and the media. At a societal level, civic education is influenced by institutions, processes, and values in domains such as politics, economics, education, and religion. Each of the framing questions for the case study is related to one or more of the societal level influences or to one of the carriers in the model.

The model is grounded in a conceptual approach for understanding human development formulated by Urie Bronfrenbrenner (1988) that sees development as an outcome both of individual characteristics and of processes operating at different levels of proximity to the individual. According to Bronfrenbrenner's theory, the carriers of civic education who interact directly with individual students are part of the microsystem context of development; the social institutions, processes, and values constitute the macrosystem, which can influence both the microsystem and the individual student. The model also reflects the situated cognition theories of Jean Lave and Etienne Wenger (1991).

Lessons Learned

For each of the first-generation projects, the focus was on developing indicators in as short a timeframe as possible.[3] The CCC Feasibility Study selected competencies for which instruments already existed; IALS applied an existing conceptualization and methodology; for the human capital project, the request was to develop indicators based on existing data. Providing information in the form of indicators to the policy community quickly was of paramount importance.

As a result of the need to produce indicators rapidly, new developments in the theoretical and conceptual issues were not at the forefront of these efforts. For example, the CCC Feasibility Study devoted scant attention to conceptualizing or defining the term "cross-curricular competencies" or to the competencies measured and their interrelationships with each other. The IALS and the Human Capital Indicators Project were based on theoretical and conceptual work that had taken place over many years and was not the focus of the projects. Further, the studies operated independently of each other with minimal conceptual and organizational coordination related to selecting and defining competencies and without an organizational structure to facilitate continuing development. Individual initiatives and particular national inter-

---

[3] This discussion of first-generation projects is based on Salganik et al., 1999.

ests rather than an overarching strategy largely determined the process of definition and selection of competencies.

Notwithstanding the low priority of theory and conceptualization and the lack of coordination among the projects, the ideas advanced have much in common and much that represents both an emerging consensus and innovation in indicator development. Each of the studies adopted a broad conception of competencies and outcomes of education. The ideas covered in the CCC Feasibility Study stretch across curricular boundaries and are viewed as skills for life rather than for success in school. Whereas traditionally literacy was conceptualized as a dichotomous characteristic (either one is literate or one is not), IALS viewed it as a continuum spanning from basic to advanced skills. Further, the literacy concept proposed in IALS includes performing tasks based on a wide range of printed materials used in everyday life, rather than school-based material. Human capital as presented in the HCI report is made up of multiple components acquired both in and out of school that contribute to economic productivity of individuals and is conceptually distinct from attainment in formal education, the traditional measure. Taken together, these studies reflect three innovative ideas with respect to conceptualizations of indicators of learning outcomes:

- Desired outcomes of education are broader than the acquisition of subject-related knowledge typically taught in schools.

- Acquisition of competencies – i.e., learning – extends beyond the school context.

- Learning is preparation for life.

These studies also succeeded in providing a great deal of information for policy-makers and in generating interest in indicators of learning outcomes beyond the field of education.

The more recent second-generation studies reflect the common ideas established through the earlier efforts and have built on what was learned from them about indicator development. The conceptualization of self-regulated learning in PISA is an extension of the self-concept notion from the CCC Feasibility Study. Problem-solving in PISA selected an approach more appropriate to a cross-national assessment as a result of lessons learned from problem-solving in the CCC study. The IEA Civic Education Study also built on the CCC Feasibility Study. It introduced outcome measures that do not have "correct" responses, and it developed a theoretical model that relates the individual to his or her social environment. ALL built on IALS by expanding the range of competencies addressed; reading literacy in PISA built on the notion of reading literacy used for IALS and expanded it to reflect the notion of reading for reflection and for active participation in society. In addition to their work related to particular competencies, these studies have made two important contributions relevant to building an overarching framework of competencies: the ALL Overarching Framework, which proposes an integration of approaches based on employability skills and ideas from the discipline of psychology; and PISA's conception of literacy, which grounds it in the individual's ability to achieve his or her purposes in different areas (e.g., reading literacy, mathematical literacy, scientific literacy).

These advances have come as a result of increased emphasis placed on conceptualization of learning outcomes, on the involvement of the scientific community, and on international collaboration. For example, Kirsch (1998) explains that the formulation of reading literacy for PISA developed through the interaction of three components: the framework (which expresses how reading literacy is defined and measured), the practical constraints (other design elements of the survey such as length of time for the assessment), and constituencies (who will make use of the data). Each study relied extensively on dialogue and exchange among experts with different scientific and policy perspectives. Smaller-scale studies using a variety of methodologies contributed empirically based insights as the development progressed (see, for example, Ducret & Lurin, 2000; Peschar et al., 1999). This participatory process at the international level was a crucial element of building shared meaning for the concepts being developed. It may seem obvious, but is nonetheless important to note explicitly, that each of these studies devoted several years to developing their measurement frameworks and instruments.

Thus, the second-generation studies have built on the consensus and innovative aspects of the earlier ones by investing considerable effort in conceptual work and development of measures grounded in well-established theory. Within the next few years, policy-makers can expect to have information about many learning outcomes that has not been available at the international level in the past. In addition, the data from the studies will be available for substantial empirical, analytical efforts aimed at contributing to clearer conceptualization and better measurement of the outcomes in the future. Finally, PISA and ALL represent programmatic long-term efforts that provide an organizational structure for coordinated continuation of the work. (Discussions are ongoing for establishing a schedule for periodic assessments of civic competencies.)

While the empirical studies have been working to sharpen the concepts and measurement behind indicators of learning outcomes, DeSeCo has focused on the overall theoretical and conceptual foundations for the concept of competence and for key competencies. A number of issues raised in DeSeCo and reflected in this volume may be relevant to future empirical efforts. These include, for example, the high importance attached to competencies in the social domain and to autonomous behavior, and the recognition that there are levels of competence that develop only during adulthood. DeSeCo has also placed key competencies in the context of normative viewpoints, and proposed that they are applied in multiple spheres of life and provide a benefit to society as well as individuals. These are ideas that would need to be discussed further in the context of empirical work on indicator development and could contribute to broadening their policy relevance. Last, the concept of competence itself – with its focus on multi-faceted entities structured around demands of life – could help to provide a structure for how different learning outcomes relate to each other (for example as components of competencies or as sub-competencies needed for other competencies), as well as a means to conceptually link learning outcomes to a broad range of policy issues relevant for life in a modern, democratic society. As the effort to strengthen the theoretical and conceptual foundations of key competencies continues, findings from empirical studies – including analyses of PISA, ALL,

CivEd, as well as smaller-scale studies using both quantitative and qualitative methodologies – will constitute an important input to the discussion.

References

Adult Literacy and Lifeskills Survey. (1999). *Frameworks: Working Drafts.* Briefing materials for National Study Managers meeting, Luxembourg.

Baumert, J., Fend, H., O'Neil, H. F., & Peschar, J.L. (1998). Prepared for life-long learning: Frame of reference for the measurement of self-regulated learning as a cross-curricular competency (CCC) in the PISA project. Paris: OECD.

Becker, G. S. (1964). *Human capital: A theoretical and empirical analysis, with special reference to education.* Chicago: University of Chicago Press.

Binkley, M., Sternberg, R., Jones, S., & Nohara, D. (1999). An overarching framework for understanding and assessing lifeskills. In *Frameworks: Working drafts.* Briefing materials for Adult Literacy and Lifeskills Survey National Study Managers meeting, Luxembourg.

Bronfrenbrenner, U. (1988). Interacting systems in human development. In: N. Bolger, C. Caspi, G. Downey & M. Moorehouse (Eds.), *Persons in context: Developmental processes* (pp. 25–49). Cambridge, England: Cambridge University Press. Carroll, J. B. (1993). *Human cognitive abilities: A survey of factor-analytic studies.* New York: Cambridge University Press.

De Neufville, J. I. (1975). *Social indicators and public policy: Interactive processes of design and application.* Amsterdam: Elsevier Scientific Publishing Company.

Dossey, J., Csapo, B., de Jong, T., Klieme, E., & Vosniadou, S. (2000). Cross-curricular competencies in PISA: Towards a framework for assessing problem-solving skills. In Organisation for Economic Co-operation and Development, *The INES compendium: Contributions from the INES networks and working groups* (GA[2000]12). Paris: OECD.

Ducret, J., & Lurin, J. (2000). *Problem solving skills in adults: A qualitative study.* Geneva: Service de la recherche en éducation (SRED).

Gal, I., Tout, T., van Groenstijn, M., Schmitt, M.J., & Manley, M. (1999). Numeracy Framework. In *Frameworks: Working Drafts.* Briefing materials for Adult Literacy and Lifeskills Survey National Study Managers meeting, Luxembourg.

Horn, J.L. (1994). Fluid and crystallized intelligence, theory of. In R.J. Sternberg (Ed.), *Encyclopedia of human intelligence* (Vol. 1, pp. 443–451). New York: Macmillan.

Kirsch, I. (1998). *The PISA framework for assessing reading literacy.* Draft report revised from meeting of PISA Reading Functional Expert Group, Liège, Belgium.

Kirsch, I. & Jungeblut, A. (1986). *Literacy: Profiles of America's young adults.* NAEP Report No.16-PL-01. Princeton, New Jersey: Education Testing Service.

Lave, J., & Wenger, E. (1991). *Situated learning: Legitimate peripheral participation.* Cambridge: Cambridge University Press.

Organisation for Economic Co-operation and Development (1991). *Handbook on international education indicators* (CERI/INES (91)17). Paris: Author.

Organisation for Economic Co-operation and Development. (1992). *Education at a glance.* Paris: Author.

Organisation for Economic Co-operation and Development. (1997). *Prepared for life.* Paris: Author.

Organisation for Economic Co-operation and Development. (1998). *Human capital investment: An international comparison.* Paris: Author.

Organisation for Economic Co-operation and Development. (1999). *Measuring student knowledge and skills.* Paris: Author.

Organisation for Economic Co-operation and Development & Human Resources Canada. (1995). *Literacy, economy and society.* Paris: Author.

Organisation for Economic Co-operation and Development & Human Resources Canada. (1997). *Literacy skills for the knowledge society.* Paris: Author.

Organisation for Economic Co-operation and Development & Statistics Canada. (2000). *Literacy in the information age: Final report of the International Adult Literacy Survey.* Paris: Author.

Organisation for Economic Co-operation and Development. (2000). *Measuring student knowledge and skills: The PISA 2000 assessment of reading, mathematical, and scienticfic literacy.* Paris: Author.

Peschar, J. L., Veenstra, R., & Molenaar, I. W. (1999, October). *The construction of instruments in 22 countries for the PISA main study 2000: Final report to OECD.* Paper presented at the Network A Meeting Echternach, Luxembourg.

Salganik, L. H., Rychen, D. S., Moser, U., & Konstant, J. (1999). *Projects on competencies in the OECD context: Analysis of theoretical and conceptual foundations.* Neuchâtel: Swiss Federal Statistical Office.

Sternberg, R. J. (1985). *Beyond IQ: A triarchic theory of human intelligence.* New York: Cambridge University Press.

Sternberg, R. J. (1997a). *Successful intelligence.* New York: Plume.

Sternberg, R. J. (1997b). Successful intelligence: A broader view of who is smart in school and in life. *International Schools Journal, 17,* 19–31.

Torney, J., Oppenheim, A. & Farnen, R. (1975). *Civic education in ten countries: An empirical study.* New York: Halsted Press.

Torney-Purta, J., Lehmann, R., Oswald, H. & Schulz, W. (2001). *Citizenship and education in twenty-eight countries: Civic knowledge and engagement at age fourteen.* Amsterdam: International Assocation for the Evaluation of Educational Achievement (Eburnon).

Torney-Purta, J., Schwille, J., & Amadeo, J. (Eds.) (1999a). *Civic education across countries: Twenty-four national case studies from the IEA civic education project.* Amsterdam: Eburon.

Torney-Purta, J., Schwille, J., & Amadeo, J. (1999b, December). *The IEA civic education study: Expectations and achievements of students in thirty countries.* ERIC Clearinghouse for Social Studies/Social Science Education (EDO-SO-1999-10). Washington, D.C.: U.S. Department of Education.

Trier, U. P. (1992). *Non-curricular bounded socio-cultural knowledge and skills: Some remarks and proposals.* Paper presented at the INES Network A meeting, Oslo, Norway.

U.S. Department of Education. (1993). National Center for Education Statistics. *Adult literacy in America: A first look at the results of the National Adult Literacy Survey.* Washington, D.C.

Chapter 2

Defining and Selecting Competencies: Historical Reflections on the Case of IQ

John Carson

Introduction

What can an historian and science studies scholar contribute to the Organisation for Economic Co-operation and Development (OECD) project *Definition and Selection of Competencies: Theoretical and Conceptual Foundations* (DeSeCo)? The goal of the project is to provide a resource for the process of defining, selecting, and measuring the competencies necessary for individuals to lead a successful and responsible life and for societies to face the challenges of the present and the future. Certainly historical sources can provide little direct data that might help identify those competencies or measure them more precisely. But perhaps a cautionary tale, drawn from the not-too-distant past, might shed light on some of the challenges involved in such a project and some of the work necessary to realize it in whatever terms it is taken up. The DeSeCo Project is not without precedents; indeed, attempts to establish standards in the physical and biological sciences have a long history. In the social sciences, however, such endeavors are of more recent vintage. One of the first major attempts to define and measure a key human competency was the work done at the turn of the century in Britain, France, Germany, and the United States on mental measurement, efforts that resulted in the production and dissemination of the modern notion of intelligence, the IQ, and of the instruments to assess it.

Just to mention the term IQ, of course, is to send up warning flags for many readers. Arguably the first truly standardized universal measure in the mental sciences, it has been a source of controversy almost from the moment it was first proposed by the German psychologist Wilhelm Stern and then subsequently adopted and championed by the American mental tester Lewis M. Terman. To some, the IQ test signifies precise scientific measurement of a basic biological feature of the human mind that accounts in large measure for individual competency in a range of domains, while for others, IQ's hereditarian, elitist, and racializing connotations demonstrate vividly that the process of scientific universalization is one of the imposition of white, male, Euro-American standards on the entire world. Even to point this much out is to provide at least one cautionary lesson for the DeSeCo Project: the articulation of universal competencies cannot easily be disengaged from powerful political and moral concerns about the very nature of any such program, especially one initiated by elite

Western institutions such as the OECD. While it is clear that the DeSeCo Project is aware of the example of IQ, it might still benefit from an examination of the history of IQ's production. An investigation of the way in which IQ came to be established and deployed, with varying degrees of success, throughout the West, and then the subsequent effects it had once established, may provide some important general insights into the DeSeCo Project's goals of defining and selecting key competencies.

To condense and schematize a complicated history, the first successful psychological technique for quantifying differences in individual mental ability came early in the 20th century. In response to a request from a governmental commission on children lagging behind in school, French psychologist Alfred Binet and his colleague Théodore Simon developed a psychological instrument, the Binet-Simon Intelligence Scale, designed to reveal deficiencies in overall intellectual ability. Created in 1905 and subsequently revised in 1908 and 1911, the Binet-Simon consisted of an individually administered set of tasks whose final output was a number assessing the subject's mental age: his or her intellectual level as compared to the norms for all others of the same age group. Not only did this number allow test-takers to be compared to each other according to the presumed degree of their intelligence, but it suggested as well that intelligence itself was something singular and quantifiable.

Especially with the advent of the 1908 revision, the Binet-Simon scale became the standard against which all further developments in the field were compared. Numerous improvements were proposed during the 1910s, culminating in Terman's 1916 revision of the scale, the Stanford-Binet, which almost immediately came to dominate the practice of mental measurement. One of Terman's most important innovations was to introduce the concept of the intelligence quotient (IQ), a ratio of mental age to chronological age that he adopted from Stern. Before mobilization for World War I, intelligence testing was restricted largely to psychological research and some clinical applications. During the war, however, a new way of administering mental tests, by groups, was developed and its successful application to 1.75 million U.S. Army recruits introduced intelligence testing on a large scale to the general public. In the postwar period, many schools and industries, especially in the United States and Britain, turned to testing as an efficient means of assessing students and staff. New instruments continued to be developed, so that by the end of the 1920s intelligence and its assessment had become well entrenched throughout the U.S. and parts of Europe.

There are four aspects of this history of IQ and its tests to which I would like to draw attention, springboards that may prove useful for discussing some of the issues raised by the DeSeCo Project: 1) the identification of competency as a problem and a need for a standard; 2) the process through which the measurement of IQ was developed and gained widespread acceptance; 3) the social embeddedness of measuring IQ; and 4) the potential impact of such testing and measurement on individuals and societies.

Identifying the Need for a Standard

To begin with the most basic question: in what sense, if any, was it necessary to establish a standard such as IQ at all? As many of the legion of critics of IQ testing would suggest, the world might actually have gotten along decidedly better if IQ had never been constructed and then ensconced in such a transportable technology as the intelligence test. The problems it was meant to solve, some would argue, either did not really exist – the menace of the feebleminded comes to mind[1] – or else could have been better approached by using different methods, ones taking into account the multitude of ways in which people perform cognitively in the world. From such a perspective, psychologists and other experts got swept up in turn-of-the-century worries about eugenics, degeneration, the purity of the race, the maintenance of the elite, and the like, and saw in the methods of science the possibility of producing an objective measure of human competency that would allow for the efficient reorganization of the social world.[2]

In terms of the DeSeCo Project, therefore, one might begin by asking whether there really is a problem of competence at all in the early 21st century. Is it clear that people feel suddenly less competent, or *are* less competent, or that competency is something that a vast majority of the inhabitants of the planet are lacking? While national or international surveys might be one way of at least partially answering these questions, such surveys could also exacerbate them, provoking worries that otherwise might not have arisen, as IQ testing seemed to do in the United States during the 1920s vis-à-vis questions about the national intelligence.[3] One might also ask what sort of work is being done by casting competency as a significant social problem. Who is gaining and who is losing by the politics of that move? What kinds of strategies and resources are being mobilized, and what kinds are being deflected? For example, it is possible that at the beginning of the 21st century, questions of the differential access to information and capital, the imbalance in basic health care provisioning, the rise in international environmental threats, the implications of globalization, and the inequities in food distribution are far more pressing problems than the differential access to forms of competency – or perhaps not. But it is an issue that seems critical to the agenda of any project such as DeSeCo. What sort of problem is competency and how pressing is it?

Part of the reason that competency is seen as an issue of such potentially immense significance at the present moment may be that there is a presumption in much of the literature that this is a time of intensely rapid technological change which is radically reconfiguring the social-economic worlds in which competencies must operate, and that 21st century citizens must be able to adapt themselves to this new reality. There is now a virtual celebration of just what a dramatically changing, different, vital, vola-

---

[1] See, for example, Rafter, 1997.
[2] The literature on eugenics, degeneration, and the rise of scientific racism in the late nineteenth century is enormous. See, for example, Hawkins, 1997; Kevles, 1986; Kraut, 1994; Nye, 1984; Pick, 1989; and Stepan, 1991.
[3] On the intelligence and democracy debates in the United States in the 1920s, see Gould, 1996; Cravens, 1978; and Degler, 1991.

tile, out-of-control, life-is-a-constant-struggle world we live in. It is announced every day, and many of us seem to live it in every part of our lives. But from an historian's perspective, it must be pointed out that people at the end of the 19th century, with the invention of the telegraph and telephone, felt that way; people in the middle of the 19th century, with the great technological transformations associated with the steam engine and the railroad, felt that way; and people in the late 18th century, with the first rumblings of the Industrial Revolution, also felt that the world was changing in ways and at speeds that were almost unimaginable. So it seems clear that part of what needs to be done is to step away from a wholesale embrace of this language of constant flux and consider first, what consequences ensue by imagining the world along these particular lines. What is being accomplished by saying that we now live in the midst of a series of technological revolutions that will completely transform the ways we live? One function of such a characterization, to take the cynical view, is that it makes the stock of corporations like Microsoft go up. While not the whole of the picture, this view does reflect one part of the reality, which is that certain people gain and others lose from promoting particular visions of what the future holds. As compelling as the life-as-constant-change representation of early 21st century life may be, there are also other ways of looking at this complicated, complex, and variegated world, ones which may, for example, concede that there are areas of rapid change but also insist that there are places of enormous stability, and all kinds of mixtures in between.

Thus, a whole series of possible understandings of life can be envisaged. We who are academics by and large live in a postmodernist moment, and so the tendency is to see it as variegated, multiple, rapidly changing, identity-is-fractured, as a world where computers and electronic mail and the whole variety of techno-baubles constitute the warp and woof of the reality in which we live; for many of us, it is a kind of de-centered, virtualized space. But that is only one of a number of scenarios we could project onto the planet at this moment that would be consonant with the lives of a significant fraction of its inhabitants. In fact, in many ways the postmodern version may well be the least appropriate for the simple majority, were it to be a question of sheer numbers. So however the world is to be represented, it is in some sense a choice that itself involves particular simplifications and complexifications, the plausibility of which will depend in part on the cultural place where those doing the choosing stand. As such, there is a politics involved, for each representation of the world will open certain avenues and possibilities and remove others.

To return to the IQ example, from the perspective of the social engineers of the early 20th century, the world was unquestionably an unruly, chaotic place that needed to be rendered orderly, efficient, and comprehensible. Objects such as IQ and its tests helped to accomplish this task, by allowing for a simple and efficient method of ranking individuals in terms of their overall intellectual capacity. As a result, the world did become partially reconfigured, made in some sense more rationalized and orderly, with consequences good and bad rippling out in all directions. Educational opportunities, for example, were opened to certain individuals and groups who previously had been routinely excluded, while at the same time these benefits were denied to others in a more thorough way than had ever before been possible. For others living at exactly the same moment, however, a much different reality was experienced, one in which the predations of industrial capitalism, or the excesses of Western colonialism, or the unpredictabilities of rural life were most salient. Such individuals and groups may or may not have felt that there were issues of competency fundamental to their lives, but it seems clear that if they did, the kinds of competencies needed in their worlds would have been far different from those most important in the world experienced by the social engineers. It is not that one was real and one was false, but rather that multiplicity may be unavoidable, that there may be an enormous number and variety of micro-cultures jostling into each other at any given moment. Thus, in addition to determining whether indeed there is a problem of competency at the beginning of the 21st century, it seems relevant also to consider what vision of society is being represented and thereby created and sustained.

Development and Acceptance of IQ Measurement

The second aspect of the history of IQ I will discuss is the historical development of IQ testing. It is important to underscore that the IQ version of intelligence, the tests invented to measure it, and the practices developed to keep it robust did not emerge whole and ready to operate, but were rather the final products of prodigious and difficult effort that spanned decades and involved thousands of researchers, teachers, administrators, and individual test takers. It took work to construct IQ, and to build it in such a way that it could seem able to traverse diverse continents, cultures, and time periods. While it is easy to imagine the large amount of effort involved in building the IQ test, another part of that work – the act of turning some specific set of capabilities tied to particular groups of human subjects into a universal human competency – may not be so obvious. Although it may be in some sense reasonable to say that IQ was discovered by Alfred Binet (or was it Wilhelm Stern, or perhaps Lewis Terman?), the story of its articulation and use suggests much more the language of construction: psychology did not so much identify a universal competency as make a particular competency universal.

Now if that is the case, and what is more, if such practice is routine when scientific universals are produced, then the DeSeCo Project will have to grapple with some of the implications of this process for its own program of identifying and assessing a set of key competencies. Most immediate is the charge that adopting this constructivist interpretation implies that anything goes, that any powerful agency can unilaterally foist its values on an unsuspecting public because reality is ultimately about power rather than truth. Certainly such arguments are not unknown among critics of IQ testing, nor more broadly within anti-essentialist critiques of many distinctions drawn along racial and sex/gender lines. Here, however, it may be much more pertinent to draw on work in science studies which contends that the issue is less whether universals such as gravity or evolution or the meter stick are fictional or not, as it is to realize that their universality must be propagated, not proclaimed. Cambridge University historian Simon Schaffer, for example, has argued that one of the great achievements of late 19th century physics was its creation of a "manufactory of ohms," a site where a standardized electrical unit could be produced and converted into a physical object capable of being dispatched around the world to regulate electrical practice and the electrical measurements on which it depended (Schaffer, 1992). In Schaffer's telling, the ohm did not start off as a universal standard, but was made into one; such could also be said of IQ. In the late 19th century, there may well have been as many ways to assess the mind as there had earlier been methods for measuring electricity. IQ was only one of these methods, initially visible only in very specific populations. It became universal as intelligence tests were standardized, statistical methods applied and refined, protocols and procedures reformulated, researchers in psychology and education recruited, sample populations expanded, methods of administration altered, social implications adduced, and so on. Researchers did not make up intelligence, but they did help to make it into a particular thing, a specific kind of natural object, and they did so by creating networks of people, objects, and institutions in which IQ could be meaningful and flourish.

Dropping the language of discovery and identification thus brings to the fore the dynamic and contingent nature of the process of establishing universals. It should remind those who want to establish broadly applicable competencies that there is an inescapably normative dimension to their undertakings. On the one hand, there is the normativity associated with choice: it is not nature alone that is determining which individual capabilities are turned into universal competencies, but the active agency of researchers who must not only select what will become a competency but must also determine how its propagation will be accomplished. On the other hand, there is also the normativity associated with result: the very acts of choosing and producing universals change the social landscape, often in profound ways. Making IQ meant making a world in which IQ would matter; for good or for ill many of us still live with the results of that decision today.

Thus, it would be wise for the DeSeCo Project, in its consideration of key competencies, to take into account two aspects concerning their potential universality. First, there should be a consideration of what would ideally result, imagining the best possibilities, imagining all the ways in which universals can do important work, be it providing solid grounds for meaningful comparisons, or criteria for justifying reallocation of resources, or ways of looking beyond the specifics of local situations. But second, the project should also think hard about what is actually likely to happen. Because, as we know, the gap between what is ideally imagined – and here the critiques of Enlightenment universality come to mind – versus the kind of actualities that get produced is often quite large. DeSeCo must thus consider carefully the ways in which universals are defined within particular regimes of cultural power, and should be aware that the translation of idealized competencies into everyday practice is a complicated one, not always likely to go along the lines most to be hoped. IQ has certainly not only been pernicious, but it has also undeniably been embedded within political and social agendas that have had tragic consequences for a variety of groups and individuals.

The language of construction serves an additional useful purpose by highlighting the various kinds of work it takes not only to make objects into universals, but also to keep them that way. The story of IQ is only in part one of the labor of producing a human competency and its measure. It is at least as much the saga of how IQ became integral to determinations of mental handicap, admission processes to colleges and universities, decisions about hiring or promotion, and assignments to college-bound or vocational educational tracks, to take only some American examples. Constant revision of IQ tests, continual production of validity and other research studies, stories about the IQs of Albert Einstein or Stephen Hawking, jokes in the lunchroom about a person's IQ, even debates engendered by *The Bell Curve* and other such publications elaborating the presumed social consequences of IQ differences have also contributed to the process that maintains IQ as a basic human competency (Herrnstein & Murray, 1994; Jacoby & Glauberman, 1995). Thus, having accomplished the work of selecting certain competencies and arguing for their universal applicability, only a part of DeSeCo's job will be done. Like any other objects or constructs, work will also be necessary to keep them vital and in place, especially within ever-changing socio-cultural worlds. This is especially true because of the high political charge elaborations of human competencies carry. Taking the construct, say, of basic literacy and turning that into something that can be maintained across time and space will not be easy and will require efforts that far transcend its simple definition and measurement.

The Social Embeddedness of Measuring IQ

The third aspect of the process of making competencies that should be examined is what might be termed their social embeddedness. IQ was not the only way in which intelligence was conceptualized at the turn of the century. It was a particular answer to a particular question set in a particular social order. It began as the response of a number of turn-of-the-century psychologists in France, Germany, Britain, and the United States to perceived difficulties in readily identifying the higher orders of the "feebleminded," those individuals thought to be neither profoundly mentally impaired nor of normal intellectual ability. Suffused with the ideology of science, the ambitions of social engineers, and the worries of old elites about the new industrial order, these mechanics of the mind sought to produce objective measuring instruments that could unambiguously distinguish the healthy from the deficient. The result was IQ and its tests, technologies that allowed entire populations to be ordered and arranged into intelligence hierarchies, stratifications that could then serve as the basis for an array of administrative decisions efficiently rendered. Whatever aspects of the competent mind IQ captured, they were intimately related to these specific ways of approaching the world and these presumptions about what a useful measure might entail. DeSeCo's project of identifying key competencies will inevitably find itself in a similar position. It is not any competent individual that is being imagined, but at the very least one able to function successfully in the liberal democracies and capitalist economic regimes that characterize the OECD nations.

First and foremost, such a world is one in which the individual is posited as the fundamental unit of analysis. One could readily imagine other situations where some sort of group, or community, or larger organizational unit would constitute the onto-logical reality of primary importance, but interest in collectivities of this sort is not much in evidence within the DeSeCo Project. Such a choice has important implica-tions in at least one respect, for it seems to mitigate against giving much attention to an approach to competency of much current interest within the fields of philosophy, cognitive science, and science studies: distributed competence. Within this analytic framework, it is not the individual that matters so much as the system of individuals and non-human objects that together produce the complex competencies characteris-tic of the contemporary world (see, for example, Hutchins, 1995). It is argued, for example, that the competencies necessary to produce this printed volume are not situated in the head of any single individual, but rather distributed in the bodies of authors, the capabilities of printing apparatuses, the skills of typesetters, the accuracy of spell checkers, the knowledge of editors, etc.

Historically, of course, one of the solutions to the problem of individual compe-tency has been to move it elsewhere, into machines and technology, into institutions, into normativities. That can be seen everywhere from the de-skilling within industrial technologies in the 19th century, to a whole range of ways in which computers now take on routine tasks that were once performed by copy editors, statisticians, or the mail service, to the functional differentiation of the modern corporation when com-pared with the jack-of-all-trades individual entrepreneur, to the early modern prolif-eration of etiquette manuals to enhance success in polite society. Viewed over time, competencies appear to be neither static nor necessarily inherent in individual human agents. This does not mean that the possession of particular competencies in particu-lar social settings is valueless; clearly that is not the case. But it does suggest that there are many possible kinds of solutions to the problem of a perceived lack of com-petency, and that the re-training of individuals in that competency is only one. If competencies are understood to be transmutable and mobile, social as well as indi-vidual, embodied in artifacts as well as human bodies, then the tasks of identifying, locating, isolating, and enhancing them cannot become, as it did with IQ testing, solely a matter of focusing on the isolated individual. From this broader perspective, competency may be something that exists not at all in a given person, but only in a social field. Thus any particular individual may manifest only some small part of it, but together a group of individuals may prove able to manage very complicated forms of competency. How this version of competency can be squared with the rights-bearing autonomous individual postulated by the liberal Western democracies and the DeSeCo mandate, however, is not immediately apparent.

Equally important to consider in terms of the social context that gets built into constructs such as key competencies is the pervasive tension in the Western democ-racies between celebrations of egalitarianism in one form or another and the realities of the existence of high degrees of social stratification. On the one hand, as the DeSeCo initiative itself testifies, all of the OECD nations are firmly committed to expanding opportunities within every sector of the citizenry; on the other hand, both within educational systems and life in general, people are being trained for particular functional places in highly differentiated economic and social systems. Again, the history of IQ is apposite. In one sense, intelligence testing embodies and reproduces a particular form of equality: all test takers are measured against the same standard, regardless of race, gender, class, or any other specifics of their background, and one of the justifications for testing was that it would replace arbitrary and subjective judgments open to the influence of such characteristics with an objective determination able to reveal the underlying biological reality of those being tested. And for some, testing did work that way, opening educational and employment opportunities that would otherwise have been closed to them. At the same time, however, IQ testing was also used, as is well known, to rationalize and strengthen systems of occupational and social stratification already in place, by suggesting that different levels of intelligence did and should translate into different educational opportunities and different occupational niches, as well as into more pervasive forms of discrimination.

Aware of this history, it could justly be argued that the DeSeCo Project's focus on competencies that can be acquired is precisely an attempt to avoid some of the pernicious aspects of defining human capabilities associated with IQ. Nonetheless, the mere invocation of words such as "equality" may not begin to do justice to the complications of a world in which, without fundamental changes, some people will inevitably be in lower classes than others. Whose competencies will matter, and what kind of world are these competencies meant to prepare them for? Will these competencies include those fundamental to challenging and changing the social landscape, or will they, as in the case of IQ, in the end be those that reproduce that world, that world whose analysis and measure gave rise to them in the first place?

In this vein, it might be worthwhile to consider figures such as that notorious, irascible 19th century American crank, Henry David Thoreau.[4] He and the many others of his ilk are relevant as reminders of a kind of person who, while not marginalized on economic or social grounds, nonetheless does not fit the normativities and competencies that have been laid out as socially most desirable, and indeed who may see their roles precisely to be one of criticizing the complacencies of their middle-class "competent" fellow countrymen and countrywomen. They bring to the fore the question of where the crank is likely to fit in the definitions of competency that DeSeCo is trying to develop. Can people who are deeply idiosyncratic be accommodated within models that are, by and large, attempting to acculturate the run of the population to particular regimes of truth and power and economics? Are they to be tolerated, ignored, or even obliterated, and what might happen if such outside perspectives as they represent are somehow lost? Many would argue that the most unsettling ideas and those that do the most to remake the future, come not from the center of a culture, but from its periphery. How will that periphery be taken into account, sustained, and even nourished in the project of determining norms of competency designed to help individuals adapt to particular social realities? It may well be, for example, a very important skill for individuals living in the modern interdependent cultures of the OECD nations to be able to work with each other in groups. But is

---

[4] Thoreau, like French Enlightenment writer Jean-Jacques Rousseau, was famous for his rejection of contemporary society in favor of the "purity" of nature. He was the author, among other works, of *Walden, or Life in the Woods* (1854).

someone like Thoreau, who refuses that competency, then to be deemed incompetent, or in need of further training? And if not, then how will it be decided who gets provided with what range of possibilities?

Changing the Social Landscape

This suggests the fourth and final observation to be drawn from the story of IQ and its instruments, which concerns the impact that defining key competencies might have once the work is done to put and keep them in place. If the history of intelligence testing shows nothing else, it surely demonstrates that successfully and persuasively identifying and measuring a human competency is unlikely to be a socially neutral activity. A number of the consequences that IQ testing has had on the societies that have adopted it have already been pointed out. Individuals' and groups' horizons of opportunities have been altered, educational systems have been rationalized according to its logic, justifications for political and social discriminations have been refashioned to incorporate its presumptions, and conceptions of the nature of human abilities have been reformulated in the light of its methods. Perhaps more prosaically, intelligence itself also came to be transformed, and in a sense flattened out, as the range of competing ways in which the mind was understood at the turn of the century largely gave way, especially in the United States, to quantitative, unidimensional IQ.

It is important to emphasize this power to reshape what people think and how they live not to dissuade the DeSeCo leaders from undertaking their project, but to remind them that there will inevitably be far-reaching and long-term consequences of their efforts, and that it is crucial to try and anticipate some of those consequences. Certainly the scope of the project and the number of important researchers enrolled in it almost ensures that whatever gets demarcated a key competency and however it is defined, that articulation will carry enormous weight in the field as a whole. It is also extremely likely that the DeSeCo understanding of those competencies, especially as embodied in instruments of measurement and league tables for international comparisons, will have significant influence on policy makers throughout the OECD and beyond. This suggests the need for a certain modesty in the findings proposed by DeSeCo. If there is one charge that could easily be leveled against the IQ testers in specific and social and human scientists more generally in the early 20th century, it is that their, at times, overly confident belief in the power of science to solve social problems left them too often blind to alternative interpretations of the phenomena they were observing and to the social effects that their work was actually having.

Among a number of possible strategies to keep this tendency toward hubris in check, two stand out. First, it may be wise to refuse to seek global, one-size-fits-all solutions to the question of necessary competencies for the new millennium. Partial, local, and only somewhat transportable competencies, while perhaps not as elegant nor as accommodating of comparisons as their universalistic cousins, may allow for a textured approach to life in this variegated world that has its own kind of power, while limiting some of the damage possible from all-encompassing schema developed in global cultural centers.[5] And second, it is critical to listen to voices outside of the relevant expert communities, and to do so at every stage of the project. While academics and professionals have much to offer, so too do the people who live and work in the world that shapes the competencies examined by the DeSeCo Project. What skills do they feel that they lack? What ones do they wish that they had? What ones do they think they acquire well on their own? And how do they think that any program attempting to enhance competencies should be implemented? Going beyond what experts define as the nature and problems of competence to what the people involved think themselves as they are living through their own complicated and very localized lives, while by no means a panacea, may at least restrain some of the excesses to which programs such as DeSeCo's are prone.

Concluding Observations: Toward an Historical Perspective on the Notion of Competence

The story of IQ and its tests has cast a long shadow over the project of defining capabilities in the human sciences. On the one hand, its model of a quantified measure of a basic human attribute that can be applied across cultures, continents, and time has proven enormously influential and continues to beckon as a kind of paradigm for a range of the social sciences. On the other hand, the history of the abuses that have been perceived to be carried out in its name have convinced many that the attempt to define and isolate fundamental human characteristics is inherently problematic, if not simply racist, sexist, and ethnocentric. As a result, universalistic pronouncements about human nature have largely fallen into disfavor, while the quest for interpersonal standards of measurement and comparison remains unabated. It is as part of the response to this history of potential abuse that the DeSeCo Project may be best understood. DeSeCo's focus on a language of competencies marks a decided rejection of the global presumptions that undergirded the articulation of IQ in favor of a move to a construct that implies a more limited and local conception of what people need to be successful. At the same time, DeSeCo's commitment to defining objective and measurable skills that will enhance the prospects of adapting successfully to 21st century life marks its continued belief that interpersonal and transsocietal norms of learning and development are both possible and desirable. One of the most vexing challenges for the project will be to articulate competencies that can be general enough to be used throughout the OECD and beyond while not losing the texture of the local and specific, the sense that competencies live in particular places and are for particular circumstances, and that attempts to overly universalize bring along the potential for grave consequences.

This need for humility, for want of a better word, on the part of DeSeCo concerning what can and ought to be put into place is underscored by a reading of the history of attempts to establish broadly agreed-on competencies at all. Examined from the

---

[5] For a theoretical exploration of this approach, see Haraway, 1991.

perspective of the last hundred years, what one would not see is a static process of identifying and then refining a set of human attributes deemed fundamental to issues of competency. Rather, whatever else is clear, it is certainly the case that the determinations of what key competencies are and what they are presumed able to do can change dramatically over time. No set of definitions will ever remain vital if cast into stone, and none will be deemed successful if it fails to incorporate into its very core a sense of dynamism, the ability to change as new circumstances dictate. The history of the use, misuse, rise, fall, and rise again of intelligence and its tests clearly testifies to the volatile nature of such determinations. It suggests that a project that took account of history seriously would, if nothing else, be sure that it saw all determinations and articulations of competencies as provisional, momentary, and continually open to modification. When the time for measurement comes, the trick will be to create instruments that can reveal such competencies without reifying them.

References

Cravens, H. (1978). *The triumph of evolution: American scientists and the heredity-environment controversy, 1900-1941*. Philadelphia: University of Pennsylvania Press.

Degler, C. N. (1991). *In search of human nature: The decline and revival of Darwinism in American social thought*. New York: Oxford University Press

Gould, S. J. (1978). *The mismeasure of man*. New York: Norton.

Haraway, D. J. (1991). Situated knowledges: The science question in feminism and the privilege of partial perspective. In D. J. Haraway (Ed.), *Simians, cyborgs, and women: The reinvention of nature* (pp. 183–201). New York: Routledge.

Hawkins, M. (1997). *Social Darwinism in European and American thought, 1860-1945*. Cambridge: Cambridge University Press.

Herrnstein, R. J., & Murray, C. (1994). *The bell curve: Intelligence and class structure in American life*. New York: The Free Press.

Hutchins, E. (1995). *Cognition in the wild*. Cambridge, MA: MIT Press.

Jacoby, R., & Glauberman, N. (Eds.). (1995). *The bell curve: History, documents, opinions*. New York: Times Books.

Kevles, D. J. (1986). *In the name of eugenics: Genetics and the uses of human heredity*. Berkley, CA: University of California Press.

Kraut, A. M. (1994). *Silent travelers: Germs, genes, and the "immigrant menace"*. New York: Basic Books.

Nye, R. A. (1984). *Crime, madness, & politics in modern France: The medical concept of national decline*. Princeton, NJ: Princeton University Press.

Pick, D. (1989). *Faces of degeneration: A European disorder, c.1848-c.1918*. Cambridge: Cambridge University Press.

Rafter, N. H. (1997). *Creating born criminals*. Urbana, IL: University of Illinois Press.

Schaffer, S. (1992). Late Victorian metrology and its instrumentation: A manufactory of ohms. In R. Bud & S. E. Cozzens (Eds.), *Invisible connections: Instruments, institutions, and science* (p. 23–56). Bellingham: SPIE.

Stepan, N. L. (1991). *"The hour of eugenics": Race, gender, and nation in Latin America*. Ithaca, NY: Cornell University Press.

Chapter 3

Concept of Competence: A Conceptual Clarification

Franz E. Weinert

Definitions of the Concept of "Competence"

In general, we know what the terms "competence," "competencies," "competent behavior," or "competent person" mean, without being able to precisely define or clearly differentiate them. The same can be said for terms such as "ability," "qualification," "skill," or "effectiveness." The use of these terms as synonyms is reflected in dictionary entries as well. For example, competence is defined in Webster's dictionary as "fitness or ability." Words given as synonyms or related terms are "capability," "capacity," "efficiency," "proficiency," and "skill."

If one considers the Latin roots and historical variations in meanings ascribed to competence, it is also understood to mean "cognizance" or "responsibility." This concept of competence is and has been used in very specific and arbitrary manners in biology, immunology, jurisprudence, and in some other academic disciplines, which will not be further elaborated in this chapter.

Restricting our focus to the use of the term competence in philosophy, psychology, linguistics, sociology, political science, and economics still yields a wide variety of definitions. Nonetheless, in all of these disciplines, competence is interpreted as a roughly specialized system of abilities, proficiencies, or skills that are necessary or sufficient to reach a specific goal. This can be applied to individual dispositions or to the distribution of such dispositions within a social group or an institution (e.g., a firm).

Over the last few decades, competence has become a fashionable term with a vague meaning not only in public use, but also in many social sciences. One could even refer to a conceptual "inflation," where the lack of a precise definition is accompanied by considerable surplus meanings. A typical illustration of this can be found in a report given by an advisory committee for technology and innovation appointed by the German Chancellor. The report states:

> Competence can generally be understood as knowledge times experience times power of judgment. Knowledge is the necessary foundation of competence, and experience is the habitual way one deals with acquired and continuously changing knowledge. Power of judgment is a criterion for the independence of knowl-

edge and its use. Thus, competence is always more than just knowledge or just experience (BMBF, 1998, p. 10).

Specific competencies mentioned in this report included: economic, technological, technical, and methodological competencies; social competencies; creativity and innovation skills; and mobility and flexibility combined with persistence, reliability, and precision. In some respects this report is typical of many current publications. Although the term competence is used to refer both to high-achieving individuals and successful social groups that master specific tasks and reach important goals, it is at the same time always concerned with the necessary learning dispositions that are available to individuals and/or the members of social groups and that must be used to solve demanding problems.

The variety of meanings given to the concept of competence is seen not only in its many uses, but also in the construction of terminology to express competence, such as media competence, business competence, traffic competence, age competence, and also cognitive, social, motivational, personal, etc., competencies. It is not possible to discern or infer a coherent theory out of these many uses. There is no basis for a theoretically grounded definition or classification from the seemingly endless inventory of the ways the term competence is used.

One will be equally disappointed if one restricts the search for a common core to only scientifically based definitions of the concept of competence. There are many different theoretical approaches, but no single common conceptual framework. What follows is a descriptive list of seven different ways in which competence has been defined, described, or interpreted theoretically.

General Cognitive Competencies

Competencies can be understood as cognitive abilities and skills. These include all of an individual's mental resources that are used to master demanding tasks in different content domains, to acquire necessary declarative and procedural knowledge, and to achieve good performance. Cognitive competencies can be conceived as general intellectual abilities with strong and stable inter-individual differences.

The prototypical approaches that focus on general competencies include psychometric models of human intelligence, information processing models, and the Piagetian model of cognitive development. Psychometric approaches understand intelligence (competence) as a system of more or less content and context-free abilities and aptitudes (Carroll, 1993). They provide the cognitive prerequisites for purposeful action, good reasoning, successful learning, and effective interaction with the environment. In information-processing approaches, intelligence (or general competence) is understood as an "information processing machine" whose general system features (i.e., processing speed, working memory capacity, or processing capacity) allow it to acquire an endless variety of specific knowledge and skills. The Piagetian approach also assumes general cognitive competencies. However, in this ontogenetical view, psychologically organized adaptation processes also take a central role. They engender a universal sequence of developmental stages that lead to increasingly flexible and abstract knowledge and action competencies (Piaget, 1947; see also Parrat-Dayan & Tryphon, 1998), which are also adaptive to concrete environmental conditions (Cellérier & Inhelder, 1992).

Specialized Cognitive Competencies

A second theoretical approach focuses on the categorization and characterization of specialized cognitive competencies. Specialized cognitive competencies refer to clusters of cognitive prerequisites that must be available for an individual to perform well in a particular content area (e.g., chess playing, piano playing, automobile driving, mathematical problem-solving, trouble-shooting in complex systems, etc.). The domains of specialized competencies can be very narrowly defined (e.g., chess competency) or very broadly and openly defined (e.g., diagnostic competencies in medicine).

We know, at least in the case of excellent chess players, that neither general memory capacity, extreme intelligence, nor excellent problem-solving skills are decisive for high performance. Rather, the cognitive competence of chess masters and club players, in contrast with beginners, stems from a system of specialized skills and routines, based on thousands of chess configurations stored in memory ("memory chunks"). This is an example of a *learned competency* that of course may itself depend on greater or lesser abilities in acquiring this expertise (Charness, 1991; Gruber, 1991).

Although the surface performance skills and the cognitive prerequisites for chess are quite different from those for other areas of expertise (e.g., medical diagnosis), the types of necessary underlying cognitive competencies are comparable. For example, in both chess and medical expertise, mental networks of content-specific knowledge, skills, and routines are more important than general cognitive abilities. These specialized competencies require long-term learning, broad experience, deep understanding of the topic, and automatic action routines that must be controlled at a high level of awareness (Patel, Kaufman, & Magder, 1996).

An overview of research on performance-specific concepts of cognitive competencies suggests that this approach has strong advantages over ability-centered definitions of competencies because of its theoretical base and pragmatic applications. In particular, the performance-specific approach allows scientific analyses of competencies to consider the necessary learning prerequisites for development of expertise (Leplat, 1997).

The Competence-Performance Model

One of the most influential theoretical paradigms in competence research is derived from the distinction between competence and performance used by the linguist Noam Chomsky (1980). Chomsky understood linguistic competency as a universal, inherited, modularized ability to acquire the mother tongue. A limited system of inborn linguistic principles, abstract rules, and basic cognitive elements (competencies) combined with a specific learning process allows each normal human to acquire the mother tongue, including the ability to create and understand an infinite variety of unique, grammatically correct sentences (performance). Linguistic competency thus underlies creative, rule-based language learning and language use.

Chomsky's linguistic competence model, admired and cited, but also criticized and challenged, is frequently used in the cognitive sciences, especially in psycholinguistics and in cognitive developmental psychology. In addition, many models have incorporated single components of the competence-performance model, including the ideas of: (1) domain specificity, (2) an inborn system of modularized principles and rules, (3) rule-based learning, and (4) performance whose quality depends not only on universal principles, but also on learning experiences and the learner's/actor's current situational context.

Across linguistics, philosophy, and psycholinguistics, the use of the terms related to "competence" has acquired a range of meanings differing somewhat from Chomsky's original theoretical meaning, and has been applied to an expanded set of phenomena. In theories of speech, this broader concept was seen as a semantic and pragmatic change in the definition of linguistic competence, characterized as an integration of psychological, sociological, and ethnological approaches (Hymes, 1967). Especially influential examples are theories of communicative competencies and communicative acts (Habermas, 1971, 1981; Wunderlich, 1971). In a similar theoretical context, further variants of the competence concept include hermeneutic-analytical, rhetorically persuasive, poetic, and aesthetic competencies.

Currently, the concept of competence has been expanded even further with concepts such as "social competencies" and "emotional competencies" (Weber & Westmeyer, 1998). In these examples, "competence" has replaced an earlier, intelligence-based concept (social intelligence: Cantor & Kihlstrom, 1987; emotional intelligence: Goleman, 1995). Weber and Westmeyer (1998) suggest using "social" or "emotional competence" rather than "social" or "emotional intelligence" because "these concepts have...the advantage that assessments can be carried out in a concrete, substantive context and measures can be described, thus allowing statements about what competence is" (p. 4).

Chomsky's basic dual model of linguistic competence and performance has been generalized extensively in modern developmental psychology to characterize the ontogenesis of numerical, spatial, physical, social-psychological and other areas of domain-specific knowledge.

Modifications of the Competence-Performance Model

The competence-performance approach was energized with the postulation of a competence-moderator-performance model (Overton, 1985). In this model, it is assumed that the relation between competence and performance is moderated by other variables, for example, cognitive style, memory capacity, familiarity with the task situation, and other personal variables.

Within developmental psychology, another modification of the competence-performance model, even more influential than Overton's moderator model, involved a conceptual differentiation of competence into three components (see Gelman & Meck, 1992; Gelman & Greeno, 1989; Greeno, Riley, & Gelman; 1984, and also Sophian, 1997). These three components are:

- conceptual competence, which refers to Chomskian rule-based, abstract knowledge about an entire domain;

- procedural competence, which refers to the availability of procedures and skills that are necessary to apply conceptual competencies in concrete situations;

- performance competence, which refer to having all the skills required to evaluate the relevant features of a problem, so that suitable solution strategies can be selected and used.

Greeno, Riley, and Gelman (1984) refer appropriately to the last two components of competence as a "logic of planning."

This last competence-performance model, enriched with a differential psychology perspective, has been criticized for focusing only on cognitive aspects, and not on the socially transmitted, individual perspective of the actor (Elbers, 1991). Catherine Sophian (1997) commented that this model exclusively addresses the influences of competencies on performance (behavior), and ignores the shaping of competencies through performance.

Cognitive Competencies and Motivational Action Tendencies

The close relation between cognitive competencies and motivational action tendencies was "discovered" by R. H. White in 1959. In an influential article, he defined competence as an "effective interaction (of the individual) with the environment... I shall argue that it is necessary to make competence a motivational concept, that there is a competence motivation as well as competence in its more familiar sense of achieved capacity" (White, 1959, p. 317).

White postulated an intrinsic need to deal effectively with the environment (see MacTurk & Morgan, 1995). This need is characterized by an "effectance motivation" that is closely tied to personal "feelings of efficacy." There are a variety of self-concept models that span the continuum between adopting more cognitive or more motivational definitions of competence. These models concern knowledge and beliefs about one's own learning and performance. An individual's system of knowledge and beliefs is formed through experience with one's own competence in achievement situations, and influences performance and achievement through expectations, attitudes, and interpretative schemata. For all models of the self-concept, it is important to separate concepts at the trait level (personal self-concept as a stable, relatively persistent belief-value system) and the state level (current, task-specific self-concept).

Hierarchical models of the self-concept (e.g., Epstein, 1973) differentiate the concept according to levels of generality. The top level is a highly generalized, overall self-concept (e.g., "a highly self-confident person"). The next level concerns self-evaluation in different, but still general areas (e.g., self-concepts of physical attractiveness, social standing, intellectual capacity, personal achievement, and morality). Lower levels include further differentiation. For example, the self-concept of achievement is comprised of more specific self-concepts for different performance domains such as mathematics, foreign languages, sports, rhetoric, and so on. Subordinate to these are yet more finely differentiated self-evaluations for specific competencies within a performance domain (e.g., arithmetic versus geometry versus calculus in the mathematics domain, or persuasive rhetoric versus story telling versus public speaking in the speech domain).

In addition to the self-concept, an especially influential theoretical construct for describing subjective experience of personal competence, there are two other constructs that are relevant to the analysis of competencies and competency use. These are the achievement motive and personal control beliefs. Important features of achievement motivation include the strength, direction, and origins of an individual's need to experience competence through excellent performance. This need can be inferred from hope of success or fear of failure, and from intrinsically or extrinsically caused motivational states. Stable personal control beliefs include the extent to which the self is experienced as the cause of actions and action results, and attributional style – the personal explanations for success and failure.

Objective and Subjective Competence Concepts

Analogous to the general differentiation of competencies into cognitive and motivational aspects, Sembill (1992) distinguished between objective competence (performance and performance dispositions that can be measured with standardized scales and tests) and subjective competence (subjective assessment of performance-relevant abilities and skills needed to master tasks and solve problems – for a comprehensive overview, see Sternberg & Kolligian, 1990).

The concept of subjective competence can be further differentiated into:

- heuristic competence (a generalized expectancy system concerning the effectiveness of one's abilities across different situations – generalized self- concept);

- epistemological competence (beliefs and confidence that one possesses domain-specific skills and knowledge to master tasks and problems within a specific content domain – domain-specific self-concept);

- actualized competence (momentarily experienced, subjective self-confidence that one possesses the abilities, knowledge, and skills believed necessary for success in a concrete learning or performance situation – current or dynamic actualized self-concept) (Stäudel, 1987).

Action Competence

Unlike conceptualizations of competence that accentuate either cognitive or motivational aspects, action competence includes all those cognitive, motivational, and social prerequisites necessary and/or available for successful learning and action. The concept of action competence has been applied especially in the analysis of the necessary and sufficient conditions for success in meeting task, goal, and success criteria in selected fields of action. The following components are frequently included in action competence models:

- general problem-solving ability

- critical thinking skills

- domain-general and domain-specific knowledge

- realistic, positive self-confidence

- social competencies

The theoretical construct of action competence comprehensively combines those intellectual abilities, content-specific knowledge, cognitive skills, domain-specific strategies, routines and subroutines, motivational tendencies, volitional control systems, personal value orientations, and social behaviors into a complex system. Together, this system specifies the prerequisites required to fulfill the demands of a particular professional position, of a social role, or a personal project (Boyatzis, 1982; Lévy-Leboyer, 1996).

In this theoretical perspective, the concept of action competence is primarily or exclusively attributed to individuals – which is the usual psychological perspective. Other approaches to concepts of action competence are more socially centered. What this means is not only individual social knowledge, but team skills. In the last few decades, there has been increased attention to group competencies and institutional competencies, especially in sociology, ethnology, and economics. Performance demands and goals are set for social groups, teams, firms, communities, states, and cultures, as well as for individuals. The issues addressed from this perspective include asking which competencies must be available to all members of a social group, an institution, or a society, and which competencies can be complementarily available. In this approach as well, competencies are usually goal- or task-specific and include team competencies, social attitudes, appropriate habits and belief-value systems, as well as cognitive expertise.

Key Competencies

Similar terms such as key competencies, core competencies, key qualifications, and core skills have recently become popular in the social sciences and in educational policy. The concept of key competence is, however, no less vague or ambiguous than the concept of competence. Clear and well-reasoned distinctions between the two concepts are either arbitrary or nonexistent. Within the last few years over 650 different key competencies have been suggested just in the German literature on occupational training. These competencies range from such constructs as creativity, logical thinking, problem-solving skills, achievement readiness, independence, and concentration abilities, to foreign language skills, communication skills, and media competencies.

There are two motivations for the search for key competencies: (a) the well-founded assumption that competencies acquired in school and vocational settings are learned and used in context-specific ways (e.g., within a discipline, within a vocation, within a company), and (b) most activities over the life course take place in a variety of social and vocational contexts. This has led to the search for context-independent key competencies that are equivalent in their use and effectiveness across different institutions, different tasks, and under varying demand conditions.

Why is the concept of key competence so attractive? The term generally refers to multifunctional and transdisciplinary competencies that are useful for achieving many important goals, mastering different tasks, and acting in unfamiliar situations. For many teachers and politicians there is also the promise that a curriculum overloaded with the many competencies necessary for life in the modern world can be reduced by transmitting a limited number of key competencies.

Regardless of how much academics and practitioners agree on the formal criteria for defining key competencies, there are large disagreements about which competencies should be classified as key competencies. If one considers the tasks and demands that most people face today in modern societies and whose mastery brings personal success, one can identify the following as frequently mentioned key competencies in the available literature: oral and written mastery of the mother tongue; mathematical knowledge; reading competency for rapid acquisition and correct processing of written information; mastery of at least one foreign language; media competence; independent learning strategies; social competencies; and divergent thinking, critical judgments, and self-criticism. If one identifies and defines key competencies within a normative-philosophical and socially critical frame of reference, one derives for instance those key competencies characterized by Canto-Sperber and Dupuy (Chapter 4).

Regardless of whether one chooses a reality-based or a philosophical-normative perspective to identify key competencies, there are eight issues which always require attention:

- Key competencies follow no strict formal definitional constraints. Competencies and key competencies are defined at very different levels of universality, generality, and abstraction. It is often noted that very abstractly formulated key competencies need to be specified into subcompetencies. Such scientific plans have often failed in psychology, however. The underlying multilevel models can be logically reconstructed, but not validated psychologically. The different degrees of abstraction mean, therefore, a fundamental asymmetry in competence research – high abstraction: intellectually brilliant, pragmatically hopeless; low abstraction: pragmatically useful, intellectually unsatisfactory.

- A related but independent question concerns the frame of reference within which key competencies are defined. Philosophical ideas about the nature of human-kind, or ideas about the good life and a desired society, or expectancies about present human life and social demands, may be used to identify competencies and key competencies. There is a strong danger that the necessary skills for a success-ful everyday life, social and personal effectiveness, or professional success will be trivialized when compared to normatively anchored universal competencies. Nevertheless, if one wants to go beyond an individual's adaptation level to the world of today with its limited possibilities of further development, and change the world by providing people with the appropriate competencies, it is necessary to choose a normative starting point, and not an empirical one, when defining key competencies.

- Key competencies are always complex systems of knowledge, beliefs, and action tendencies, that are constructed from well-organized domain-specific expertise, basic skills, generalized attitudes, and converging cognitive styles. Without at least hypothetical structure and process analyses, key competencies can easily become catchwords which refer only to desired states.

- Frequently cognitive abilities, cognitive styles, and emotional qualities are de-scribed as constituent components of key competencies. There are large individ-ual differences in these psychological features and it is doubtful whether they can be modified through learning, and to what degree; whether deficits can be com-pensated for; and whether people can indeed change in the required direction. If this question remains unasked or unanswered, there is a danger that an academic discussion of key competencies will trivialize the already enormous inter-individual differences and could lead to a surge of individual discrimination.

- Frequently dangerous illusions about the possibilities and limitations of sociali-zation and education are tied to the concept of key competence. Many scholars suggest to an incredulous public that to learn a lot it will no longer be necessary to acquire a large amount of world knowledge, expertise, and competencies or to work hard. In the future, it will be sufficient, so the argument goes, to possess some key competencies, to have learned how to learn, and to acquire some media competence so that necessary information can be acquired at any time in an elec-tronic form. This will create an attitude of self-confidence that one can always appropriately and creatively react to all difficult situations in life. Modern cogni-tive psychology would tell us that such an educational model is not only a utopia, but also mostly nonsense.

- The more general a competency or strategy (i.e., the greater the range of different types of situations to which it applies), the smaller the contribution of this com-petency or strategy to the solution of demanding problems. Over the last decades, the cognitive sciences have convincingly demonstrated that content-specific skills and knowledge play a crucial role in solving difficult tasks. Generally, key com-petencies cannot adequately compensate for a lack of content-specific competen-cies (Weinert, 1998).

- In the lively discussions of the meaning of systematic versus situated cognitions, it has been demonstrated that general competencies have virtually no practical utility alone. Rather, specific knowledge, embedded in experience, is required to successfully implement available competencies for solving specific practical problems.

- For many key competencies, the question is whether they can be acquired through planned instructional programs, and how. A typical example is critical thinking: although there are special training programs for this key competency (Halpern, 1998), their construction and efficiency remain scientifically controversial.

Metacompetencies

Although frequently subsumed under the concept of key competence, it is important to separate the concept of metacompetence on theoretical and practical grounds. Spinoza (1632–1677) used a sophisticated formulation to remark that to know something also means to know what one knows. This captures the everyday experience that people are more or less aware of what they know and what they do not know; they know their own intellectual strengths and weaknesses; and they know what to do to use available skills and knowledge to solve a variety of tasks, to acquire missing skills, or to judge from the start that there are no chances of success in solving a specific task. Further, not only can we estimate our own performance possibilities and necessary prerequisites, but we can also use these "naive" judgments to guide our actions. This knowledge about knowledge is called metaknowledge, and the ability to judge the availability, use, and learnability of personal competencies is called metacompetence (Nelson & Narens, 1990).

Better learning and performance does not arise just from knowing and doing more. Given similar conditions, those who know more about themselves and who are able to put this knowledge to practical use are likely to perform better than others when solving difficult tasks and problems. Based on this insight, research on metacognition, especially studies of the development of metacognitive competencies in childhood and adolescence, has received a great deal of scholarly attention over the last decades. A short summary of the research results shows the following:

- One basic prerequisite for the acquisition of metacompetencies is the ability to introspect about one's own cognitive processes and products, available from the third year of life on and increasing with age. Introspection is the psychological condition that allows the awareness of ongoing processes of learning, memory and thinking, personal experience about available knowledge and abilities, and the generation of increasing "metaknowledge" about necessary, available, missing, or currently not possible personal competencies. The natural growth of experience-dependent metacompetencies does, however, require school-based support. The observation of one's own and others' learning during instruction, learning-related demands and feedback from the teacher, and the transmission of effective problem-solving strategies during instruction considerably enriches children's metacognitive knowledge.

- Metacognitive knowledge, combined with personal awareness of actions, allows diverse forms of unconscious but goal-directed behavioral control. Thus, in addition to declarative metaknowledge, there is the development of procedural metacompetencies. These include automatized but potentially conscious skills in planning, initiating, monitoring, evaluating, and manipulating one's own cognitive processes and task-specific actions.

- Metacognitive competencies include both declarative and procedural metaknowledge. Declarative metacompetencies include experience and knowledge about different task difficulties; knowledge about one's own abilities, talents, skills, and cognitive deficits; knowledge about learning, problem-solving, and action regularities; knowledge about effective strategies for learning, remembering, problem-solving, and trouble-shooting; and knowledge about techniques for mastering diverse tasks with available cognitive competencies, compensating for missing knowledge, and for setting realistic goals (see also components of "successful intelligence" as described by Robert Sternberg, 1996). Procedural metacompetencies are necessary for using metacognitive knowledge and insight to optimize task-directed behavior. They include all those strategies for organizing tasks and problems to make them easier to solve (e.g., organizing a task into a meaningful structure; breaking a text into smaller units that are easier to encode; marking and underlining important points to make them easier to remember; constructing memory cues and using them later). They also include the use of effective cognitive aids and tools (e.g., graphics, pictures, analogies); the application of cognitive resources in task-relevant ways and at an appropriate level of difficulty; and the continual registration and evaluation of performance progress. To summarize, metacognitive competence is expertise about oneself as a knower, learner, and actor.

- Many empirical studies show that the quantity and quality of relevant metaknowledge affects learning, memory, and problem-solving performance more than chronological age, and is a better indicator of mental development in childhood or general intelligence in adulthood. There are also beneficial effects of metaknowledge on performance when this knowledge is not explicit, but available as tacit knowledge and can be measured only indirectly. At this point, we still do not know the cognitive mechanisms that are responsible for the relationship between metaknowledge and performance.

- Even a brief characterization of metacompetencies illustrates that the construct and related phenomena are very broad and diverse. To be able to use knowledge about one's own knowledge requires mastering many facts, incorporating a variety of diverse experiences, and acquiring different strategies, operations and problem-solving heuristics (see Nuthall, 1999). It also requires a realistic level of self-confidence. Although one can distinguish metaknowledge from motivational and volitional processes analytically, it is not possible to do so empirically in concrete tasks. This means that what we measure is always a conglomerate of metacognitive judgments, feelings of efficacy, and volitional control beliefs.

• The variety and number of metacognitive competencies and their variable relations to cognitive, motivational, and volitional variables are important causes for the failure of many metacognitive training programs. However, the phrase "learning to learn" is one of the hottest catch phrases in current educational theory and educational policy. The core of learning to learn is the acquisition of individual learning competency, that is, the ability to carry out self-guided learning (see Boekaerts, 1999). One set of prerequisites for this ability is declarative and procedural metacognition. However, the same rule holds for metacognitive processes as for key competencies: the more general a metastrategy, the lower its effectiveness in guiding concrete learning and thinking processes. Thus, it is necessary to acquire many specific metacognitive competencies for use in different domains. However, the available teaching and learning models underlying school practices have tended to fall short in realizing the goals of metacognitive competence acquisition. This is because teaching and learning focus on the products of learning (knowledge) and not on reflection about learning processes and their optimization (metacognition).

Difficulties in Conceptualizing Competence

Given the number and variety of ways in which competence has been defined, it is necessary to thoughtfully decide which aspects, constituents, and components are appropriate in order to use the concept theoretically and/or practically, and which can (or must!) be ignored. To facilitate this, this section will briefly describe ten problems that arise from different definitions of competence.

Identifying Cognitive Competencies

Competence and competencies should be understood primarily as the mental conditions necessary for cognitive, social, and vocational achievement.

Which cognitive competencies are there?

An exhaustive definition of competence would have to include all the intellectual abilities, content-specific knowledge, skills, strategies, metacognitions, and action routines that contribute to learning, problem-solving, and achieving, in various ways. Such a definition would mean that the concept of competence covered all of a person's cognitive resources, that is, all those mental conditions that underlie individual performance, intra-individual performance changes, and inter-individual performance differences at any given point in time. The advantage of such a broad definition is also its greatest disadvantage. One would be confronted with a problem not yet solved in the 100-year history of scientific psychology: a complementary classification and performance-specific integration of ability and knowledge. There is neither a theoretical nor a practical solution to this problem at this time.

Which cognitive competencies does one need to meet demands?

The answer to this question does not require considering all cognitive resources, but it does require a classification of those demands, problems, and tasks for which individuals need special cognitive prerequisites. A comprehensive psychological theory of human abilities (which does not exist!) is not necessary for this approach, nor is a comprehensive, sociological classification of environmental demands. What is required is a prototypical, typical, and/or specific characterization of classes of performance demands, performance criteria, and indicators of competencies. There is a good deal of scientific information available: curriculum theory, measurement models, task profiles for many vocations/positions (often defined as a set of action competencies), and task profiles for typical life situations (e.g., economic, administrative, and political activities; interaction with mass media; leisure behavior; travel expertise; social conventions; etc.) and for specific action fields (e.g., bank consultant, games such as chess, sales skills, etc.).

Intellectual Abilities

As already noted, many academics use the cognitive concept of competence to refer to primary intellectual abilities, rather than to learned skills, knowledge, and strategies. This view considers competence as a system of basic mental abilities. If one considers the most important characteristics of intelligence (genetic roots, a distribution of abilities according to a normal curve, stable inter-individual differences over long periods of life, independence of intellectual abilities, and domain-specific knowledge), it seems theoretically and pragmatically expedient to restrict the concept of competence to domain-specific learning and domain-specific skills, knowledge, and strategies.

David McClelland (1973) suggested such an approach, focused on learned, domain-specific competencies that can be changed by experience, in his article "Testing for Competence Rather Than for Intelligence." He criticized traditional uses of intelligence on conceptual and methodological grounds (arguing that they were of limited predictive validity, e.g., of long-term prediction of professional success). The scientific alternative he suggested was the measurement of specific competencies. He urged that tests to be developed be valid in the sense

> that scores on them change as the person grows in experience, wisdom, and ability to perform effectively on various tasks that life presents to him... Some of these competencies may be rather traditional cognitive ones involving reading, writing and calculation skills. Others should involve what traditionally have been called

personality variables, although it might better be considered competencies (McClelland, 1973, p. 8ff).

Examples of such variables included communication techniques, composure (response delay), moderate goal-setting, and the development of a sense of self.

McClelland's theoretical approach to competence was initially discussed and enthusiastically endorsed in the psychology literature (Spencer & Spencer, 1993), although it has since been substantially criticized. Two main problems are accentuated: (a) "A fundamental problem with McClelland's research was his failure to define the concept of competence" (Barrett & Depinet, 1991, p. 1019); (b) McClelland's suggested methodology of the "behavioral event interview" did not improve prediction of professional success over traditional intelligence tests. These criticisms, however, did not question the basic utility of defining competence as specific performance dispositions, because the use of the competence concept is often more to diagnose rather than predict individual learning success and inter-individual performance differences.

Relevance of Chomsky's Linguistic Theory

The conceptual tradition begun by Chomsky has had a strong theoretical impact. Competence is understood in a strict domain-specific (linguistic) sense as a universal, species-specific, and inherited ability to acquire and creatively use language, with little room for individual differences. This theoretical approach takes its scientific weight from the fact that it offers an explanation for why all children acquire their mother tongue in the first years of life, often despite a non-optimal speech environment. However, there is controversy in linguistics and developmental psychology about what count as valid and testable regularities for speech acquisition, what the relationship is between competence and performance, and how to interpret observable individual differences in the mastery of the mother tongue. Chomsky's conceptual framework is difficult to translate onto the acquisition of other psychological phenomena (knowledge acquisition, memory development, etc.), because the separation of competence and performance is relatively arbitrary. In addition, from a developmental psychological perspective, inter-individual differences in intra-individual change are the focus of scientific and pragmatic interest – a theme that is fundamentally ignored in the Chomskian tradition. Because of this and other reasons, the competence concept as proposed by Chomsky is not appropriate for non-linguistic purposes.

Influence of Context on Performance

Most definitions of competence are centered on the individual, and fail to consider the ecological, social, and task-specific contexts in which performance occurs. Fischer, Bullock, Rotenberg, and Raya (1993) questioned such a definition of competence as a general performance disposition, independent of context:

Skill level is a characteristic not only of a person but also of a context. People do not have competencies independent of context... Traditional conceptions of competence and performance fail because they treat competence as a fixed characteristic of the child, analogous to a bottle with a fixed capacity. Performance factors are seen as somehow interfering with this capacity... Our research shows that children do indeed have stable levels of competence when domain and degree of support are held constant across assessment contexts (p. 113f; see also Samurçay & Pastré, 1995).

Because systematic variation of assessment contexts is not possible or is extremely limited (e.g., one can vary task difficulty by embedding the same problem in familiar and less familiar contexts), finding an appropriate measurement procedure is not only a technical problem, but is a scientific precondition for the measurement of inter-individually and inter-institutionally comparable competencies through valid performance indicators.

Learning and Performance Domains

Frequently, domain-specific and domain-general competencies are not distinguished in scientific models of competence concepts. Because the cognitive sciences have not yet been successful in developing theoretically acceptable definitions, comprehensive taxonomies, or appropriate criteria to differentiate domains, it may not be useful to burden the definition of competence with a classification of learning and performance domains.

Which Competencies Should Be Included or Excluded?

The concept of competence refers not only to content-specific, task-specific, and/or demand-specific performance dispositions, but also to specific functional competencies (e.g., memory competencies, problem-solving competencies, and learning competencies). Although many learned skills and strategies as well as general intellectual abilities or capacities play a central role in such functional competencies, it is nonetheless better to exclude this class of cognitive functions from a pragmatically oriented definition of competence. There are two important reasons for this. First, mental functions are part of the basic cognitive apparatus and as such are not learned prerequisites for reaching specific performance goals. Second, although there are many training programs for learning to learn and general problem-solving skills, transfer of this training to content-specific tasks or novel contexts is questionable (Loarer, Chartier, Huteau & Lautrey, 1995).

There is no doubt that the decision to exclude general intellectual abilities (but not specific skills and strategies that may be related to them!) has pragmatic and theoretical advantages and disadvantages. In addition, it is difficult to draw the boundary between general cognitive functions and many cognitive competencies. Thus, the suggestion is to exclude such general thinking abilities or learning capacities, but not to exclude, for example, critical thinking competencies or competencies related to learning-specific tasks. What is important is to distinguish systems of primary cognitive abilities and learned, demand-specific, cognitive competencies.

Competence, Key Competence, and Metacompetence

The concepts of competence, key competence, and metacompetence are not clearly differentiated in everyday language or in scientific use. This is especially problematic in educational contexts because these three constructs are often used to describe different levels of content specificity and functional importance.

If one considers the entire spectrum of cognitive performances that are necessary, for example, for a member of a particular society, a student of a particular class, or for practicing a particular profession, one would need to construct an enormous number of necessary domain-specific competencies to cover each particular demand. The large number of learning objectives can be somewhat reduced:

- if an individual possesses knowledge, skills, and/or strategies that are appropriate to organize and reorganize available competencies in adaptive and flexible ways (metacompetencies);

- if an individual possesses competencies that can be successfully applied across a maximum number of different tasks (key competencies, core skills).

Objective and Subjective Approaches

An overview of the different definitions showed that the competence concept is used in scientific terminology

- for cognitive prerequisites for specific performances (objective approach)

- for performance-relevant motivational tendencies and expectations (subjective approach)

- for cognitive and motivational/volitional prerequisites for successful action and learning (combination of an objective and subjective approach in the concept of action competence)

- for referring to cognitive competencies and competence-related motivational attitudes and volitional skills

There are two primary reasons for tying cognitive and motivational attributes of competencies together conceptually:

- First, performance in specific situations depends on more than cognitive prerequisites – it also depends on motivational influences. If one wants to infer properties of individual competencies from inter-individual performance differences, one has to account for motivational factors by varying assessment conditions or by statistically controlling for motivational variables measured separately.

- Second, the long-term development of competencies (and expertise) depends to a great extent on the number of available learning opportunities and on the amount of deliberate practice (Ericsson, Krampe, & Tesch-Römer, 1993). Motivational incentives presented by the environment, stable individual attitudes, and volitional skills are important factors in this regard.

Measurements of Action Competence

It would not be useful to restrict attention to cognitive and metacognitive competencies if one is concerned with success in broad fields of action across a variety of tasks (e.g., in school, in social institutions, or in a profession). Thus, action competence includes an extensive configuration of cognitive and social competencies, motivational tendencies, and volitional skills. Comparative measurements of individual action competencies are, however, more complex. They require that suitable scales to measure relevant cognitive competencies and related motivational attitudes be available or constructed ad hoc. Any concept of action competence constructed from different components must then be validated with appropriate success criteria.

Longitudinal Studies

As noted above, competencies are understood to include learned cognitive performance dispositions and complementary metacognitive strategies for successful mastery of task demands. Individual competencies and inter-individual competence differences are always a confounded result of inherited talents, developmental regularities, general environmental influences, and the quantity and quality of specific learning opportunities. Even an approximate separation of the different causal influences is impossible without costly longitudinal studies.

However, an analysis of available longitudinal studies as well as available twin and adoption studies shows that arguments for a strong genetic determination ("nature") are just as untenable empirically as arguments for a strong environmental determination ("nurture"), regardless of how much these positions are popularized in the press:

- Hypotheses of a broad genetic determination of cognitive development (e.g., Jencks et al., 1972; Herrnstein & Murray, 1994) are strongly contradicted by available empirical findings – even though genetic differences strongly influence the development of cognitive competencies. The general effects of environmental differences are especially relevant to schooling: "There are important school effects...and...it is clear that school effects can be very substantial, indeed" (Rutter, 1983, p. 13).

- Hypotheses of radical environmentalism are also empirically untenable. This is especially true for the utopian expectation that all students can achieve the same level of learning if instructional quality is improved overall and if individual students are provided an optimal time to learn (Bloom, 1976).

Part of the lack of theoretical clarity and resulting controversy is due to the fact that two developmental phenomena with different regularities are frequently confused in the literature (Weinert & Schneider, 1999). One of these phenomena concerns intra-individual development of cognitive competencies, for which the intensity of cumulative learning, the quantity of learning opportunities, and instructional quality are important variables. The other phenomenon concerns the origins and regularities of inter-individual differences in the development of cognitive competencies. From about the fifth year of life on, there are large stabilities in these inter-individual differences that are caused by a mixture of (sometimes co-varying) genetic differences, differences in early childhood facilitation, and the application of the Matthew Principle to cumulative learning ("who already has, gets more") (Weinert & Helmke, 1997).

It is important to note that, in interpreting empirical results, general abilities and qualities of knowledge are increasingly intertwined over the course of the development of competencies throughout life (Sternberg, 1998; Weinert & Helmke, 1998).

All in all, the development of domain-specific competencies appears to be a process of cumulative learning, in which inter-individual differences in developmental speed and in performance level remain relatively stable, even under favorable social and instructional conditions. The concept of competence combines stable cognition abilities and personal features, different learning outcomes, belief-value-systems, and changeable attitudes in a mixed relation, so that it is often unclear what is normatively desirable and what can be realistically achieved.

Concluding Remarks

Clearly, the conceptual problems with competence, key competence, and metacompetence reside in the fields of the social sciences. I will thus defer from giving a unified definition and limit myself to some pragmatic conclusions concerning the use of the concept of competence.

First, this concept refers to the necessary prerequisites available to an individual or a group of individuals for successfully meeting complex demands. The (psychological) structure of a competency derives from the logical and psychological structure of the demands.

Second, it should be used when the necessary prerequisites for successfully meeting a demand are comprised of cognitive *and* (in many cases) motivational, ethical, volitional, and/or social components.

Third, the concept of competence implies that a sufficient degree of complexity is required to meet demands and tasks. Those prerequisites that can in principle be fully automatized can also be characterized as skills. The boundary between skill and competencies is fuzzy.

Fourth, learning processes are a necessary condition for the acquisition of prerequisites for successful mastery of complex demands. This means much must be learned, but cannot be directly taught.

Fifth, key competencies and metacompetencies should be conceptually differentiated. Key competencies should be invoked only when a competency is used to master many different, equally important demands of everyday, work-related, or social life. Metacompetence should only be used to refer to declarative or procedural knowledge about one's own competencies.

A consideration of these minimal criteria for a pragmatic definition of the concept of competence has practical rather than theoretical utility. I consider this utility to be sufficiently large to use the concept in the future.

There is, nevertheless, a strong danger that academia, policy, and education will find themselves helplessly lost in Paul Valery's Dilemma: Everything that is simple is theoretically false, everything that is complicated is pragmatically useless. Is there a successful strategy for joining together large normative strides with the necessarily small empirical steps required to develop a scientific basis for the concept of competence? At the moment, we do not know, but we should nonetheless give it a try.

References

Barrett, G. V., & Depinet, R. L. (1991). A reconsideration of testing for competence rather than for intelligence. *American Psychologist, 46*(10), 1012–1024.

Bloom, B. S. (1976). *Human characteristics and school learning*. New York: McGraw-Hill.

BMBF (1998). *Kompetenz im globalen Wettbewerb* (Competence in a global competition). Bonn: Bundesministerium für Bildung und Forschung.

Boekaerts, M. (1999). Self-regulated learning. *International Journal of Educational Research, 31*, 443–457.

Boyatzis, R. E. (1982). *The competent manager: A model for effective performance*. New York: John Wiley & Sons.

Cantor, N., & Kihlstrom, K. F. (1987). Social intelligence: The cognitive basis of personality. In P. Shaver (Ed.), *Review of Personality and Social Psychology* (Vol. 6, pp. 15–34). Beverly Hills, CA: Sage.

Carroll, J. B. (1993). *Human cognitive abilities: A survey of factor-analytic studies*. New York: Cambridge University Press.

Cellérier, G., & Inhelder, B. (1992). *Le cheminement des découvertes de l'enfant*. Paris: Delachaux.

Charness, N. (1991). Expertise in chess: The balance between knowledge and search. In K. A. Ericsson & J. Smith (Eds.), *Toward a general theory of expertise: Prospects and limits*. Cambridge: Cambridge University Press.

Chomsky, N. (1980). Rules and representations. *The Behavioral and Brain Sciences, 3*, 1–61.

Elbers, E. (1991). The development of competence and its social context. *Educational Psychology Review, 3*, 73–94.

Epstein, S. (1973). The self-concept revisited: Or a theory of a theory. *American Psychologist, 28*, 401–416.

Ericsson, K. A., Krampe, R. T., & Tesch-Römer, C. (1993). The role of deliberate practice in the acquisition of expert performance. *Psychological Review, 100*, 363–406.

Fischer, K. W., Bullock, D. H., Rotenberg, E. J., & Raya, P. (1993). The dynamics of competence: How context contributes directly to skill. In Wozniak, R. H. & Fischer, K. W. (Eds.), *Development in context: Acting and thinking in specific environments.* Hillsdale, NJ: Erlbaum.

Gelman, R., & Greeno, J. G. (1989). On the nature of competence: Principles for understanding in a domain. In L. B. Resnick (Ed.), *Knowing, learning, and instruction* (pp. 125–186). Hillsdale, NJ: Erlbaum.

Gelman, R., & Meck, E. (1992). Early principles aid initial but not later conceptions of number. In J. Bideaud, C. Meljac, & J. P. Fischer (Eds.), *Pathways to numbers: Children's developing numerical abilities* (pp. 171–189). Hillsdale, NJ: Erlbaum.

Goleman, D. (1995). *Emotional intelligence: Why it can matter more than IQ.* New York: Bantam Books.

Greeno, J. G., Riley, M. S., & Gelman, R. (1984). Conceptual competence and children's counting. *Cognitive Psychology, 16*, 94–143.

Gruber, H. (1991). Qualitative Aspekte von Expertise in Schach. Dissertation. Munich: Ludwig-Maximilians Universität.

Habermas, J. (1971). Vorbereiten der Bemerkungen zu einer Theorie der kommunikativen Kompetenz. In J. Habermas & N. Luhmann (Eds.), *Theorie der Gesellschaft oder Sozialtechnologie* (pp. 101–141). Frankfurt: Suhrkamp.

Habermas, J. (1981). *Theorie des kommunikativen Handelns* (Vol. 1 and 2). Frankfurt: Suhrkamp.

Halpern, D. (1998). Teaching critical thinking for transfer across domains. *American Psychologist, 53*, 449–455.

Herrnstein, R. J., & Murray, C. (1994). *The bell curve.* New York: The Free Press.

Hymes, D. (1967). Models of the interaction of language and social setting. *Journal of Social Issues, 23*, 8–28.

Jencks, C., Smith, M., Acland, H., Bane, M. J. Cohen, D., Gintis, H., Heyns, B., & Michelson, S. (1972). *Inequality.* New York: Basic Books.

Leplat, J. (1997). Regards sur l'activité en situation de travail. *Contribution à la psychologie ergonomique.* Paris: PUF.

Lévy-Leboyer, C. (1996). *La gestion des compétences.* Paris: Les Editions d'Organisation.

Loarer, E., Chartier, D., Huteau, M., & Lautrey, J. (1995). *Peut-on éduquer l'intelligence? L'évaluation des effets d'une méthode de remédiation cognitive.* Bern: Peter Lang.

MacTurk, R. H., & Morgan, G. A. (Eds.). (1995). *Mastery motivation: Origins, conceptualizations, and applications.* Norwood, NJ: Ablex.

McClelland, D. C. (1973). Testing for competence rather than for "intelligence." *American Psychologist, 28*, 1–14.

Nelson, T. D., & Narens, L. (1990). Metamemory: A theoretical framework and new findings. *The Psychology of Learning and Motivation, 26*, 125–173.

Nuthall, G. (1999). Learning how to learn: The evolution of students' minds through the social processes and culture of the classroom. *International Journal of Educational Research, 31*(3), 139–256.

Overton, U. F. (1985). Scientific methodologies and the competence – moderator – performance issue. In E. Neimark, R. Delisi & J. Newman (Eds.), *Moderators of competence* (pp. 15–41). Hillsdale, NJ: Erlbaum.

Parrat-Dayan, S., & Tryphon, A. (1998). Jean Piaget. *De la pédagogie.* Paris: Editions Odile Jacob.

Patel, V. L., Kaufman, D. R., & Magder, S. A. (1996). The acquisition of medical expertise in complex dynamic environments. In K. A. Ericsson (Ed.), *The road to excellence* (pp. 127–165). Mahwah, NJ: Erlbaum.

Piaget, J. (1947). *La psychologie de l'intelligence*. Paris: Colin.

Rutter, M. (1983). School effects on pupil progress: Research findings and policy implications. *Child Development, 54,* 1–29.

Samurçay, R., & Pastré, P. (1995). La conceptualisation des situations de travail dans la formation des compétences. *Education Permanente, 123,* 13–31.

Sembill, D. (1992). *Problemlösefähigkeit, Handlungskompetenz und emotionale Befindlichkeit*. Göttingen: Hogrefe.

Sophian, C. (1997). Beyond competence: The significance of performance for conceptual development. *Cognitive Development, 12,* 281–303.

Spencer, L. M., Jr., & Spencer, S. M. (1993). *Competence at work: Models for superior performance*. New York: John Wiley & Sons.

Stäudel, T. (1987). *Problemlösen, Emotionen und Kompetenz*. Regensburg: Roederer Verlag.

Sternberg, R. J. (1996). *Successful intelligence*. New York: Simon & Schuster.

Sternberg, R. J. (1998). Abilities are forms of developing expertise. *Educational Researcher, 27(3),* 11–20.

Sternberg, R. J., & Kolligian, J., Jr. (1990). *Competence considered*. New Haven: Yale University Press.

Weber, H., & Westmeyer, H. (1998). Die Inflation der Intelligenzen. *Vortrag gehalten auf dem 41. Kongreß der Deutschen Gesellschaft für Psychologie*: Dresden, 28.9.–1.10.1998.

Weinert, F. E. (1998). Vermittlung von Schlüsselqualifikationen. In S. Matalik & D. Schade (Eds.), *Entwicklungen in Aus- und Weiterbildung - Anforderungen, Ziele, Konzepte* (Beiträge zum Projekt "Humanressourcen") (pp. 23–43). Baden Baden: Nomos.

Weinert, F. E., & Helmke, A. (Eds.). (1997). *Entwicklung im Grundschulalter*. Weinheim: Psychologie Verlagsunion.

Weinert, F. E., & Helmke, A. (1998). The neglected role of individual differences in theoretical models of cognitive development. *Learning and Instruction (Special Issue), 8(4),* 309–323.

Weinert, F. E., & Schneider, W. (Eds.). (1999). *Individual development from 3 to 12: Findings from the Munich Longitudinal Study*. New York: Cambridge University Press.

White, R. H. (1959). Motivation reconsidered: The concept of competence. *Psychological Review, 66,* 297–333.

Wunderlich, D. (1971). Pragmatik, Sprechsituation, Deixis. *Zeitschrift für Literaturwissenschaft und Linguistik, 1,* 153–198.

Editors' Note

This first draft of this chapter was written in German and translated into English. Subsequent revisions were made in English.

Chapter 4

Competencies for the Good Life and the Good Society

Monique Canto-Sperber
Jean-Pierre Dupuy

Theoretical Background and Normative Orientations

We address the issue of the skills and competencies necessary for individuals to lead a successful and responsible life and for society to face the challenges of the present and the future from the perspective of philosophy. As we construe it, philosophy starts with description, but is mainly concerned with bringing out the conditions of possibility and conceptual definition as well as the normative assessment of the objects it considers. Our philosophical standpoint is argumentative and rationalistic. Such a brand of philosophy has been overwhelmingly illustrated throughout the history of philosophy and is currently practiced all over the world, not only in English-speaking departments of philosophy. It could be called analytical philosophy, provided that it be understood more as a style of philosophizing rather than as a reference to a particular type of philosophy. In that general sense, being analytical in philosophy entails resorting to arguments and counter-arguments, theoretical models, and thought-experiments rather than systems building. One can be analytical while inscribing one's thoughts in the context of ancient philosophy or in the framework of contemporary philosophy.

We come from different theoretical backgrounds. One of us is currently working on moral and political issues from historical and conceptual points of view. The other's present practice is related to the theory of mind and the corresponding field of "cognitive science." Both perspectives are relevant for tackling the questions that have been posed to us. The general issue – that capacities are required to lead a meaningful and successful life – pertains to normative and cognitive reflection.

In keeping with our respective backgrounds, this present contribution draws upon both philosophy of mind, and moral and social philosophy. It is located at the meeting point of these two sets of disciplines. The research currently done in both fields informs and enriches our conception of the issue at hand. The relevance of these fields can be argued as follows.

Philosophy of mind is concerned in principle with the age-old problem of the faculties of the mind: human understanding, learning, memorizing, problem-solving, intuition, concept formation, etc. A great deal of contemporary philosophy of mind is also closely linked with the developments of cognitive science (cognitive and developmental psychology, artificial intelligence, neuroscience, linguistics). It has inherited from the latter a conception of skills and competencies that purports to be appropriate both to human beings and machines. "Having a skill" is thus reinterpreted as being able to follow abstract rules or algorithms and bringing them to bear on basic data that result themselves from a decomposition of the environment into recognizable elements.

This algorithmic and constructivist rendering of human expertise has become very influential in all quarters of our societies. It pervades, in particular, the design of our educational systems and it seems to us that most of the programs carried out by the Organisation for Economic Co-operation Development (OECD) and other international institutions to date reflect this conception. Even if such a perspective can be helpful in some respects, it bears serious limitations. In our view, much more is involved in human skills and competencies, and justice must be done to the irreducible dimensions of intuition and common sense (no wonder these dimensions have been the very ones that artificial intelligence has been unable to emulate). Our orientation here is very much in keeping with the critiques that have been leveled at the current state of cognitive science from the viewpoint of phenomenological research[1] and also with the tradition of social philosophy illustrated by names such as Michael Polanyi, Michael Oakeshott, Friedrich Hayek, and others (Hayek, 1960, 1973, 1988; Polanyi, 1951, 1958; Oakeshott, 1962, 1975, 1983).

Over the last thirty years, moral philosophy has developed numerous reflections related to the notion of a human life. This preoccupation is explicit in virtue ethics, moral psychology, and theory of goods. It involves a practical interest in the possibility of leading a good life and a theoretical concern with the definition of values that make a human life meaningful. It raises questions regarding the understanding of the goodness of life (and the conditions without which a life cannot be meaningful or good), and the definition and assessment of the goods comprised in the good life. It also deals with the structural constraints (due to psychological limits or external circumstances) placed on the attainment of these values and goods or on the achievement of a meaningful life.

Virtue ethics is in part a revival of some Greek preoccupations transformed by the need to address the difficulties of modern moral philosophy (see, for instance, Crisp & Slote, 1996; and Rachels, 1998). It has tried to overcome the limitations of previous analytical ethics and has also put forward criticisms of imperative moral philosophy (grounded in the notions of obligation and duty). Both utilitarianism and Kantianism, as representatives of imperative moral philosophy, have put the emphasis on the characteristics of action (maximization of happiness for all, in the case of utilitarianism, or conformity to moral law, in the case of Kantianism) which can account for its moral status. In contrast, virtue ethics has stressed the necessity to resort to an attractive philosophy (based on the notion of informed tendency or desire towards the good) and to shift the emphasis from the intrinsic features of action to the determination of agent (his beliefs, desires, feelings, inner dispositions, and skills). It has fo-

---

[1] See, for instance, Dreyfus, 1979.

cused on the notion of virtue, understood as both a disposition and a competency to act, but also to judge and feel in an appropriate way in a particular situation. These kinds of competencies are obviously required to lead a good life. In that regard, a great deal of reflections concerned with inner capacities and competencies to act rightly can be drawn from the current development of virtue ethics.

Virtue ethics are also greatly enriched by the standpoint of moral psychology. The link between psychology and ethics concerns questions of pleasure and pain, happiness, self-realization, and human needs. There is extensive literature on hedonism, affective and cognitive stages of maturation functionally congruent with human nature, and the good life. All these considerations tend to rely on psychological dispositions discerned in humans and to embed ethical normative criteria in psychologically regular dispositions.

Finally, as to the understanding of the good life, the reflection on goods, quite widespread in moral philosophy now, has been prompted by the necessity to go beyond the subjective mental state of contentment for the assessment of a good or meaningful life. We need a fit between our subjective mental state of contentment and the objective conditions whose presence makes our contentment appropriate. Assessing the good life is not limited to the subjective impression of contentment; it needs some objective theory of the goods involved, which bring about this mental state of contentment. The conceptions of man and society we are working with are developed against the background of these reflections currently ongoing in philosophy of mind and moral philosophy.

Conceptions of Man

Man is a "rational animal," to be sure, but this assertion must be qualified at the outset. In accordance with Hayek and other authors of the same tradition, we denounce the "fatal error" that consists of believing that reason, conscious and deliberate, can govern the life of the mind. In contrast with this kind of "constructivist rationalism," we characterize the mind as follows: The mind is made up of abstract schemata which are a kind of "habitus," dispositions to think and to act in accordance with rules (Hayek, 1988). Hayek writes:

> What we call mind, is not something that the individual is born with, as he is born with his brain, or something that the brain produces, but something that his genetic equipment (e.g., a brain of a certain size and structure) helps him to acquire, as he grows up, from his family and adult fellows by absorbing the results of a tradition that is not genetically transmitted (1988, p. 22).

This absorption that constitutes learning takes place through imitation. The history of civilization is precisely that of the transcendence of innate responses by cultures and traditions, which impregnate the mind due to the faculty of imitation.

Human knowledge is at once fundamentally practical and fundamentally abstract. That is because it is embodied in the abstract schemata that compose the mind and it manifests itself through the rules that guide our actions, quite often without our realizing it. It is a knowledge made up of *savoir-faire*, of "know-how," as opposed to a propositional knowledge, one which "knows that," to employ Gilbert Ryle's classic distinction (Ryle, 1946). Or, to cite two other thinkers writing in the same spirit, it is "tacit" knowledge in Michael Polanyi's sense, "traditional" knowledge in Michael Oakeshott's sense (Polanyi, 1951, 1958; Oakeshott, 1962, 1975, 1983). In order to function in the physical and social world, we need to adapt to a mass of singular facts that are utterly impossible for us to grasp in their totality and their interrelations. As a paradox that is merely apparent would have it, only our capacity to act in accordance with abstract rules of which we have "no" knowledge, in the sense that we could not produce a theory of them, gives us the ability to accomplish this necessary feat. If, every time we acted in the world, we had to reason in the manner the "constructivist rationalists" require, proceeding from clear and distinct premises in syllogistic fashion, we would be unable to function unless we were gods endowed with the gift of omniscience. What saves us is our capacity to imitate. That is what permits us to "absorb" the rules of the "tradition" to which we belong. And these rules, the fruit of collective experience, constitute a body of knowledge that is at our disposal even though we are unable to render it explicit.

"Tacit" knowledge truly is knowledge, but of a kind that is "not conscious." We know the rules that constitute our mind inasmuch as we are able to recognize them. The recognition in question is analogous to what in artificial intelligence is called "pattern recognition." Every human being has, for example, a linguistic competency that allows him to articulate a potentially infinite number of well-formed sentences. He immediately recognizes any mistake in syntax. But he will often be at a loss to present the motivation for his judgment in the form of deductive reasoning. This type of knowledge may be called unconscious because it is incorporated in the mind and not produced by it.

Man is a normative being. Even in the simplest conversations, we are not only passing on information, not only working out what to believe about things, events and people, but we are also deciding how to think and feel. People ask such questions as "What should I do?", "What should he have done?", "Where are the limits?", "Had I better...?", etc., which are basic normative questions. It is difficult to conceive of any deliberation or reflection that would not be guided by normative questions of this kind. They shape the examination of life, even if they draw on the materials of common thought and speech. People live by norms, and they have attached to these norms specific beliefs (about what is right, required, or good, but also about what is properly human, or about what would be rightly approved of by other people) and feelings (resentment towards the person who does not act rightly, or guilt about oneself), as well as mental attitudes (approbation or disapprobation, for instance).

A great deal of human behavior can be understood as the expression of this relationship to norms. Internalization of norms does not suppose a lack of autonomy. It involves adopting a kind of "internal attitude" (Hart, 1961) (accepting the worth of a behavior, feeling guilt or resentment in case it is lacking, and willingly sanctioning the one who does not act properly), because the act selected by the norms is rationally evaluated, autonomously accepted, and thought of as being of value for its own sake. The presence of norms is especially important for a moral philosophy in which moral behavior does not consist mainly in forming maxims, following rules, or performing calculations, but in having the competency to behave rightly. An important part of this competency-formation process is linked to the internalization of norms.

A human being is a normative being in another aspect. Human beings are engaged in activities which have ends and whose achievement requires the appropriate means. The ends of these activities and the means selected to meet them are subject to normative assessment. In so far as normative questions can be raised about the general design of one's life, questions such as "Was I right to do that?", "Knowing the consequences of what I did, should I have done it?", "Why did I take this path to reach this aim?", involve the capacity to have a normative perspective over one's own life. They suppose the ability to practice some kind of distancing from the immediate activities in which we are engaged and to step back from one's current needs and desires, looking at them from afar.

Conceptions of Society

Our conception of society combines a Hayekian social epistemology and philosophy with a Rawlsian[2] conception of the good society as well-ordered and governed by principles of justice (Hayek, 1973; Rawls, 1972).

In keeping with the concept of complexity which we shall introduce below, we take society to be a complex automaton, in a sense that renders compatible the two following assertions: 1) society results from the actions of the people who compose it; 2) society escapes them because it is (infinitely) more complex than they are.

The social order is a "spontaneous order" that no will wished for, that no consciousness conceived in its complete specification. This type of order is located between the natural and artificial types of order, in the same way that the absorption of tradition through imitation is located "between instinct and reason." It is an emergence, a composition effect, a system outcome. This leap in complexity when going from the local to the global level makes it possible to talk about self-organizing or "autopoietic" systems. Obviously, one does not want to make the "social" system out to be a subject endowed with consciousness and will. The "knowledge" mobilized by the system is irremediably distributed over the entire set of constituent elements, and it cannot be synthesized in a single place that would contain the system's "absolute knowledge" of itself. There is truly a form of "collective knowledge" even though it cannot be attributed to a collective subject of any kind. It is knowledge without a subject, embodied in norms, rules, conventions, values, and institutions of which a large part are incorporated in individual psyches, in the form of abstract schemata.

Taking society to be a self-organizing system does not mean that one considers it to be inaccessible to conscious and willful human intervention and shaping. To some extent, the "rules of the game" can be agreed upon and set up, in particular in the political and judiciary domains. Society is "well-ordered" when its basic social institutions are governed by principles of justice that everyone accepts and knows others accept. We assume, in addition, that the basic institutions of a democratic, just, and

---

[2] The compatibility between these two views is not evident and must be worked out carefully (Dupuy, 1992).

stable society are such that they induce its members to have a desire to act as the principles of justice require.

This conception of society and the normative aspect of human beings and the form of rationality that can be ascribed to it account for the general definition of what the good life is, the understanding of competencies and the selection of five key competencies.

Premises of a Successful Good Life in Various Spheres of Life

Reflection on the nature of the good life and how to live is not a prerogative of philosophers. Nonetheless, such a reflection belongs in the province of philosophy for several reasons[3]: it is a classical philosophical topic and philosophers have exercised their minds on the issue of "how should I live?" They have defined the conditions without which it is difficult to speak of a good life; they have discriminated between the different forms of contentment and satisfaction which are involved in the good life; they have listed the various kinds of goods (subjective goods, objective goods, individual goods, community goods) that account for the goodness of life. In this regard, philosophers can give insights into the constituents of the good life and the ways they can be combined. They contribute to shape a reflective point of view from which the objective value of the goods involved in the good life can be assessed. But philosophers are not to be themselves exemplars of good lives. The question of whether philosophers are supposed to live up to the expectation of the good life is irrelevant.

In what follows, we will not refer explicitly to particular theories of past or present philosophers. In conformity with the DeSeCo Project, we will limit ourselves to the case of industrialized and democratic societies. In the corresponding cultures, the notion of a life plan makes sense and does not carry with it any substantial weight, given a general orientation toward the future, and a fairly high social mobility which gives most people a good chance of changing plans over a lifetime. Even if a philosophical blueprint is thoroughly patent in our reflections, we do not suppose philosophical expertise on the part of the agents but only a willingness and ability to endorse a reflective attitude. The analysis we provide is not dependent upon any ontological or epistemological commitment. It goes without saying that our perspective is secular and anthropocentric. We are concerned with facts that make a life a good life, and that have human significance. We do not conceive of the good life for human beings as depending on living in conformity to a moral order permeating reality. The goodness of life is not the realization or at least the approximation of some ideal that exists independently of it. Good lives are taken to depend on human effort; nothing else but human action is relied on in trying to achieve it. Our perspective is also pluralistic, in the sense that we do not describe one particular good life but the general

---

[3] See Griffin, 1986; Kekes, 1995; and Becker, 1992.

requirements of the good life. Even if the admission of the existence of a set of stable features that define human condition thus establishes necessary requirements which any reasonable conception of the good life must meet, simply meeting them is not enough. There are many forms good lives may take beyond these necessary requirements. Even the idea of universal, constant human characteristics is not incompatible with human diversity and the notion that many different good lives are conceivable. Forms of the good life that meet these requirements are many. Achieving a good life is hard; it requires constant struggle against adversity and fortune. These adversities are inherent in the human condition. Competencies for the good life can provide some resources (in terms of attitudes, beliefs, feelings) to cope with this fact of adversity.

Before trying to define what a good life is, it could be useful to understand what the requirements for a meaningful life are. The meaning of life depends on the capacity individuals have to achieve the ends they value and to shape their desires, deliberations, decisions, and actions into a more or less cohesive pattern directed toward these achievements. Several considerations are involved in the assessment of this capacity. First, it depends on the value of ends and ideals that give orientation to a human life. Ideals can be harmful or unattainable. A life focused on an ideal that is impossible to achieve or even to make one's own will not be even moderately meaningful. Second, it depends on the worth of the activities individuals are engaged in. In the frame of a meaningful life, there might be activities which are intrinsically worthless or have only instrumental value. However, it would be difficult to conceive of a life as meaningful if activities lacking in intrinsic value dominated. Third, a meaningful life requires a relative consistency of desires. If desires are distracted toward different directions or are incompatible, forms of satisfaction will be difficult to attain. Fourth, aims, beliefs, and desires are taken to express a minimum of autonomy of the subject and reflect a self-directed engagement. They proceed from the fact that we reflect on ourselves and on the world and discover what matters to us.

Against such a background, let us try to answer more specifically the question which has been posed to us: What is a personally and socially worthy life in modern, complex, and democratic societies?

We start with some kind of uncontroversial description. A good life involves the capacity to lead a successful and responsible life, a productive life for understanding and acting in different areas and meeting everyday challenges in all relevant fields of life found in a democratic society. These different fields are (1) *life at home* – family life and private interpersonal and community relations which allow for personality development and general personal satisfaction; (2) *life in the economy* – the capacity to become a responsible worker, with active economic participation, successful participation in the labor market and labor practice; the ability to play a role in economic institutions within a competitive economy, which brings economic benefits to individuals; (3) *life in political society* – political and social participation; the capacity to get involved in a well-functioning public social network and to handle social communication in a multicultural society with a minimum level of social cohesion.

All healthy members of the human species have many of the same physiological needs and capacities. There are also psychological similarities shared by all human beings. They do not differ in their psychological aspirations to go beyond necessity, to do what is necessary for survival, and to aim at a condition in which they have leisure, choices, alternatives. We are alike in the capacity to learn from the past and plan for the future. We have a view, though never clearly articulated, about what we want to make out of our lives. We have the capacity to think, remember, imagine, have feelings and emotions, and to restrain ourselves. Contact with other people is part of human life; most of the time we depend on it. We live in a network of close relationships in which we cooperate, compete, and share. The satisfaction of our needs and the establishment of these relationships require social life. Social life allows for the emergence of conventional practices, rules of coexistence, and social restrictions on what we can do.

For most of the goods or values that make a life good, it is a factual question to ask how far they are derivable from the invariant traits that define the human condition. These values are objective because their status is independent of what anyone believes about them. Furthermore, our subjective mental state of contentment is not enough for the assessment of a good or meaningful life. We need some criterion of adequacy between our subjective mental state of contentment and the objective conditions whose presence makes our contentment appropriate. Assessing happiness is not limited to the subjective impression of contentment; it needs some objective theory of the goods involved that bring about this mental state of contentment.

The deliberation which goes on in determining what kind of objective values are at the center of a valuable human life involves a kind of reflective assessment which first separates the values from confusing appearances, and then shows that values are the sorts of things that give life point and substance when we step back far enough from our everyday concerns. In this report, we will not go into the details of deliberation of these sorts, and will limit ourselves to propose what could be a tentative list of the main values that account for the good life. These values are consistent with any major moral theory. They involve a conception of human beings partly free from appetite and taste, capable of assessing ends, and of choosing those ends which deserve to be chosen. These values are:

- accomplishment – the good which consists of the realization of the things we value; it is distinct from mere achievement and its value does not come merely from gaining praise;

- the elements of human existence – choosing one's own course through life and having a life which is properly human; included are values of autonomy, liberty, and humanity;

- understanding – knowing about oneself and one's world is part of the good life; we value the fact of being in touch with reality, and of being free of ignorance and error;

- enjoyment – we value pleasures, the perception of beautiful things, and the satisfaction we derive from day-to-day events;

- deep personal relations – they have a value independent of the pleasure and benefit they give.

These values are the necessary requirements of all good lives. In a sense, we can say that good lives are the same for all, even if the conventionally recognized forms these values take can be manifold. According to the cultural context, these values can take the shape of desirable professions, prized talents, acceptable balance between political involvement and private life, work and leisure, competition and solidarity; they can attribute worth to independence, creativity, honor, success, comfort and privacy.

The human condition in which these goods can be reached and lived by is shaped by facts of human vulnerability and by limitations of strength, intelligence, and rationality. Such a condition makes individual effort all the more crucial, but in order to make that effort efficient, we need skills. It is through skills and competencies that we find the right way of making reasonable choices among possibilities, a way of making reciprocal adjustment between our conceptions of the good life and perceptions of what makes human efforts appropriate and suitable. We need the capacity to apprehend the meaning of achievement.

The capacities required for the good life are the capacity to satisfy psychological and physiological needs, the capacity to establish close relationships with other people, the capacity to have a real and rewarding private life, and the capacity to deal with the social order and to make the goods we derive from it our own goods. The good life is a regulative ideal. In each circumstance, it depends on what goods would best suit our character and circumstances, what importance we should assign to them, how much evil we should risk and tolerate in order to enjoy the goods we want.

What Are the Competencies for the Good Life?

What kinds of competencies are indispensable for the good life? Which skills play a significant role in the ability to manage individual and political life? What is the theoretical basis and rationale for the selection and definition of such competencies?

First, we will try to clarify the significance of the terms and issues at stake. The terms of "key competency" or "core skill" seem to have multiple, flexible, and vague meanings. Many other words (key qualification, fitness, ability, capacity, efficiency, proficiency) can be used to mean apparently the same thing, namely a mixture of knowledge, behavior, attitude, and values. They all designate the possession of some skill in order to learn something, to do something, or reach an aim. They involve creativity, ability for innovation, mobility, flexibility, endurance, reliability, and precision.

The theoretical and pragmatic conceptualizations of competencies are mainly from psychology of development. To grasp its meaning, it is important to distinguish competency from the notions of

- literacy (understood in an inclusive way, meaning prose literacy, document literacy, quantitative literacy); literacy goes from the most basic decoding skill to the ability to understand complex ideas in a written text;

- numeracy;

- survival kit, understood as the set of basic skills and fundamental knowledge required for the survival of individuals or of democratic society and the continuation of community; they are the common, bottom-line goals of all compulsory educational systems;

- theoretical knowledge or propositional knowledge.

By "competencies for the good life," we mean kinds of competencies which are not reducible either to literacy and numeracy or to basic knowledge and propositional knowledge. In a very general fashion, the kind of competency we are interested in pertains to some kind of know-how and could be described as a mix of conceptual and practical competencies. The constituents of these competencies for the good life could be spelled out in the following way:

- conceptual competencies, which can be classified either as general conceptual competencies (conceived of as a context-free or content-free ability, including cognitive preconditions for purposeful action and reasonable thinking, dealing with the environment, and involving information-processing paradigms and rule-based knowledge over a whole domain) or as specific cognitive competencies, conceived of as a special cluster of cognitive prerequisites, content-dependent abilities.

Conceptual competencies, either general or specific, are supplemented by

- procedural competencies, which encompass the availability of procedures and skills necessary to apply the conceptual competency in concrete situations;

- motivational competencies, which are the capacities to be involved in effective interaction with the environment and to provide an appropriate motivational attitude;

- action competencies, which involve the psychological prerequisites for successful performance; they include problem-solving capacities and skills for critical thinking; they are forms of practical intelligence: the capacity to grasp the relevant characteristics of a problem and to select and employ a suitable strategy.

These three kinds of volitional skills are the result not only of cognitive capacities but also of hereditary talent, developmental regularities, environmental influence, and quantity and quality of special learning opportunities.

Several points have to be stressed regarding this general characterization of competency for the good life.

These competencies for the good life are general cognitive and emotional abilities and dispositions that are used in a variety of situations. A competency spans different contents. The conceptual constituent of competencies is often related to content.

These competencies show an ability to learn from unforeseen situations and circumstances and to cope with life situations. They include a dimension of learning (e.g., knowledge) and a dimension of motivation (since they refer to values, attitudes, beliefs, habits, emotions, and psychological constructions which regulate learning).

Cognitive, conceptual, and propositional knowledge are certainly not the only parameters, nor even the most important ones.

These competencies are not a cognitive goal. They are not curriculum-bounded knowledge or skill, but cross-curricular competencies (included in multiple-subject areas across the curriculum). They are an education outcome, not a school outcome. They are manifest in both formal education and everyday life.

The definition of such competencies involves the general issue of the relationship between cognitive or conceptual competencies and competencies linked to performance and dependent upon a situation. We assume a strong interaction between both conceptual competencies, on one side, and procedural, motivational, and action competencies, on the other side. There is a shaping of competence through performance: long-term development of a competency depends on opportunities and past performances. The very formation of cognitive competencies is influenced by memory capacity and familiarity with the task situation.

These competencies are formed through individual experience; they influence the form of expectations, attitudes, and perceptual schemata. They depend on the talents and achievement dispositions of the individual (these form the objective side of such competencies) and on the personal assessment of one's ability and skill (this is on the subjective side).

These competencies require subjective assessment, which provides the necessary relevant knowledge about oneself and self-related beliefs. Competencies for the good life require concepts related to the self (self-esteem, self-efficacy, beliefs, and expectations of what one is able to come to terms with and is motivated to achieve). Such self-concepts can be general or related to different areas or attitudes (effective motivation, feelings of efficacy for a special task). They involve the subjective experience of one's competence. They are related to introspection and awareness.

These competencies include a form of implicit competency which is central in action planning, in the monitoring of one's actions, in the self-evaluation of one's actions and of its results, in the managing and correcting of one's actions. It is, so to speak, a form of metacompetency, which is not in the form of a context-dependent knowledge (core skill, planning skill), but is suitable for the mastering of many content-specific tasks. In a declarative form (explicit, verbalized), it is knowledge of one's knowledge, knowledge about one's ability. It depends upon the degree of self-confidence and upon the availability of volitional skills (attention, concentration). It helps transform a general skill into a content-specific skill.

These competencies are mainly person-oriented. But they can be viewed too as a characteristic not only of a person but also of a context.

These competencies are to a degree specifically related to our modern world (teamwork, some kinds of practical cognition, computer familiarity).

These are the general features of competencies required for the good life. In what follows, we identify, define, and characterize five key competencies that we take to be applicable to a wide variety of domains, independent of the cultural context (to the extent that it remains consistent with the general characterization of a well-ordered society we gave above), and independent also of any particular period of life. Once again, we are dealing with the complex setting-up of projects and plans that requires effective action, the capacity to learn from past deeds and to take account of future outcomes. In order to meet these conditions, we had to situate the five key competencies at a sufficiently high level of generality and abstraction. Indeed, every key competency listed below can be seen as a cluster or constellation of elementary skills and sub-competencies. It might be more illuminating to construe it as a dimension in a five-dimensional abstract space where each particular skill, ability, or capacity takes its place. A given elementary skill or ability, therefore, may pertain or may be attached to several if not all of the key competencies. For example, the capacity to trust others is a crucial component of the skills required to take an active part in local political life and has a cooperative dimension to be sure (indeed, we take it as the epitome of the cooperative competency). However, the normative, perceptive, and complexity dimensions have a bearing on it as well. This example can be generalized: skills are components of higher order skills which themselves are components of still higher order skills, etc. One can assume that the set of skills has therefore a network structure, in which each node can be located in the five-dimensional space defined by the five key competencies. As philosophers, we take up the issue at a very fundamental level.

Our contention is that it is only by resorting to such an abstract characterization that it is possible to achieve the desired result, namely to reach an identification of competencies independent of culture, context, personal characteristics, including age, gender, social status, professional activity, etc. Let there be no misunderstanding. That this identification of key competencies is independent of these parameters does not entail that the latter play no role in the production and development of these competencies, nor in the very specific forms they take on here and there. Indeed, culture, context, age, etc. are all factors of production of key competencies. For instance, protestant cultures tend to be more favorable to the development of cooperative skills than catholic ones; older age seems to make it harder to maintain a sufficient level of the competencies required to cope with the complexities of the social and technological world; conversely, youth makes it harder to be normatively competent; etc. Moreover, the asserted independence does not preclude the fact that different activities or tasks, associated with different values of the key parameters (context, age, etc), will require a different mix of key competencies. For example, it is likely that the learning of democratic values on the part of adolescents will require a higher dose of narrative and normative competencies (e.g., through the identification with role models) than those demanded of an older and more experienced person, etc. The weights relative to the particular mix of key competencies required for a given task in a given context can only be determined by empirical studies.

The five key (constellations of) competencies are

- competencies for coping with complexity
- perceptive competencies
- normative competencies
- cooperative competencies
- narrative competencies

It is our conjecture that one arrives at such a list, in its present form or in a roughly equivalent one, if one takes into account the philosophical background expounded above. Let us stress again, in particular, our commitment to (1) the idea that the goods and values which make up the goodness of life are to a large extent independent of the way people feel about them; in this sense, they are objective; (2) the notion that the good life requires a reflective perspective.

The five key competencies include cognitive elements mingled with motivational, procedural, and practical skills. None of them is reducible either to theoretical or propositional knowledge. They constitute forms of *know-how*, rather than forms of *know that*. To a certain extent, they can be learned.

The settings and social institutions relevant for the development of these competencies are school, family, conversation, association, reading, political life, and cultural life. The competencies can be learned in all kinds of activities in which a minimum reflective attitude is present. But it is essential to emphasize that these competencies, or desired outcomes of education, are broader than the acquisition of subject-related knowledge typically taught in schools. They extend beyond the school context and encompass the notion of preparation for life. Not only learning outcomes, not only skills needed for work, but skills needed for life. They are non-curricula bounded socio-cultural knowledge and skills.

We are confident that each of these key competencies can lend itself to the elaboration of quantifiable indicators. We refer in passing to a number of experiments in cognitive psychology that can easily be translated into tests conducive to such an elaboration. However, given our philosophical perspective, we have given priority to conceptual and theoretical issues.

Let us add that none of these key competencies presupposes either a very high degree of cognitive intelligence or a very high level of education. They constitute the dimensions of practical intelligence.

Five Key Competencies

Competencies for Coping With Complexity

These competencies, as we construe them, command the whole gamut of human expertise. Their constellation makes up a metacompetency of sorts. In a sense, all particular skills come under this heading as soon as they are properly understood. This metacompetency consists first in understanding their real nature and performing in a way that takes full advantage of it. It is assumed that this understanding is crucial not only for educators and skill teachers but for the skills-bearers themselves as well as for society at large.

The first step is to define and understand the concept of complexity. The opposite of "complex" is not "simple" (many actions and tasks are both simple and complex, like riding a bicycle, cooking, or carrying on a conversation), but "complicated." It was John von Neumann (1966) who launched the notion of complexity into the scientific area in the framework of his study on automata, natural and artificial. Given a non-complex machine, it is easier to describe what it is capable of doing than to describe the machine itself. Beyond a certain critical threshold of complexity, however, the opposite is true: it is easier, infinitely easier, to conceive the machine than to describe completely its behavior. What a complex object is capable of is (infinitely) more complex than the object itself. The matrix is (infinitely) transcended by its progeny. Or again: the simplest model of a complex object is the object itself. To be complex is to be capable of becoming more complex. By contrast, a complicated mechanism is reducible to its individual components and to their rules of composition. What makes it complicated is just the large number of such components and the intricacies of those rules.

As predicted by von Neumann, the concept of complexity has come to play a momentous role in most scientific disciplines, from mathematics to biology. Many researchers in these fields have stressed the pedagogical role of a well-known class of very simple (although non-linear) mathematical models capable of generating a surprisingly rich, varied, and complex phenomenology. According to these scientists, children should get acquainted with the properties of these models at an early stage through the manipulation of formal objects or the participation in educational games in or outside schools. Should they be implemented, these recommendations would introduce a revolution in the teaching of mathematics and sciences with far-reaching implications well beyond those brought about, a few decades ago, by the introduction of "modern" mathematics in the classroom. So far, these recommendations have remained a dead letter (see May, 1974).

The philosophical implications of the concept of complexity are no less important. Mechanical (analytical, computational, algorithmic) reason turns out to be capable of bootstrapping and transcending itself into a form of intuitive reason irreducible to it. Most of the tasks we perform by way of coping skillfully with our everyday environment, including the simplest ones, are complex. If we have acquired expertise, we do not perform tasks by applying rules to the basic features of the situation at hand. The novice and the advanced beginner do just that, but they are in the process of learning the relevant skills. Hubert and Stuart Dreyfus have distinguished five stages in the acquisition of a new skill: novice, advanced beginner, competent, proficient, and expert. The remarkable feature in this process is the evolution from the application of abstract rules toward using past experience in concrete situations to guide action, from the mechanical toward the intuitive, from *the know that* toward the *know-how*, or, as Dreyfus and Dreyfus put it:

> the progression from the analytic behavior of a detached subject, consciously decomposing his environment into recognizable elements, and following abstract rules, to involved skill behavior based on an accumulation of concrete experiences and the unconscious recognition of new situations as similar to whole remembered ones (1986, p. 35).

We suggest that it is possible, in light of this, to reconsider the results of the 1994–1995 International Adult Literacy Survey (IALS). At times, surprisingly high percentages of the tested populations have been categorized as being unable "to understand and employ printed information in daily activities, at home, at work, and in the community – to achieve one's goals and to develop one's knowledge and potential" (OECD & HRDC, 1997, p. 14). In principle, then, these people shouldn't be able to manage in their most basic, daily activities. Now, when one examines the tests they had to go through, one realizes that a number of them were framed in "knowing that," context-free, and abstract terms. The subjects' failings are by no means sufficient to infer that the same people would not *know how* to find their way about in their own, familiar world. A good case in point is the celebrated "selection task" devised by the English cognitive psychologist P. C. Wason (See Johnson-Laird & Wason, 1977). A great majority of subjects are shown to be quite incompetent in understanding and handling *modus tollens* (i.e., the inference from "If p then q" to "If not q then not p") when they have to apply it to an abstract task. However, when the same logical task is presented in a meaningful context and in terms familiar to the subjects from practical experience, about 75 percent of them give the correct answer. The capacity to recognize patterns already encountered in past experience is the major component of most skills, rather than the capacity to follow rules and apply them to known facts (Margolis, 1987).

There are two kinds of contingency and uncertainty in human affairs. The first stems from the fact that human beings are complex agents; the second, from the fact that, sometimes, they are "trivialized" and lose their complexity altogether (See von Foerster, 1987). In the latter case, the agents are rigidly, univocally coupled to one another and to their environment. The resulting collective phenomena combine paradoxically two seemingly contradictory traits: they are highly predictable from an external vantage point, but the agents within are powerless to control them. The uncertainty, therefore, is not cognitive, but practical. What emerges at the collective level takes on the figure of Fate, although it is but the resulting effect of the agents' actions and reactions (many traits of the current ecological crisis meet this description). The former case of uncertainty is very different and inherent to human condition and the fact of freedom. If freedom exists, two consequences follow at the same time: human affairs are intrinsically contingent and, to a large extent, unpredictable, but by their very freedom, the agents are able to make sense of, and ascribe meaning to their affairs (on meaning, see the section on narrative skills below) and, to some extent, to shape them according to their will and desires.[4]

The intellectual and practical ability to deal with contingency is part of the agent's complexity and capacity to cope with complexity. There is a political side to this capacity: the humble recognition that human reason is not the master in its own house and that there is more knowledge and wisdom in norms, values, institutions, etc., than in any individual mind – although these norms, values, etc., lie in no other place than people's minds. However, there is a stringent condition for this to be true: the contingency of the world must result from the complexity of the agents rather than their lack of complexity. Now, it must be acknowledged that a good deal of the contemporary human world, especially in its technological dimensions, is more com-

---

[4] One could appeal, here, to a cybernetical notion, Ross Ashby's "Law of Requisite Variety" (1958).

plicated than complex. Think, for example, of the impenetrability of most modern tools. As Ivan Illich once put it:

> Industry has surrounded people with artifacts whose inner workings only specialists are allowed to understand... This type of design tends to reinforce a non-inventive society in which the experts find it progressively easier to hide behind their expertise and beyond evaluation. The man-made environment has become as inscrutable as nature is for the primitive. At the same time, educational materials have been monopolized by school (1971b, p. 26).[5]

The same could be said of the economy. The "flexibility" that is required of many workers looks much more like the (unlikely) capacity to adjust to an economic world that is unpredictable because of its extreme complication rather than the complexity both required to cope with a complex world and fostered by it. This leads us to stress the dangers of too individualistic an approach to skills. What makes the agents skilled, competent or not, has at least as much to do with the characteristics of their world as with their personal qualities.

Perceptive Competencies

We use the word "perceptive" in the sense it has in the received English translation of Pascal's concept of *esprit de finesse* (the perceptive mind) as opposed to *esprit de géométrie* (the mathematical mind). As Pascal puts it in *Pensées*:

> The difference between the mathematical mind and the perceptive mind: the reason that mathematicians are not perceptive is that they do not see what is before them, and that, accustomed to the exact and plain principles of mathematics, and not reasoning till they have well inspected and arranged their principles, they are lost in matters of perception where the principles do not allow for such arrangement... These principles are so fine and so numerous that a very delicate and very clear sense is needed to perceive them, and to judge rightly and justly when they are perceived, without for the most part being able to demonstrate them in order as in mathematics; because the principles are not known to us in the same way, and because it would be an endless matter to undertake it. We must see the matter at once, at one glance, and not by a process of reasoning, at least to a certain degree... Mathematicians wish to treat matters of perception mathematically, and make themselves ridiculous... The mind...does it tacitly, naturally, and without technical rules (cited in Dreyfus, 1979).

We stressed before that coping with complexity requires the capacity to recognize patterns, to establish analogies between whole previously experienced situations and new ones, and to use patterns to guide activity in the world. This competency is not sufficient to find our way about in daily situations. We cannot afford to ignore the very details that make situations different from one another and individualize them. However, the limitations of human cognition make it impossible to take into account every such detail. Cognition and practical intelligence are not in general the applica-

---

[5] See also his *Deschooling Society* (Illich, 1971a).

tion of rules to facts if only because it is utterly impossible to grasp all the facts. Hence the necessity of a different set of skills that allows us to discriminate between the more or less relevant elements of a situation. We have to appreciate the relative importance of details in view of our aims (i.e., to identify, combine, weigh, and ponder the various considerations that constitute a situation).

A similar skill bears, not on the details of the situation, but on the concerns we bring to it. As David Wiggins puts it:

> No theory, if it is to recapitulate or reconstruct practical reasoning even as well as mathematical logic recapitulates or reconstructs the actual experience of conducting or exploring deductive argument, can treat the concerns an agent brings to any situation as forming a closed, complete, consistent system. For it is of the essence of these concerns to make competing, inconsistent claims. (This is a mark not of our irrationality but of *rationality* in the face of the plurality of ends and the plurality of human goods). The weight of the claims represented by these concerns is not necessarily fixed in advance. Nor need the concerns be hierarchically ordered. Indeed, a person's reflection on a new situation that confronts him may disrupt such order and fixity as had previously existed and bring a change in his evolving conception of the point or the several or many points, of living or acting (1998, pp. 231–232).

Most of these skills are embodied in what we call *common sense*. The apparently irremediable obstacles artificial intelligence has found in its way while trying to solve what its practitioners dub the "frame problem" (i.e., the discrimination between what in a situation is relevant and what is not) is proof to the fact that common sense is not reducible to mechanical or algorithmic reason.

Practical intelligence requires several skills that fall naturally under this heading: sensitivity to context; background/foreground distinction; the capacity to make a detour.

Stupid is the person who does not adapt her conduct to the circumstances and the changes thereof, for instance, who does not adjust her way and style of speaking to the context of the conversation she is engaged in, the identity of her interlocutors, etc. Inhuman seems to many the moral agent who sticks stubbornly to a would-be "categorical imperative," such as "Thou shalt not lie" even in a situation in which his self-righteousness will lead to disastrous consequences.

The capacity to discriminate between relevant and irrelevant features of a situation or of a change of situation presupposes the capacity to identify the salient traits against a background of general, undifferentiated knowledge. This capacity supposes the ability to go back and forth, to go close to the problem and far from it to determine and select the elements which remain salient in as many perspectives as possible.

Practical intelligence is characterized by the capacity to make detours to better attain one's ends: the ability to take a roundabout path if it will allow one to reach one's destination faster; to refrain temporarily from consuming and invest so as to augment one's overall consumption; to refuse a good opportunity in order to take advantage of a better opportunity later, and so on; or, as Leibniz put it, the capacity "to step back in order to leap forward" (*reculer pour mieux sauter*).

Normative Competencies

Normative competencies are expressed by the capacity to ask questions related to norms, assessments, goods, values, meanings, and limits, such as "What should I do?", "What should he have done?", "Where are the limits?", "Had I better...?", etc. People use normative expressions along with specific beliefs and feelings. Deliberation and reflection about one's actions are often guided by normative considerations. The fact that these considerations are internalized does not prevent rational assessment and autonomous acceptance. Insofar as rightness of action is not reduced to the conformity to rules or calculation of outcomes, a normative competency is required. Its familiar manifestations are normative questions, deliberations, justifications of actions, or decisions and assessments of states of affairs, actions, behaviors, on limited or general matters.

An epistemological issue can be raised. Normative skills are not observable entities. The only facts that can be observed are actions, behaviors, or choices which are taken to be the effects of such a competency. But the very definition of these effects involves a general idea of what a normative competency is. On the other hand, a normative competency does not necessarily lead to specifiable types of action; it does not manifest itself in any specific type of action. We cannot begin with examples of actions or behaviors and go on to ask: What is it about these actions and behaviors that make them the effect of a normative competency? Ascribing a normative competency to an agent supposes in this agent the embodiment of a lasting pattern that makes true a subjunctive conditional such as "given a general description of the appropriate type of action required, given normal circumstances, if the agent had any opportunity to act, thus he would typically tend to act that way." Even if people act wisely at least some of the time, it is not enough for ascribing a normative competency to them. They have to predictably and regularly act wisely in the appropriate situations; it has to be an enduring pattern of their lives.

Nevertheless, history, literature, personal experience, and autobiographical evidence provide countless examples of people acting normatively. So we can ask what is it about these actions that connects them to the exercise of normative skills, to some sort of deliberation involved in the normative questions "What should I do?", "What kind of life am I leading?", etc. The identification of actions issued from a normative competency and the very definition of this competency will be based on the intuitive meaning of these questions and assumptions and will go beyond intuitions to understand the complexities involved. In other words, it will be immediate understanding deepened by analysis.

First, normative competencies are a kind of judicial and critical power. Asking questions like "Was I right to do that?", "Knowing the consequences of what I did, should I have done it?", "Why did I take this path to reach this aim?", involves a critical perspective over one's own action. Normative competencies equate the capacity to judge rightly with the ability to determine what should be done in particular situations in order to make life better. They presuppose choice, deliberation, and are guided by some conception of what could be better or worse in the long run. A normative competency is a psychological capacity which involves higher mental processes (such as second order desires, or desires about desires) (Frankfurt, 1988) and enables those who have it to judge rightly in important matters. To act wisely requires types of actions which will vary with the countless situations upon which people are called to exercise normative wisdom. Normative wisdom requires some kind of immediate insight and discernment; in that regard it cannot be identified with considered judgment or with sound judgment (which involves a great variety of types of action which have to be weighed against each other). Normative competencies depend not just on the nature of the action and the situation, but on the beliefs and character of the agent, and on his particular conception of what makes up a good life.

The assessment of ends of particular actions and of the means chosen to meet them pertains to normative competencies as does the evaluation of the appropriateness of means for the achievement of such ends. Normative skills lead to a skilled conduct of human affairs. They involve a practically oriented knowledge and a capacity for judging rightly in matters related to life and conduct. Normative wisdom manifests itself as the just judgment about the relevance of knowledge as to action.

In that regard, normative competencies require the capacity

- to select the relevant features of a situation which is to be described (such a selection is not arbitrary because it is guided by our normative commitment which calls attention to generally evident and accessible features of a situation);

- to choose proportionate means to reach given ends;

- to appreciate the various possibilities offered;

- to endorse some kind of knowledge of what is good and what is bad; normative competencies imply using that knowledge to evaluate situations.

Secondly, the exercise of normative skills gives its typical form to the reflection on human life. To reflect on one's own life or on the life of other people involves some conception of what a good life should be. The questions that reflective people cannot avoid putting to themselves – "How should I live?", "What should I do in this concrete situation, given my overall view of what a good life should be?" – suppose some hard critical thought and a willingness to question much that one has taken for granted. Normative thought is an implicit guide to this sort of reflection. It helps a reasonable person to make a life for herself. It is understood as the virtue of reflection over one's whole life, once we can step back from our everyday concerns. In that respect, it is different from moral virtues and from other kinds of wisdom. Any normative competency requires also some notion of what is likely to be lasting and important, desirable, prized, and admired, and a valued conception of the good life we want to achieve. It is a reflective and critical capacity, not linked to any specific form of the good life. This normative skill involves a critical scrutiny of the conception of the good life. It aims at the development of a life that not only seems to us to be good, but of a life that really is good.

In this respect, normative competencies could be characterized by the capacity

- to step back from our immediate concerns; this requires not only a reflective overview, but also a distancing of the judgment from the context;

- to look forward with an eye to the evaluation of what kind of person we want to become, and to orient individual human efforts to live a good life;
- to construct on an individual basis the framework of a good life and to discover which values are important to us through reciprocal adjustment between the moral traditions we live by and our individuality;
- to use knowledge of principles regarding some contingent aspects of the good life;
- to evaluate what is right or wrong in conduct from the perspective of life as a whole and to define critical human values (such as tolerance);
- to evaluate human actions and decisions from the perspectives of the good life and of values, with some notion of the limits and opportunities which define the boundaries of human lives;
- to manifest autonomy, which requires the possession of a sound self-concept and the ability to translate states of consciousness into acts of the will: decision, choice, and action; this capacity defines the good life as a life of will and action; it supposes too the unification of the multiple and often conflicting elements of action (dispositions, motives, needs, appetites, etc; deliberation and practical wisdom characteristic of deliberative rationality; the principle of autonomy that resolves itself in choices).

Normative competencies make life better, and the lack thereof make it worse. For the formation and development of normative competencies, it is natural to turn to literature, cinema, life experience, as they bring about knowledge of that which is worth valuing and of that which is worth doing. Normative skills do not pertain to an egoistic conception of action; genuinely good conceptions of life include caring about the welfare of other people. Last, even if they were inborn, normative competencies of that kind would still have to be acquired, they would need to be developed to make the resulting judgment reliable. We make a good life by living well.

Cooperative Competencies

Many evils in our world stem from a lack of cooperative skills. In keeping with our Rawlsian framework, we take society to be a "cooperative venture for mutual advantage," "typically marked by a conflict as well as by an identity of interests" (Rawls, 1972, p. 4). Social agents often find themselves caught up in structures of interaction which have the following characteristics: If everyone sets out to maximize her or his own self-interest regardless of others' self-interest, they end up in a situation that is disastrous for everyone, or, at least, in which everybody comes out less well-off than if they all had acted otherwise. Their inability to handle their conflicting interests results in their having to forsake the benefits of social cooperation. The so-called "prisoner's dilemma" (PD) which plays a prominent role in Game Theory analyses of moral philosophy is but one structure of this kind.

It would be wrong-headed to blame this inability on people's selfishness (i.e., on a lack of moral qualities such as altruism or benevolence). For instance, in the PD case, almost three times more people cooperate when they are ignorant of the others' moves than when they know that the others have cooperated (see Shafir & Tversky, 1993). If cooperation depended on altruism, it should be the other way around. What happens is that our not knowing what the other person does, does not block the capacity we may have of universalizing the maxim of our action, by asking: "What would happen if everyone acted as I do?" A decisive factor seems to be, then, the faculty to put ourselves in the place of others and to see the world, including ourselves, through their eyes. In cognitive science, this capacity to form representations about someone else's representations is dubbed "meta-representational."

The capacity to *trust* other people comes naturally under this heading. It is well recognized today that trust is the decisive "social capital"[6] that accounts for differences in productivity, social well-being, and vitality across the nations of the world (much more decisive than, in particular, worker skills) (see, for instance, Fukuyama, 1995; and Peyrefitte, 1995). Trust is by essence a self-fulfilling representation or expectation. If you do not trust other people, it will turn out that they are not trustworthy or, at least, you will forsake the opportunity to test their trustworthiness. A trusting agent, in a PD-like structure, will reason as follows: "If I were to cooperate, I would be in a world in which the others are trustworthy, and I should expect them to cooperate," thereby universalizing the maxim of her action.

The capacity to put oneself in the other's place, which is the ethical move par excellence, is not an unmixed blessing. It is also, in turn, the source of personal and social evils due to the decentering from the self toward others that it brings about in the agent: invidious comparisons (Rousseau), feverish competitive spirit (Tocqueville), etc. A traditional way of coping with the ambivalent nature of the capacity under consideration is to have the agents' relationships mediated by values, norms, institutions. It is not so much in the specific, other person that you put your trust as in the common world you share with her. Since Keynes, economists, for example, do not hesitate to speak in terms of "trust in money" or "trust in the future" (or even, as written on the greenback, "in God we trust").

Economists and sociologists argue that in addition to skills and knowledge – which they contend represent today a more decisive capital than land, factories, tools, and machines – social capital as represented by the ability to cooperate with others makes up an increasing portion of human capital (See Coleman, 1988; and Fukuyama, 1995, p. 10). This implies that the ability to cooperate is neither skill nor knowledge. We object to this categorization which makes sense only if one construes skills in the rule-governed, algorithmic way we previously denounced, and if one reduces knowledge to the kind of knowledge which any individual mind at any given time consciously manipulates. Actually, we "know" (in this latter sense) very little of what makes us cooperate, and it is this very "ignorance" that contributes mostly to our coordinating successfully. As Hayek argued provocatively:

---

[6] The phrase "social capital" meaning "the ability of people to work together for common purposes in groups and organizations" was coined by the American sociologist James Coleman in "Social Capital in the Creation of Human Capital," (Coleman, 1988).

It is largely because civilization enables us constantly to profit from knowledge which we individually do not possess and because each individual's use of his particular knowledge may serve to assist others unknown to him in achieving their ends that men as members of civilized society can pursue their individual ends so much more successfully than they could alone (1960, p. 25).

The accumulation of social capital is mainly a cultural process. Trust is grounded in habit rather than in the rational calculation of the consequences of one's actions. For instance, when trust is present in a network business organization, its members

follow an informal set of rules that require little or no overhead to negotiate, adjudicate, and enforce. The moment that trust breaks down...relations have to be spelled out in detail, unwritten rules codified, and third parties brought in to resolve differences (Fukuyama, 1995, p. 342).

The same could be said of various sectors of social life, from "street democracy" (the way anonymous agents relate to each other in daily life) to the political arena. None of this implies that the ability to cooperate with others through trust is not a skill and, for instance, that it cannot be learned, nurtured, or enriched. Becoming a trustful and trustworthy person requires habituation to the moral norms of one's community. It presupposes that one believes in the rationality of the tradition to which one belongs, that one agrees to follow rules of conduct dictated by that tradition, although one is quite unable to predict the consequences of doing so and measure the benefits one can derive from it. It is, in a sense, a leap of faith which requires the acquisition of social virtues like loyalty, honesty, dependability. On the other hand, it is a capacity that we improve by practice, by correcting our errors over time. In brief, developing in our children a sense of "critical rationalism," not oblivious of the virtues of tradition, seems a much better course than inculcating upon their minds the tenets of "constructivist rationalism" if one is to cultivate their cooperative skills.

Narrative Competencies

Narrative competencies depend upon the human capacity to tell stories. They are mainly a way of making sense of what happens in life. They require the capacity to work out patterns of consistency that have to emerge from the complex heterogeneity of human life. They also encompass the ability to imagine alternative possibilities, endings or unfolding, or "counterfactual scenarios" as cognitive psychologists call them.

The basic capacities required for the exercise of narrative skills are partly the same as for the formation of normative skills. They suppose the capacity to detach ourselves from what happens, to distance ourselves from the continuous flow of events in order to understand their meaning and to make sense of what they are, and to be able to anticipate and foresee the long-term effects they will have. They require the ability to construct and conceive schematic, practicable, revisable plans, for one episode of life or for our whole life.

A narrative competency supposes having a strong sensitivity to the situation one is involved in as well as the capacity to perceive the modifications of such a situation. To exercise narrative skills, the agent must be sensitive enough to detect the uncertainty of life and its resilience, which are the very characteristics of the human background against which a general meaning and a form of unity have to be found. Narrative competencies aim at devising a way of fitting the heterogeneous elements of life into a coherent pattern. Finally, they require the capacity to go backwards and forwards within the limits of human life, giving meaning to the entirety of life as a whole, as well as to the various episodes of this life. The design of one's own life will be lacking in substance if it is not enriched by the diversity of various episodes that have in most cases a distinctive character. On the other hand, understanding the episodes of human life will be incomplete if they are not understood in a larger context of life in general. What seems without meaning when we focus on a temporal slice of life will turn out to be meaningful when we take a larger view.

Required by narrative competencies, these basic capacities will be used in a different fashion from the way they are used in perceptive or normative skills. The point is not asking "What should I do?", "What should I have done?", but, "What is the meaning of what happens?", "In what way was what I did meaningful?", "How can I make a consistent episode out of what happened?", "What kinds of ordering, what forms of mutual dependence, consistency, and intelligibility can I find within these events?" In order to exercise one's narrative imagination over other possibilities, one can ask, "If this or that had occurred, would I have acted in a different way?" and "If I had acted in a different way, would this have happened?" This dwelling upon various possibilities exercises the imagining of alternative situations, which is a major aspect of narrative competencies. The intellectual capacity to make sense of something and to conceive of different possibilities which are equally meaningful enables the individual to work out the best possible scenarios according to which his acting will be consistent and intelligible. Viewed in that way, narrative competencies pertain to a set of competencies that contribute to the shaping of deliberation and decision.

Narrative skills are not self-indulgent capacities, too concerned with particulars and with their relation to the self. Along with the workings of imagination, narrative competencies can give a vivid portrayal of alternatives in all their consistency and singularity. Although wedded to particular characters, events, and situations, they can be used in a way of impartial assessment of facts and probabilities. They work along with the active and selective aspect of perception. They are well suited to the work of deliberation, linking observations, reasoning and imaginings, making a cohesive unit from many heterogeneous elements.

In that way, narrative competencies suppose a special kind of understanding, a form of knowledge or comprehension of the meanings of things, events, and experience. They aim at building episodes in which soundness or completeness are to some extent achieved. This criterion is epistemic; it implies some consistency and intelligibility. This special competency could be illustrated by the ability required of the reader of detective stories (who tries, before reaching the end, to establish the missing episodes, to construe motives of actions, to conceive of plausible courses of action which led to the murder), or the people who like to play games of the "who done it?" kind (finding the doer, starting with a limited set of clues) or other games such as "find the differences" (establishing as many similarities as possible in order to find the elements which do not fit); "find the one which does not belong" (construing the rules of formation of a set, which apply to every element of that set but one single item); "complete the series" (finding the law according to which a series is constituted and being able to extrapolate it) or "find the missing elements" (construing the law of a series in spite of the lack of some elements).

Finally, narrative competencies are involved in the capacity to conceive of projects which are valuable enough to warrant the claim that the mere potential to pursue such projects gives value to one's own life. They help in the selection of the roles and goods that will be sufficient to give one's life meaning no matter how small the role one plays or how remote or ambiguous the consequences.

The importance of this widely ignored competency can be brought out in various domains. It is required in social interaction, to deal with others' behavior, to forecast one's own behavior and others' too, and to guess what they will be doing. It is necessary to build a kind of plausibility in order to make events and actions intelligible to oneself and to others. Narrative competencies are also required in order to have some insight into what a possible course of action could be, given a description of actions and events. Construction of intelligibility of past and present events and of plausibility of events to come is a very important aspect of the way human beings deal with the world. Narrative competencies are specially required in order to know how to behave in situations with limited information. In this case, rationality is constrained, but it can be exercised more fully when it is enhanced by the activity of narrative skills working out anticipations and finding missing links.

Narrative competencies are also required for social communication. Making stories intelligible to oneself is the first step to communicating them. Narrative skills are analytical skills, but at the same time they are also communication skills. They contribute to the finding of stylistic devices such as pictorial language which tends to activate the feelings and imagination of the people we communicate with. Narrative competencies work with rhetoric and eloquence.

Lastly, narrative competencies are required for self-understanding and self-interpretation. Such an activity (i.e., interpreting oneself) is a very important aspect of human life in our contemporary world. Narrative skills lead to hermeneutic skills; they are a way of finding the meaning of one's own (his) story by telling it, making sense of it, and interpreting it. Furthermore, the way one tells to oneself one's own stories is one of the major forms of interpreting oneself, and of making this interpretation available to oneself and to other people too.

References

Ashby, R. (1958). Requisite variety and its implications for the control of complex systems. *Cybernetica, 1*(2), 1–17.

Becker, L. C. (1992). Good lives: Prolegomena. *Social Philosophy and Policy, 9*(2), 15-37.

Coleman, J. (1988). Social capital in the creation of human capital. *American Journal of Sociology, 94*, 95–120.

Crisp, R., & Slote, M. (Eds.). (1997). *Virtue ethics.* New York: Oxford University Press.

Dreyfus, H. (1979). *What computers can't do.* New York: Harper Colophon Books.

Dreyfus, H. L., & Dreyfus, S. E. (1986). *Mind over machine: The power of human intuition and expertise in the era of the computer.* Oxford: Basil Blackwell.

Dupuy, J. P. (1992). *Le sacrifice et l'envie.* Paris: Calmann-Lévy.

Frankfurt, H. (1988). *The importance of what we care about.* Cambridge: Cambridge University Press.

Fukuyama, F. (1995). *Trust. The social virtues and the creation of prosperity.* New York: The Free Press.

Griffin, J. (1986). *Well being: Its meaning, measurement and moral importance.* New York: Oxford University Press.

Hart, H. L. (1961). *The concept of law.* Oxford: Clarendon Press.

Hayek, F. (1960). *The constitution of liberty.* London: Routledge & Kegan Paul.

Hayek, F. (1973). *Law, legislation and liberty,* (Vol. I, Rules and Order). London: Routledge and Kegan Paul.

Hayek, F. (1988). *The fatal conceit.* Chicago: University of Chicago Press.

Illich, I. (1971a) *Deschooling society.* New York: Harpers and Row.

Illich, I. (1971b) Education without school: How it can be done. Four educational networks. *The New York Review of Books, 15*(12), 25–31.

Johnson-Laird, P. N., & Wason, P. C. (1977). *Thinking: Readings in cognitive science.* New York: Cambridge University Press.

Kekes, J. (1995). *Moral wisdom and good lives.* Ithaca, NY: Cornell University Press.

Margolis, H. (1987). *Patterns, thinking and cognition: A theory of judgment.* Chicago: University of Chicago Press.

May, R. (1974). *Stability and complexity in model ecosystems.* Princeton, NJ: Princeton University Press.

Oakeshott, M. (1962). *Rationalism in politics, and other essays.* New York: Basic Books Publishing Company.

Oakeshott, M. (1975). *On human conduct.* Oxford: Clarendon Press.

Oakeshott, M. (1983). *On history and other essays.* Oxford: Basil Blackwell.

Organisation for Economic Co-operation & Development and Human Resources Development Canada. (1997). *Literacy skills for the knowledge society.* Paris: OECD.

Peyrefitte, A. (1995). *La société de confiance.* Paris: Editions O. Jacob.

Polanyi, M. (1951). *The logic of liberty: Reflections and rejoinders.* London: Routledge and Kegan Paul.

Polanyi, M. (1958). *Personal knowledge: Towards a post-critical philosophy.* Chicago: University of Chicago Press.

Rachels, J. (Ed.). (1998). *Ethical theory 2: Theories about how we should live.* New York: Oxford University Press.

Rawls, J. (1972). *A theory of justice.* New York: Oxford University Press.

Ryle, G. (1946). Knowing how and knowing that. *Proceedings of the Aristotelian Society, 46*, 1–16.

Shafir, E., & Tversky, A. (1993). Thinking through uncertainty: Nonconsequential reasoning and choice. *Cognitive Psychology, 24*(4), 449-474.

Von Foerster, H. (1987). Conjecture and its demonstration. In H. Atlan, J. P. Dupuy, & M. Koppel (Eds.), Von Foerster's Conjecture: Trivial machines and alienation in systems. *International Journal of General Systems, 13*, 257–264.

Von Neumann, J. (1966). *Theory of self-reproducing automata.* Urbana, IL: University of Illinois Press.

Wiggins, D. (1998). *Needs, values, truth* (3rd ed.). New York: Oxford University Press.

Chapter 5

Ambiguity, Autonomy, and Agency: Psychological Challenges to New Competence

Helen Haste

"Future Competencies" – Some A Priori Considerations

Any projections to the future rest heavily on two features of the present that are usually taken for granted and unquestioned:

- *values* that are currently held in high regard, deemed to be desirable attributes of the individual, and instrumental for the common good; and

- *deficits* that are perceived to need remedying. Such perceptions of deficit may reflect a comparison – explicit or implicit – with some past era of supposed stability or competence, in which case they will be part of a rhetoric of the "slippage" of skill, knowledge, or values. On the other hand, they may be defined as new deficits that accrue from rapid technological developments which require new practical, cognitive, and social skills.

Projections to the future are, therefore, inevitably parochial and time-bound. Hindsight shows us that all exercises in futurology date extremely fast. This may be a consequence of technological change: Some skills suddenly become irrelevant; others turn out to be in actuality much more easily acquired than had been feared. But there can also be unexpected consequences of large-scale value change; for example, in the course of only a decade, ecological values have become as mainstream a moral issue as the more traditional individualistic attributes of honesty, compassion, or responsibility, and now appear on the "wish list" of bodies devising moral education packages.[1]

---

[1] For example, the National Forum for Values in Education and the Community (1996). This document spells out four areas of values statements that reflect a "workable consensus," based on consultation, of values that could form the basis for moral and social values education. These are society, the self, relationships, and the environment.

Defining Competencies

As Weinert has pointed out in his comprehensive overview of the concept (Chapter 3), a competency is more than a domain-based "skill." It must involve *self-regulation, monitoring,* and *initiative-taking,* in the use and in the development of the skill. It must incorporate *adaptation* – both to innovation and to continuity. Competence implies effective interaction and agency in relation to the physical, social, and cultural world. It implies effectiveness not only in performance, but in the interpretation of context and meaning. Competencies include knowing what it is that one *needs* to know – and what one does not need to know. Such understanding comes from recognizing the context in which one's skills function in effective interaction with the environment. In Weinert's terms, this is a metacompetency; I would argue that unless it is embedded in such a metacompetency, a domain-based skill cannot be defined as a competency.

There is a further important dimension of metacompetence. Acquiring a new competency has a major effect on how we are able to interpret and make sense of our world, and on our interaction with it. When we have a particular skill, it is not just that we can use it as part of our agency in acting upon the world. Those skills and competencies provide us with metaphors for how we *can* interact with the world, and therefore, of the possible relationships between the person and the world. We can see this clearly in historical examples of the effects of technological change on our cultural practices and on how we think.

The invention of clockwork transformed not only our management of time, but even more important, our metaphors for the mechanical process, *and* for our relationship with nature. Clockwork (mechanical) models replaced organic models – even of the human body, and of the role of God in the universe (see Bassalla, 1988; Merchant, 1980; and Haste, 1994). Currently, we are adjusting to the enormous effects of having instantaneous electronic communication and universal access to knowledge, both of which have become possible not just through the invention of the computer, but through our increasingly skillful competency with the computer and our increasing use of it in so many areas of our lives.

Psychological research is extremely rich in data that illuminate the concept of competence. I have chosen not to do a comprehensive review of this work, but to draw selectively on key points from it. My starting point will be to elucidate three rather different models that underpin perspectives in psychology which also reflect cultural and philosophical positions about what it means to be "competent" and how we might achieve it. I am, therefore, asserting that our definition of competence is driven not only by the perceived needs of our culture, but by our assumptions about psychological processes.

Models of "The Competent Human"

The three models reflect different theoretical emphases in psychology, and have different implications for the *values* associated with competencies, for explanations of why *certain attributes are functionally adaptive* (and therefore, deemed competent), and for the mechanisms associated with the development of competence.

I will explore each model in relation to the competencies and skills that are implied, the locus of adaptation, and how the tension between innovation and continuity is dealt with. I will also look at the relationship, implicit and explicit, between individual and social processes.

The Puzzle Solver

This model values individual cognitive functioning. It is based on an assumption that rational decision-making is both a *value*, and an *attainable goal*. It follows that "non-rational" reasoning or behavior constitutes a *competence deficit*. It also implies that there is one "right" answer that can be arrived by linear logical processes, and by excluding distracting or distorting factors – a model of convergent rationality, hierarchical decision trees, and closed-solution problem-solving of the kind that, in the field of engineering, control theorists call "open loop-closed solutions."[2]

This model is implicitly uncomfortable with the kind of problems in which there are several routes to solutions, where, for example, feedback loops and multiplex iteration are involved, and where there are a number of possible – and equally useful – outcomes. It is inherently intolerant of ambiguity, uncertainty, and the kind of model associated, in control-theory terms, with "closed loop-open solution" problems, or with "fuzzy logic" (McNeill & Freiberger, 1993). An extensive challenge to the psychological universality of this form of problem-solving comes from Eleanor Rosch's work on *family resemblance* (Rosch, 1978), which questions the assumption that normal cognition involves hierarchical categories of thinking, by showing that, in fact, people deal very comfortably with non-linear categorization.

The Puzzle Solver model focuses primarily on individual cognitive action taking place in isolation – "inside the head" problem-solving by the individual agent. It largely ignores social interaction or cultural processes, both in the etiology of competence and in the exercise of competencies.

The Story Teller

This model of psychological functioning emphasizes social and linguistic processes. Accordingly, competence is manifested in interpretation and decoding of both linguistic and paralinguistic cues. Underpinning this model is a hermeneutic approach

---

[2] For an elaboration of this, see Gosling, 1994.

to meaning, in which narrative, sign, symbol, and rhetoric are the core features of cultural transmission and meaning making.[3]

The model focuses on the mechanisms by which language, social interaction, and cultural behaviors enact and reproduce expectations and norms. These mechanisms facilitate the individual's growing competence as a member of the culture – not only practical performance skills and tool use, but the understanding of their social meaning (see Rogoff, 1990; Cole, 1995; and Harré & Gillett, 1994). Much attention is paid in the exposition of this model to the "apprenticeship" process by which such competencies are scaffolded, and to the ways in which the growing individual decodes, interprets, and manages discursive processes.

The Tool User

This model reflects an interesting convergence of the emerging (and controversial) fields of evolutionary psychology and cultural psychology, particularly the work of Vygotsky (e.g., Vygotsky, 1978; Van Der Veer & Valsiner, 1994; and Werstch, 1998). The central idea is that we encounter our world actively *through* our tools, and these encounters shape how we make sense of, and become competent in interaction with, our world. This contrasts with the concept of "tool use" often implicit in the Puzzle Solver model in which the tool is the *passive mediator* between what is represented inside the individual's head (the "plan") and the external world. The Tool User model in contrast sees the tool (including language) as a *part of an active dialogue* between the individual and the environment (see Wertsch, 1998).

The competencies associated with the Tool User model are far from being merely the skilled manipulation of the tool; they include metacompetencies, particularly (as defined by Weinert, Chapter 3) integration of how the tool changes the way one *can* interact with the world. Having a new skill/tool does not only make it possible to complete more successfully a task already attempted or planned; it opens up new ways of transforming our relationship with the world. The tool is a *prosthesis* for the human body *and mind*, not just a mediating aid. One might say, Tools R Us.

This is often reflected in metaphor. Earlier I referred to the importance of the invention of clockwork in transforming how people interacted with the world and how this interaction created new ways of understanding and making sense of the world. There is extensive research on the effect of the computer on our conceptualization of brain function, thinking, and mind in general. Gigerenzer and Goldstein (1996), for example, demonstrated how the computational model of mind emerged from people's experience of, and interaction with, their technology.

The confluence of evolutionary and cultural psychology in the Tool User model comes out of the shared concept that our evolutionary and cultural history depends on *interacting with* tools. *With* tools, new cognitions and new social practices became possible; *through* tools, the growing individual learns not only the necessary competencies of the culture, but also the cultural significance and salience of those compe-

---

[3] The educational implications as well as the theoretical are explored in Bruner, 1996.

tencies, and the metaphors that those competencies provide which serve as explanatory frameworks for dialogue and, indeed, for innovation.

These three models can be presented as conflicting theoretical positions which have very different assumptions and focus on very different aspects and interpretations of performance. Current debates in psychology reflect such conflicts. However, for present purposes it is useful to consider each as offering a different insight on a necessary and adaptive competency which, in taking such an overview, we might decide to value and foster. By spelling out the differences, I highlight the fact that no list of "ideal" competencies comes free from philosophical, theoretical, and, indeed, empirical baggage.[4]

Below, I will justify a list of competencies that I regard as being essential in the immediate future, and which could possibly be universally relevant, although cultural contexts would determine exactly how they are manifested. This will be based on a more elaborated discussion of the three models presented above.

Tensions Between Innovation and Continuity

I argue first that a superordinate, or first order, metacompetency in the modern world is *the management of innovation (novelty) and continuity.* There is an enduring tension, but one that is particularly salient at this historical point in time, between sustaining continuity and connection to what is established, known, familiar, and supportive, and dealing with novelty and innovation, which involves the acquisition of new skills, changing perspectives, creating new associations, and becoming part of new communities.

This tension is manifested in numerous ways. Let us explore three as illustrations: the problem of the *canon,* the *rapid introduction of technology,* and the question of *autonomy.*

The Canon

Is there a body of knowledge, a repository of the "essential" elements of culture, that every child should know? If we choose to believe that there is, we must ask why. What is the purpose of a canon of knowledge? The concept of a canon reflects very precisely one aspect of the tension between continuity and innovation: whether one is perpetuating enduring wisdom and skill in order to preserve the culture by reproducing it in the next generation, or whether one believes that this particular body of knowledge equips the young not only to carry on the traditions, but to face the challenges of novelty and innovation.

The educators of imperial Britain, for example, were definitely convinced that their classical education package steeped their charges in the richness of heritage

---

[4] I have explored a number of these ideas extensively in Haste, 2000.

while also training them in mental discipline that would serve them well in the far-flung outposts and dangers of the Empire. Learning Latin was good for three reasons; it provided a knowledge of one's classical roots, a rigorous discipline (certainly as rigorous as mathematics) that would lay the foundation for logical thought, and finally, the linguistic basis for learning other languages.

Today, we have perhaps a greater overt appreciation of the nature of "culture" – particularly as "multiculturalism" becomes a major discourse. There is much more focus on the canon as a way of perpetuating *particular* cultural values and an understanding of cultural heritage and continuity. This is expressed both in positive and negative terms. There is concern among those who espouse certain forms of multiculturalism to avoid the dominance of a unitary "Western male" canon, and to replace it – or at least supplement it – with a canon that expresses the cultural values of minorities. For those who are wary of what they see as the implied relativism of multiculturalism, bolstering some consensual canon is seen as the bastion against fragmentation and the loss of "high culture."

Both sides, however, recognize that the content of the canon purveys values, beliefs, and worldviews, including metaphors which provide frameworks for talking about, and making sense of our experience. The canon is explicitly *a tool of cultural reproduction*; it is not just a toolkit for survival in a particular place in a particular historical period.

In Howard Gardner's book, *The Disciplined Mind* (1999), he explores these tensions, advocating what are in effect meta-canonical goals for education. These goals are in one sense highly traditional; they are *truth, beauty, and the good*. He chooses to *illustrate* these by three topics, each of which in his view allows us to access the larger and wider issues and implications. For *truth*, Gardner advocates the study of Darwin, who in his own right represents one version of the pursuit of truth – through scientific method – but whose field, evolution, is also crucial to modern debates and discourses. For *beauty*, Gardner advocates Mozart, particularly *The Marriage of Figaro,* through which one can appreciate not only the personal experience of being moved by a great work of art, but also understand the dramatic and musical intricacies – and from this understanding, appreciate also the basis of art and craft in other areas, and the values surrounding art. For *the good*, by which Gardner means morality, he advocates an understanding of the Holocaust, because, as he says, "if the Holocaust is mostly an account of unprecedented human evil, there are scattered incidents of goodness and heroism even in that grim chapter" (Gardner, 1999, p. 17).

Gardner anticipates the obvious criticism that his examples are not only culture- and time-bound, but also reflect his personal idiosyncratic tastes and interests. But his key point is that the very universality of the three goals of truth, beauty, and the good allow for a transcendent consensus, within which any culture (or historical period) will find its own appropriate examples.

Gardner highlights an important distinction between offering an educational path to the young that specifically reproduces an existing culture, and offering an agenda through which the young individual comes to understand the world and want to change it. Gardner's aim is that young people should understand the world through the work of those who have "studied it most carefully and lived in it most thoughtfully," which will enable them to "monitor their own lives in terms of human possibilities, including ones that have not been anticipated before" (Gardner, 1999, p. 20). The metacompetencies that he advocates are *means* of understanding, rather than the *content* of what is understood.

The Rapid Introduction of Technology

We find a second tension between innovation and continuity in the rapid introduction of new technologies and the acquisition of necessary skills. There are those who want to take a future-oriented view and ensure that the members of the next generation are hyper-skilled in the most advanced technology, probably at the expense of more "traditional" skills. Some do so on the grounds of future national commercial interest; some are more concerned about the survival of the young individual in the marketplace.

Does any child need to learn to hand-write today? Are not keyboard skills more essential – and easier to learn – and therefore more motivating? Even as I write this, I am aware that within a couple of years keyboard skills themselves *may* have become redundant as voice-operated technology becomes universal. In which case one might come to the devastating conclusion that children no longer need to learn any *manual* craft of "writing" at all, which does follow logically from taking a wholly innovation-oriented perspective. Yet, what are the justifications for continuity? What traditional skills are necessary, particularly in areas where technology has superseded much human practice? What is the justification, the rationale, for keeping certain skills alive?

One justification is survival – if the technology breaks down, can I still write a note to my cleaning person, for example? Less frivolously, we have seen the supposed "decline" of mental arithmetic in the face of the universal calculator. Of course, we say, children should learn their tables (if not the mysteries of long division). But we recognize that they need to do so in order to have a conceptual understanding of number, not just in case they mislay their machinery.

A stronger argument for teaching a traditional skill is not in order to use it as an alternative, but because through understanding how something is done, or made, I will be able to transfer such knowledge to other domains. For example, there are many ways that one can learn how to visualize, and work in, three-dimensional space. One domain is sculpture, another is dressmaking. A third is surgery. We might think it odd to teach surgery to medical students by getting them to make their own lab coats – yet there is a certain craft logic to this. A graduate student at my university, Dawn Woodgate, is investigating visualization particularly in relation to veterinary surgery, and she has found that interviews with sculptors and with people who sew have illuminated the concept greatly.

A common justification for teaching traditional skills is that they bring one "closer" to the material. The burgeoning do-it-yourself industry is testimony to people's willingness to get involved in the hands-on creation of their immediate environment. It is the challenge of making one's own impact on the physical world, in ways that high-tech interaction does not.

In Britain, most children have courses in craft and technology subjects. It is left rather vague as to whether this is a hangover from the days when schools laid the foundation for "trades" skills to be later supplemented by apprenticeships, or whether craft and technology are part of a general training in transferable skills. If you can manage the manual tasks at school, you will have the confidence to extend this to new skills. So it is a matter of the skill of acquiring skills. Another possible agenda is that through craft one can access creativity, something closer to art, with the aim of giving each child a sense of making something unique. This aim relates to an agenda of building self-confidence and personal growth, rather than simply acquiring useful skills.

I have dwelt at some length on this because I think it is useful to see just how the tensions between innovation and continuity pan out in the domain of technological education. In the discussion of training related to information technology, we see an orientation to the future needs of the individual and of society (though increasingly the skills are becoming essential to market survival). We see traditional skills, however, as serving other purposes, mostly associated with continuity in some form, so we think it worthwhile to teach children to use sewing machines and lathes even though the majority will never do so in adult life, just as we give them experience of painting and modeling irrespective of their artistic talents.

The Goal of Autonomy

The third tension between innovation and continuity is manifested in our conceptions of autonomy. It may at first sight seem curious to treat autonomy as parallel to the knowledge canon or issues of technological innovation, but my argument is that we take for granted the desirability of "autonomy" as a personal or educational goal just in the same way as we may take for granted the desirability of teaching Shakespeare.

My position is based on a perception that Western culture equates innovation with resisting a collective conservatism. In such a context, individualistic values and the psychological competency to "think for oneself" and "resist social pressure" are valued and fostered. Autonomy therefore is seen as the expression of moral and intellectual maturity; paradoxically, it is therefore a "traditional" Western value that serves the purposes of innovation. So apparently, we have here the perfect bridge between innovation and continuity.[5]

Recently, however, we have seen challenges to these assumptions. These challenges arise from a major shift in our perspectives about how we actually become effective participants in our culture. Rather than this being the successful outcome of

---

[5] Kohlberg's Rawlsian theory of moral development expresses this position elegantly and with extensive data. I do not query the evidence from Kohlberg's lifelong work and longitudinal research, but I would argue, as others have, that locating morality in reasoning about justice focuses on aspects of reasoning that reflect individual thinking. See review in Haste et al., 1998.

an individual developmental struggle, that in effect sees the self as a personal creation, there has been an increasing move towards conceptualizing such competencies
as arising from reflexive appreciation and management of one's membership in the
community.

There are many sources of this critique; they are as diverse as discursive psychology, Foucauldian sociology, and communitarianism. I will explore the latter because
it includes both a critique of values and a critique of the presumed psychological
model. This has two discrete elements: a *moral* position and an *ontological* position.
The *moral* position is that we should not, in the illusory pursuit of an autonomous
morality, try to deny our connection to our roots and to our interaction with others.
Indeed, the basis for morality should be our responsibilities for and to others. An effective, caring community is the foundation for fostering morality in the young, as
well as providing a supportive ethical environment. This has been explored by numerous writers, including Amitai Etzioni (e.g., 1988 and 1994) who advocate communitarianism as an *ethical system*.

However, there are other critiques that question the *ontological* assumptions behind a model of the "autonomous" human, notably Charles Taylor (1991) and Daniel
Bell (1993). Their position is that autonomy is based on an illusory picture of the
human being functioning in social isolation. Such an illusion makes us focus only on
"inside the head" cognitive processes, seeing us engaging in an ethical monologue,
and furthermore, ignoring the inevitable social, cultural, and linguistic dialogue
through which all our competencies are fostered. Taylor, for example, argues that
human life is "fundamentally dialogic... We become full human agents, capable of
understanding ourselves, and hence defining our identity, through our acquisitions of
rich human languages of expression" (1991, p. 32).

These critiques are consistent with social constructions and discursive theoretical
developments in psychology (for example, Shotter, 1993; Harré, 1998; and Harré &
Gillett, 1994), who argue that the *primary* human reality is face-to-face conversation.
If social interaction is the crucible of meaning, then learning morality (or any other
competency) happens through discourse and through social practices, both explicit
and implicit. The "meaning" of something – including the meaning of our own identity and our own morality – depends on what is comprehensible and recognized
within our social community. We are members of multiple communities each of
which offers us identity and personal meaning, and within each, different elements,
skills, and competencies are salient.[6]

There are many implications of this for the tension between innovation and continuity. Once we acknowledge the social embeddedness of meaning and practice, then
"innovation" has to be seen as dependent on the social facilitation and construction of
novelty, not simply attributed – as in the traditional individualistic model – to the
acts of solitary and heroic individuals. Recognizing social embeddedness does not
preclude the role of the individual mind but it does require careful analysis of how
the individual mind dialogically operates to promote novelty, and also, how the cultural context does, or does not, facilitate such novelty. There is extensive work in

---

[6] I have explored this more extensively in Haste, 1996.

history of science, and in sociology of science, for example, that shows how ideas flourish under certain conditions and belief systems but not others.

Applying the Three Models

How does this discussion of innovation and continuity fit in with the three models of Puzzle Solver, Story Teller, and Tool User?

As I implied earlier, the Puzzle Solver is quite closely wedded to a model of individual action and agency, and takes little account of dialogic or social construction processes. There is no a priori basis on which to predict the Puzzle Solver view of "the canon." However on issues concerned with technological change, we might expect that the Puzzle Solver's focus on finding solutions would lean towards defining *innovation* in terms of new technical skills, and *continuity* in terms of the functional value of traditional, but transferable, skills. In terms of the issue of autonomy and community, the Puzzle Solver's emphasis on individual problem-solving and internal cognition is consistent with a valorization of autonomy and with a limited attention to social contextual factors.

The Story Teller model, in contrast, places great emphasis on context, on dialogic and social processes, and on narrative and discourse. In such a framework, the canon is likely to be regarded critically, as culturally and historically restricted. The Story Teller model recognizes the function of multifaceted "stories" in producing and reproducing culture, including the need to generate a diversity of perspectives and a variety of experiences of positioning and of identity. As far as technological versus traditional skills are concerned, the Story Teller model is likely to focus on the meaning and context of a particular skill, as well as its function in promoting useful competencies. For the Story Teller, skills as such are not important; it is their context and the implications for what is possible via skills that matter. Stories of the benefits (and problems) of technological change have symbolic importance both in facilitating innovation and in sustaining continuity (see, for example, Haraway, 1991). On the issue of autonomy and community, the Story Teller model is wholly on the side of social construction and discursive practices; autonomy therefore becomes one "story" which may have certain value in defining one "heroic" identity.

The Tool User model would interpret the question of the canon very much as would the Story Teller: the body of knowledge, the ways of interpreting the world which are implicitly or explicitly made normative by that choice of "what should be known," become a tool by which the individual can interact in continuity with the past, and find metaphors and values for encountering the present and future. Consider, for example, the stylistic conventions of 18th century poetry, in which the story – anything from a battle to a love affair – was told through classical and mythological analogies. The message was, first, that this was the appropriate language of poetry. Second, such a stylistic convention assumed that every literate child of that era would share the cultural associations aroused by these allusions, and respond with the appropriate insights. Third, it assumed that 18th century life itself could be experienced and made sense of through the narratives of classical mythology.

On the issue of technology, the Tool User model goes even further than the Story Teller into an identification between the tool and the interpretation. What we *can* know, comes from how we have interacted with the world. It comes via whatever mediation through which we have actively engaged in dialogue with the world, be it through language and metaphor, clockwork, a computer, or a screwdriver. So, traditional techniques will affirm and reinforce the familiar metaphors of the culture, and give the growing child hands-on experience of established and familiar ways of relating to the world – not only skills, but *ways of thinking about* the interaction. There is extensive literature on how our mental models arise from our experience, and how we transfer those models to new situations (e.g., Gentner & Stevens, 1983; Vosniadou & Ortony, 1989; and Ortony, 1993).

On the matter of autonomy and community, the Tool User model, like the Story Teller, implies dialogic collaboration in the construction and negotiation of meaning, and therefore goes counter to the "isolated cognitive agent" image. However, there is more space in the Tool User analogy for the individual's agency in interaction with the world. Nevertheless, there is a strong emphasis on a shared community of tool-use, and in particular the social meaning and value of the use of particular tools.

Five Key Competencies

In the foregoing I have discussed aspects of what I have termed the metacompetency of dealing with the management of innovation and continuity. I will now consider five areas or domains, each of which implies a distinctive kind of competency. Within each there are specific competencies, but I intend to address the broad category, rather than produce a comprehensive list. I will also consider some educational implications.

Technological Competence

By this I mean not just a list of skills necessary to manage, for example, information technology, transportation, fixing household appliances, or whatever. If we take the Tool User model seriously, *metacompetence* in tool use is a *readiness to acquire new skills as needed, and to drop those no longer required.* Technological competence involves appreciating that one's interaction with the world will be modified, and possibly transformed, by a new technological skill. We cannot of course expect individuals or even tool-using communities to anticipate the nature of this transformation, but it is in my view a part of technological competence to be able to deal reflexively, in a coping manner, with such developments. In teaching new skills, we are inclined first to take the view "this will solve your current problem" – which is consistent with the Puzzle Solver model – rather than "this will create interesting new questions," which is consistent with both the Story Teller and the Tool User models.

It is salutary to consider just how technological advance transforms our interactions with the world, and how this frequently does not happen in the ways predicted by the technical experts. It is useful to distinguish the realm of the inventor or technical expert, from that of the user. Technical innovation is driven by many motives: responsiveness to a perceived need, the pursuit of elegant and streamlined design, the need to keep a market edge through constant refinements, the accidental or intended outcome of scientific developments (as for example the huge fallout of spin-offs from the space program's developments of new materials). It is frequently the case that the designer has a particular domain-specific goal in mind, a particular purpose for the development; it is frequently the case that the real applications of a development are far from the expert's own goals.

Why does the permeation of technological expertise into the lay world not follow the designer's path? It is because there is a tension between *assimilation* and *accommodation*, to use the concepts of psychologist Jean Piaget – or *adopt-to-adapt*, in lay terms. New technology is initially incorporated into existing practices, including social practices. The new "gadget" does an improved job on the current task – just as the word processor was initially an improved typewriter, still operated by a trained secretary. The full potential of a new invention is often not recognized; motor cars were initially rich boys' toys; the usefulness of the internal combustion engine over the horse and the bicycle only became apparent under conditions of war.[7] It is just this incorporation or assimilation of new technology into common practice that gives people the familiarity with the new tool that allows them to adapt its potential to other needs, and eventually, to accommodate their practices to that potential.

Returning to the word processor, the secretary's traditional role has become redundant as not only typewriting, but many other communication functions, are taken over by operators who treat the necessary skills as normative rather than specialized (and in consequence, this has removed the "female, low-status" label from keyboard skills). The word processor is no longer a glorified typewriter; it has become an essential workstation for communication and information retrieval. What was once a piece of specialized office equipment, operated by a particular class of skilled worker, is rapidly becoming a household necessity – often multiple – and the skills are universally required, and taught with other literacy skills to six-year-olds. Email is replacing telephone contact for large swaths of the population, but even more significant, access to the Internet is rapidly transforming how children as well as adults "learn"; the world's libraries are in every bedroom.

Another example of changing social practice in response to technological innovation is the effect of the mobile phone. The market penetration of mobile phones is dramatic; in some countries it is now over 70 percent, and the prediction has been made that by 2010 there will be very few line phones. This has happened extremely rapidly, particularly in Europe. What is the significance of this? Is it more than simply greater phone access? The key issue is that the phone has now become a prosthesis of the person; one phones a *person, not a place*. To retain privacy, one switches off a machine, rather than move rooms. As the technology of the mobile phone im-

---

[7] Bassala (1998) discusses this in detail.

proves, it will become the mobile workstation; the function of the "office" will change even further. Parents will increasingly expect to maintain contact with their children through mobile phones, which, paradoxically, could give children more safe freedom of movement than they can currently have.

Almost none of the above have involved the lay individual in much *technical* change; a relatively minor improvement in skill (for example, typing) has given lay people access to a technological infrastructure which, because of its impact on potential *social* practices, transforms how people interact with their worlds. The message of my argument therefore is that while a certain level of technological competence is essential and needs teaching universally, the real issues of *metacompetence* lie in responsive and adaptive development of the potential of these skills for changing social practices.

As I noted earlier, some technical skills have turned out to be very easily acquired – the usual commonsense quip being that one consults one's five-year-old about managing the video machine. But concentration on the *technical* aspects deflects us from two issues: technical designers are responding to their own agendas which presuppose a primacy of technical concerns rather than social concerns. In contrast, lay people adopt, and adapt, new technology to their existing lifestyles and behavior only gradually, and through a dialogue between the tool and these practices, adjust both and extend the potential of each.

Dealing With Ambiguity and Diversity

Pleas for multiculturalism, pluralism, and indeed, postmodernism, come from two very different traditions which have almost nothing in common. One tradition is based on values: we should cultivate the virtues of tolerance, justice, and consideration for others. The other tradition is based in epistemology; it is manifested in critiques which in essence challenge the assumptions about *how* we know, and how we *can* know. These are critiques of *an intellectual tradition*, of a philosophical position that privileges absolutism, positivism, and objectivism.

There is a strong tradition in Western thought that sustains this intellectual tradition and it has significant psychological consequences. The Puzzle Solver model is consistent with this, focusing on closed solutions, finding the "right" (and single) answer. In privileging problem *solving,* this model generates anxieties about ambiguity and uncertainty which become strong *and culturally endorsed* motives for finding the right answer. This promotes a tendency to cut through diversity and complexity, in the pursuit of simplicity and parsimony, and to valorize resistance to distraction and field-independent problem-solving.

But what happens when this breaks down? What happens when the boundaries are fuzzy, or when context is inescapable? How do people who have been trained in a bounded epistemology deal with the reality of an epistemologically messy world?

Historically, psychologists have mainly researched tolerance of ambiguity in the context of variation in individual attributes – looking at personality factors or cognitive style. To do this is to treat the issue as a trait model, and to focus on the management of anxiety as much as epistemological style. Increasingly, research which focuses more on generic cognitive processes shows that there are flaws in the Puzzle Solver model, which assumes that ambiguity will be disequilibrating and produce motives to reduce uncertainty. The Puzzle Solver model has not only focused on the route to a single solution, it has postulated that a *drive to consistency* is a dominant motive; this governed, for example, classic social psychological work on cognitive dissonance, and on balance theories of attitude change, as well as work in more cognitive domains (e.g., Festinger, 1957; and Heider, 1958).

First, it turns out that in practice, we are able to juggle a number of disparate and dissonant values or beliefs, and to move between different and contrasting discourses. I mentioned earlier the impact of psychological work by Rosch (1978) that questions the sort of hierarchical, linear, problem-solving models inherent in the Puzzle Solver model. Her work shows that even small children can deal very accurately with an apparently complex system of categorization based on family resemblance and prototypes. This brings into question both the universality of hierarchical taxonomic models, and also, the implicit assumption that ambiguity and dissonance are anxiety-inducing.

As I also mentioned earlier, work from a very different context, engineering, shows that the "ideal" solution may not be an "open loop-closed solution," because a great deal of "problem-solving" in the real world is concerned with physical (and social) contexts that are dynamic and fluid, and in which feedback, iteration, and cybernetic adjustments are crucial. Furthermore, there is often more than one solution that is equally useful and functional; *the closed loop-open solution* may be more functional both in engineering and in psychological terms. However, psychologists wedded to the Puzzle Solver model have tended – to date – to do less research on this.

It is not only in the field of cognition that a postulated "motive to avoid ambiguity" is under question. Social psychologists became aware early that Festinger's model of dissonance-reduction did not always apply. Under experimental conditions where people were forced to confront the inconsistencies of a situation, they did indeed respond by adjusting their minds – but as soon as researchers began to study "real life" contexts it was apparent that people were equally adept at avoiding recognition of inconsistency, or of just living with it.[8]

As social psychology has moved increasingly into naturalistic study, looking at narrative and discourse, and avoiding the artificial constraints of enforced experimental designs, it becomes ever more apparent how adept we are at dealing with ambiguity and multiple perspectives, and indeed, doing so not by denying the inconsistencies, but by managing them in complex ways. One striking study of this is the work of Michael Billig (1992) on British people talking about the Royal Family. This study comprised the analysis of conversations held in families. There were certain key dimensions. First, there are a number of different value positions on the Royal Family which are inherently contradictory – that they are expensive, an outdated luxury that drains the country's resources and so impoverishes others, they serve a useful symbolic function, do good works and perform important public services. Second,

---

[8] Roger Brown discusses this with particular wit in his classic *Social Psychology,* 1965.

there are conflicting views on their personal and moral qualities, and by implication, on their role as standard-setters; but the key point is that any one member of the Royal Family can be seen simultaneously as morally lacking and as virtuous.

A major finding was that when people talk about the Royal Family, they are talking about "family" in general. The domestic, parental, and marital problems of the Windsors are talked about as paralleling the same problems as those of the family who are being studied – or their friends. The Queen as the distressed mother with "difficult" children; Princess Diana trying to be a "good" mother to her sons; the problems of straying husbands and wives. These are stories not of a royal clan, but of the British family at large; to find such parallels is reassuring for one's story of one's own family.

Billig's work in this study, and also other work using discourse analysis techniques, for example by Jonathan Potter and Margaret Wetherell (1987), shows how people move smoothly and without any apparent anxiety from one statement to another though they seem contradictory. Their conclusion is that we operate with several parallel "discourses," each of which is subjectively internally consistent. Each tells a story that makes sense, has implicit or explicit justifications, presupposes origins or causes that sustain an explanation. Furthermore, each story is presumed to be comprehensible to those who hear it. So it is not only our internal subjective consistency that is at issue, but the assumption that others will hear our story in the same terms as we relate it. As Billig (1987) has explored more extensively in another classic work, *Arguing and Thinking,* we can distinguish between things that are taken for granted, and do not need explanation or justification, and things that are problematic, which we need to persuade others about, and so we offer explanations and justifications in our discourse. It is striking, therefore, when we find that apparent inconsistencies of values or argument not only fail to create subjective anxiety, but are deemed to be unproblematic in our own social context.

The key point is the switch of discourse; what might be a problem in one discourse (for example, providing fair educational opportunities for all social classes) becomes non-problematic in another (for example, when talking about one's own children's educational needs). What is evident is that we are very skilled in picking up the cues about which discourse is in place, and fitting in with it. Billig's study of Royal Family discourses showed how very rapid such a shift could be, virtually in the same sentence.

These are examples of data relating to our tolerance of ambiguity, and how they undermine the assumptions of the "Puzzle Solver." These data are much better accounted for by the Story Teller model. Indeed, such discursive practices are an inherent part of the narrative basis for the Story Teller model – the idea that we do not so much have "concepts" or "representations" as "stories" which simultaneously provide explanations and justifications, and convey the message.

I have shown that it is not only from psychological data that we see a loosening of, and a challenge to, models of thinking which emphasize the linear and the closed-solution; I have brought in examples from engineering, control theory, and fuzzy logic, which challenge the assumptions of the *necessity* of sharp boundaries and dualistic distinctions. These examples were from real problem-solving activities; we can look also to new ways of thinking, new metaphors, which change our perspective.

A metaphor of growing significance comes from chaos theory. I say it is a metaphor because chaos is about physics, about randomness and determinism, and about how small perturbations at a source can have very large effects. The major effect of chaos theory has been to undermine our classical assumption that what is determined can, *ergo*, be predictable. This has had great impact on physics and mathematics, but my interest is its growing metaphorical impact on other fields. The butterfly and the tornado, along with the evocative fractal imagery, have had enormous impact on popular thought. Much effort is going into finding "chaotic" processes in many other fields of science and social science. The details of these developments are not my current concern here; what I want to point out is that the Zeitgeist is deeply relevant to the question of tolerance of ambiguity. We are currently seeing sound physical and mathematical principles challenging some of our cherished tenets about reason – for example, our assumption that simple things have simple causes, and complex things have complex courses (e.g., Stewart, 1989; and Cohen & Stewart, 1994). These developments are having very wide-ranging implications for our normative assumptions about ambiguity and diversity.

So, what are the implications for competence? The Puzzle Solver model presupposes a competence that is associated with linear logic, the avoidance of distractions, and the elimination of as many variables in the situation as possible. But as we recognize the need for a more complex picture of the world, the competence required is the ability to manage diversity and dissonance in a creative and coping way, and avoid premature closure, or dissolution into relativism.

Finding and Sustaining Community Links

The third area of key competency that I want to explore takes us away from cognition and into social and personal domains. I want to explore the competencies needed to deal with the new form of "community" that we are encountering. Earlier I talked about communitarianism, and pointed out that the rise of communitarian ideas had two distinct elements: the *value* dimensions concerned with caring and responsibility for those in our community, and the rather more wide-reaching implications for how we think about *social processes in the construction of meaning*. The tenor of the *values* argument is that we need to re-create connection to a community and to ordered, supportive, social structures. The tenor of the *social process* argument rests on a theoretical framework that stresses the hermeneutic basis of our understanding of the world. Within this, a social and linguistic community is the basis for the construction of meaning.

In exploring the competencies associated with finding and sustaining community links, I shall be keeping in mind both these dimensions. First, the reality is that geographical, local community is problematic in a rapidly mobile world; what is replacing the face-to-face community is connection through "virtual" links of various sorts. Rather than immediately bewailing this development as alienating, we should be looking at ways in which such virtual communities are now part of many people's lives in industrialized countries (including, increasingly, children's lives), and at how they function already. How can they be viewed as effective support systems, and their potential for human interconnection realized? This kind of virtual supportive community exists as a sort of meta-structure in parallel with other social links forged by more traditional means of contact. What began in the academic and corporate world as an efficient means of interoffice and worldwide electronic communication is now permeating the domestic world.

There are competencies associated with these developments that we do not as yet fully understand. Research is sorely needed on how people use email and the Internet for creating meaningful virtual communities. It is a set of competencies however that will increasingly be needed – the initiation and management of contact, the cyber versions of eye contact and body language (and I do not mean typographical symbols for smiling, etc.). Do we say "hello" and "goodbye" on email, as we would on the phone?

In this area, the tensions between the three models I explored are particularly interesting. The Puzzle Solver dimension is of note; the development of electronic technology clearly had (and still has) an appeal for solving a defined problem. We have seen a move away from conventional mail ("snail mail") initially to fax but rapidly to downloaded electronic mail. Fax may turn out to be, rather like the electric typewriter, a short-lived transitional technology (even though it was actually invented in the middle of the 19th century but never developed). We have come to expect our communication – whether spoken or written – to be absolutely instantaneous and worldwide. I, like many academics, routinely communicate with people on at least two continents *nearly every single day*. I, like most others in my world, now pace my work, deadlines, and dialogues with colleagues on a time scale very different from one of even five years ago. In a curious way, we have restored through e-mail the intellectual written dialogues that used to be possible amongst scientists and others in the 19th century when there were four or five postal deliveries a day.

We recently interviewed a person for a job using a video link; he was in Wisconsin, we were in Bath. This will become routine, and a lot less expensive than air travel. But what is also significant is that, at the same time as sharing intellectual ideas, I chat with my friends via email with the coziness and intimacy that would hitherto have been associated with at least very long telephone calls. I also send departmental memos by email (never on paper) – and I expect my colleagues to read them almost immediately. Because many have modems at home, increasingly this can be a 24-hours a day, 7-days a week process, if people choose; the time boundaries of "the working day" have become fuzzy and fluid.

The Puzzle Solver model may be applied to a technical problem of rapid communication. But it is to the Tool User model that we should look for deeper illumination of social practices. Here we can see the evolution of which I wrote earlier, from *adopt-to-adapt,* or *assimilation and accommodation*. People's first experience of e-mail tends to be a parallel with telephoning (a well-practiced tool usage). The one-to-one, serial communication soon becomes enlarged as the new tool's potential becomes apparent. Group communication is easy; joining email networks allows both for the dissemination of information widely, and most important, for genuine interaction within the network. One can see the construction, evolution, and negotiation of meaning emerging. We are all engaging in virtual mini-conferences without even having to organize them. The departmental coffee room is now global. We are in dialogue with our machines and with each other, as the Tool User model explicates.

These are new competencies; we can see them emerging but perhaps as yet cannot prescribe where they will go, or what we need to propose for education in response. The issue I pose in this paper is that we recognize that competencies are emerging and changing in this domain, and that we need to look at them as part of community-building and relationship-maintenance, *not* as technical skills.

Such virtual communities are rapidly developing and require new competencies; face-to-face communities remain our primary social networks and support systems. I shall not touch on the huge research material on relationships; this would be beyond the scope of this chapter. Nor will I deal with a major problematic area: the changing patterns of family life and the need to find ways of parenting that work for diverse family models. Today we have single parents, serial parents, multiple step-parents, and we must manage sibling and step-sibling relationships. We have also new roles for grandparents who are now healthier, fitter, and at least in many industrialized countries, considerably more affluent than in previous generations. In particular, with the spread of female employment, the non-working granny is on the decline, with as yet unrealized implications for family care. We have barely begun to tackle these issues.

I will concentrate instead on some key issues relating to the larger community, and particularly to school. Work in schools has for some time demonstrated the importance of "school climate." The classic work by Rutter, Maughan, Mortimore, and Ouston (1979), *Fifteen Thousand Hours,* was a meticulous longitudinal study of twelve secondary schools in London, involving over 2000 pupils. The findings clearly showed that the characteristics of *schools as social institutions* were significant in relation to a number of outcomes such as academic performance and good behavior. These characteristics included teacher actions in lessons, expectations of pupils, conditions for pupils, incentives and rewards, and the extent to which children were able to take responsibility.

Since that study, there has been considerably more work done, which, on the whole, has confirmed these findings. At the same time, the ethos of education, at least in Britain, has changed considerably, with much greater emphasis in the last decade on criteria of achievement measured in examination results. But these findings about the development of community still stand. Contemporaneously with the Rutter et al. study in Britain, in the United States Lawrence Kohlberg was experimenting with the *Just Community* in schools (Higgins, 1991; Power, Higgins & Kohlberg, 1989). This was based on a cognitive developmental model that focused on reasoning, but it derived from Dewey's principles of democratic education and the importance of hands-on experience of sharing in decision-making. The *Just Community*, in Kohlberg's formulation, involved a social structure in the classroom in which everyone had an equal right in decision-making, including teachers (though with some minimal constraints).

The original purpose of the Just Community was to create an environment in which reasoning about moral and social issues was transparent, and in which the dialogue between adjacent stages of moral reasoning would act as a catalyst in the development from lower to higher stages. This arose from more experimental work using "Socratic dialogue" techniques which had been shown to stimulate moral reasoning development. But it became clear that the "moral atmosphere" or norms that developed in the group were just as interesting as the effect on individual reasoning. This work was done within a firmly cognitive developmental framework consistent with the Puzzle Solver model. It can, however, be interpreted within models of the social construction of meaning, and the role of dialogic processes in creating a community ethos and a form of discourse within which people make sense of their interactions and their values. Such dialogic processes have been explored in the context of the classroom particularly by Derek Edwards and Neil Mercer (1987), and developed by Jerome Bruner (1996) as a framework for thinking about education.

So, what competencies are relevant to finding and sustaining community? I have dwelt on the importance of the community environment for generating competencies in general, and particularly moral competence and selfhood (as expressed in the management of one's achievement motivation and goal direction). But a focus on *outcomes* misses the point that what is being fostered here is the competence *to be part of* a collective community, taking responsibility for that participation and the tasks shared by the community. The outcomes ensue because the children become skilled in understanding not only what is expected of them, but how to be engaged and active in the *process of production*. As I have discussed above, school climate facilitates – or impairs – competencies in judgment, in taking and sharing responsibility, and in leadership. These are transferable to other community settings; the more the child can practice both the skills and the understanding, the more he or she will be able to utilize them in a larger setting.

I began this section by discussing communitarianism, because it is in that critical context that both the values and the assumptions about psychological processes come together. Elsewhere I have developed the educational implications of this, in the context of the theoretical assumptions:

Let us recap on the principles for consideration:

• The theoretical presumption is that people are social beings who generate meaning through discourse and social interaction, and through cultural repertoires, stories and scripts transmitted by social practices and narratives.

It *follows* that:

• The desirable *goals* are values that will promote engagement with the community, and the transcendence of egoism and narrow instrumentalism; these values foster an individual sense of meaning, and a stable community.

The *procedures* to attain the goals therefore must harness these social and psychological processes.

Five principles of moral education follow:

- *Learning through language and social practice* means that values must be institutionalized and enacted as part of everyday life, so that they are experienced as taken for granted through action.

- *Fostering social identity* means telling stories and narratives about the community and culture which give meaning to one's self, explanations for why things are as they are, and recognition that these stories and accounts are shared.

- *Feeling engaged with, and connected to, others* means experiencing responsibility and caring, as giver and receiver, and making these explicit and normative.

- *Recognizing that institutions and communities have multiple covert and overt agendas,* and dealing with these, helps community members understand community processes, and fosters pluralist values.

- A *self-conscious appreciation of the hermeneutic processes which generate meaning*, gained by awareness of the community's norms, and reflection upon them, their evolution and their function; makes social processes explicit, and by making them open, facilitates the conscious generation of new norms (Haste, 1996, pp. 52-53).

These proposed competencies are, of course, within a theoretical framework that is consistent, for different reasons, with both the Story Teller and the Tool User models. The Story Teller model provides a context for valuing the importance of narrative and the construction of justifications based on cause and consequences. The Tool User model focuses our attention on the practices of social interaction and on the linguistic tools for engagement in the negotiation of meaning.

Management of Motivation, Emotion, and Desire

The recent hype over "emotional intelligence" (EI) (Goleman, 1996) that has been much taken up in the corporate world alerts us to two things. Our culture is identifying a gap in the over-rationalized, over-cognitive models of "human-ness" which currently dominate many areas of psychological theory. Secondly, and perhaps more cynically, EI is seen as contributing to the effectiveness of the "corporate person" – in leadership, team-building, decision-making, and innovation.

This reflects a shift towards taking emotions more seriously, which dates back to humanistic psychology movements of the mid-20th century. We can also see in the literature a major reworking of the psycho-dynamic concept of "desire" as a central feature of human functioning, a concept which transcends "motivation" and even subsumes aspects of planning and goal-direction that are conventionally defined (especially in Puzzle Solving models) as essentially cognitive. We have seen in the work of Richard Lazarus (1966, 1991) and others, the development of a model in which cognitive processes – in the form of appraisals – are both the stimuli for affective arousal, and the means by which the emotion is dealt with.

Challenges to the Puzzle Solver model, which eschews emotions and focuses on the cognitive, are coming from people like David Gelernter and Rosalind Picard from the Massachusetts Institute of Technology, who argue that we cannot possibly construct an adequate model of human cognition until we can incorporate emotion into it (e.g., Gelernter, 1994). In a somewhat different vein, writers from a social-construction perspective are arguing that emotion can best be understood in terms of how cultures define certain affective states and their culturally specific behavioral manifestations. This leads us to ask how we learn the shared categorization and interpretation of these experiences, rather than how we deal with "basic" or "universal" emotion (see, for example, Harré & Parrott, 1996).[9]

It is not my purpose in this paper to take an overview of the extensive research on emotion. In generating a set of desirable competencies, however, my concern is to tease out the major cultural influences on how we think about emotion in lay terms, and the problems that these create for effective functioning. The stories that psychologists tell about emotion are also the stories that our culture tells; psychological research mirrors – with varying degrees of reflexivity – the cultural stories and the cultural anxieties in this area as in any other, but a field like emotion is particularly problematic. When we unpack the psychologists' stories, we unpack the lay stories also.

Over the last century we have seen a number of contrasting ways of looking at emotion. These are found in the psychological literature, but they reflect profound and pervasive cultural beliefs:

- *emotion as disorganizing*: in brief, according to this model, the "homeostatic" or "balanced" state is to be rational and cognition-governed. It is seen as the function of psychological processes to order our world, but such ordering is threatened by emotion, which disorientates and distorts cognition and reason. Even "survival" emotions, while obviously valuable, are disruptive and their usefulness is constrained by the extent to which they are channeled into recognizably ordered behaviors and cognitions.

- *emotion as organizing*: according to this model, behavior and cognition (particularly planning) are inert without the fuel of motivation. Emotion is essentially functional.[10] Affect provides the energy for action and reason. But a vital distinction is made between "good" affect, which is properly channeled desire, and "bad" affect, which leads to undesirable behaviors and outcomes. The quality resides in the *form* of affect, not in affect itself. This model also hangs on the fundamental concept of "balance."

- *emotion as a window on enriching experience*: this model of emotion valorizes affective states as a route to truth and understanding, taking as a given that reason on its own necessarily denies a part of experience, and therefore, wisdom. Only through liberating emotion can one go beyond the obvious and particularly, beyond the frameworks for interpretation that inevitably follow from encultured

---

[9] For extensive discussion of debates in the field of emotion, see Ekman & Davidson, 1994.
[10] For an extensive discussion of this position, see Frijda, 1986.

and (over)educated reason. Emotion is deemed more free of these constraining and educating processes. "Listen to the heart" was an earlier, Romantic, version of this wisdom. In the latter half of the 20th century we saw a revival of this model in the cultivation of selfhood through reflection on feeling, and also, more extensively, through reflexivity about our interaction and connection with others. Perhaps more spurious, but salient to lay thinking, we have seen an increasing search for a "true" selfhood and "authentic" emotions.

The competencies associated with the first model of emotion have to do with the ability to use cognition to transcend, control, and dissociate emotion and emotionality from rationality. Indeed, the very *definitions* of "rational" and "cognitive," within this perspective, require the negation, and making antithetical, of emotion. Reason is *in contrast* to passion; "will" serves the purpose of maintaining the ascendance of judgment in the face of emotional threat.

The competencies associated with the second model are related to channeling affect appropriately, and managing the force and direction of affect, as well as its nature. Although heavily embedded in a cognitive approach in which emotions are seen as the product of reacting to the world in terms of one's own concerns, this approach is consistent with the traditional model of virtues, in which proper emotions are the basis of an organized, ordered selfhood, and "character." Courage, compassion, temperance, and so forth reflect the proper and effective ordering of affect by the self.

The competencies associated with the third model are self-awareness and the interpretation of one's own and others' underlying affective and motivational states. It is often argued within this framework that creativity is impossible without this perspective. Gelernter discusses this, but another relevant discussion of creative motive states is Mihaly Csikszentmihalyi's work on "Flow" (1990), a heightened state of well-being in which creativity is enhanced.

I have presented these three models of emotion, and their implied accompanying competencies, because I feel that currently it is conventional wisdom in some circles to educate the third. But without understanding the larger argument, the positions that the third model is countering, we cannot fully appreciate the significance of these competencies. All three continue to flourish in our culture. There remains, still, anxiety about the corrupting effect of emotion, and also of values. Much of the debate about issues, for example, of the "value-freedom" of science, come down to a battle between the assumptions of the first and third models.

So what competencies do I advocate? The main one *is to recognize that there are different ways of thinking about emotion.* I do not think that we can enter the present century rearing a generation which has been trained to separate emotion and reason. Such a separation, for a start, does not provide the coping strategies for dealing with anger and frustration, which are compounded in an increasingly stressful world. Nor do I think that the New Age extreme version of the third model provides a satisfactory alternative. But it is only when we take emotion seriously, and treat it neither as a romantic grail nor as a classical threat, that we can deal with it.

Agency and Responsibility

My final area of competency focuses on morality, responsibility, and citizenship, but addresses wider questions. Psychology has wavered throughout the century between seeing humans as passive and molded by experience or by other determining factors (currently evolutionary determinism is making a comeback) and seeing humans as active agents in relation to their experience. This distinction applies to models of cognition as much as it does to morality (e.g., Russell, 1996). It is useful to define both agency and responsibility. Agency implies that one can have active interaction with one's environment, including active involvement in one's own learning and development. The implication of having agency is that the individual requires a sense of efficacy and a sense of being able to take an initiative, whether this is the initiation of an act or the initiation of an interaction that will facilitate forms of tool-use leading to novel practices and concepts. It implies that the individual takes a role in constructing meaning and interpretations, even if these constructions take place through negotiation with others and in a cultural context. It does not necessarily imply autonomy, though models that do valorize autonomy will give great weight to agency also.

In a context that values "agency," "responsibility" is about being the originator of one's own perspective, about taking possession of it, and moderating it to one's own goals. To be an agent means to be empowered. To take responsibility means to recognize that one is an agent, and that one can act upon one's inclinations. Competence as defined within the framework of civic agency and responsibility has been quite extensively studied.[11] Although this work has been conducted under several theoretical approaches, some common findings can be summarized. The "competent" individual is self-sufficient, able to focus attention and plan, has a future orientation, is adaptable to change, has a sense of responsibility, has a belief that one can have an effect, and is capable of commitment. These characteristics are fostered by families that provide competent role models, give encouragement and affirmation, set goals, and assign responsibilities that are seen to contribute to the household, and by cohesive communities that give the individual responsibilities and the chance to acquire skills that contribute to the public good. In sum, to feel agentic requires experience of being able to have an effect on one's environment, either alone or more usually with others.

However, despite the usefulness of these data, "responsibility" is a complex term that needs unpacking. I have explored three different meanings of "responsibility," based on conflicting ideas of both the processes and goals of moral and citizenship education.

"Responsibility 1" I define as *duties and obligations to the community*. This means those expectations, rules, and mores that are seen to be central to the effective maintenance of community. In other words, the agenda is set by the community (or the legal system) and the educational task implied in this model is to make young

---

[11] See, for example, Call, Mortimer, & Shanahan, 1995; Colby & Damon, 1992; Fogelman, 1994; Hamilton & Fenzel, 1988; Hart & Fegley, 1995; Lenhart & Rabiner, 1995; Morris, 1992; and Paolicchi, 1995.

people aware of these obligations and duties, and foster the values and motivations that will lead to their voluntarily assuming these responsibilities. "Responsibility 1" is particularly associated with public calls for a "restoration of community values." It is a moot point as to how far the individual in this context is deemed to have "agency." One may argue that "Responsibility 1" is just another way of looking at conformity, in which case the individual is only an "agent" insofar as he or she decide whether or not to fit into expectations.

A moral tension implicit in "Responsibility 1" is the classic question of morality as the performance of proactive, pro-social action, or the avoidance of the antisocial action. Agentic proactive behavior may, on occasion, require the individual to contravene normative pressures – whether these are pressures of accepted codes, or the specific social pressures of the group. Any moral system that valorizes the performance of duty and obligation lends itself to the charge of inhibiting individual agency of, for example, the "whistle-blowing" sort.

"Responsibility 2" I define as the *sense of connection to others* which generates caring and concern. It is the corollary of an emphasis on relationships and interpersonal ties. In recent psychological discourse on moral development, it has tended to be defined mainly in terms of Carol Gilligan's critique of Kohlberg's theory of moral development, specifically that the ethical system within which Kohlberg was working, in his twenty-year study of moral reasoning among young males, privileges reasoning about justice, ignoring the ethic of care and responsibility (Gilligan, 1982). Kohlberg's ethical system owes much to Kantian thinking about morality, and has much in common with Rawls' theory of justice. However, it is not only within psychology that these positions are questioned; there is now considerable debate about care and responsibility as ethical systems that at the very least coexist with, if not supplant, reasoning based on justice (e.g., Noddings, 1984; and Hekman, 1995).

I would argue that "Responsibility 2" should not be conceptualized only as a contrast to an ethical system based on reasoning about justice. Behind Gilligan's (and others') perspectives on care and connection is recognition that the individual is embedded in a social context. Justice-based reasoning, in contrast, starts from an assumption of individual autonomy, and the need therefore to *balance* the respective rights, interests, and obligations of all persons involved in the situation, to arrive at the most "just" solution. So in the justice-based model, individuals are conceived of as separate, not as connected. The implications of the separate, justice-based, position are that moral reasoning primarily demands reflection on one's internal moral dilemmas.

Once we consider that people are inevitably interconnected, we see the management of interaction as basic both to competence and to the social construction of meaning – though this latter was not in Gilligan's original agenda. In other words, from the perspective of this present paper, we can see that "Responsibility 2" is consistent with both the *value* position and the *ontological* position of communitarianism, as I discussed earlier in the context of sustaining community. In such a context, the competencies associated with sustaining community are similar to those required for "Responsibility 2."

What of agency? A primary feature of agency in this context must be the effective negotiation of interaction, dialogue, and the social processes involved in creating meaning and shared consensus. But there is also *moral* agency, action that organizes one's self and its connections with others, towards ends that serve the mutual needs of the group, network, or community. If I am mutually responsible with and for others, I need to be able to identify how my strengths and talents can be mobilized to meet the needs of others, and I also need to be able to identify what those needs are, and how they should be met not only by myself, but by the community as a whole. At the very least, this is competence in the management of teamwork, group interaction, and of people generally.

"Responsibility 3" I define as a sense of personal commitment to carry through one's value position into action and engagement. It carries with it the implication of personal efficacy and competence, as well as motivation. "Responsibility 3" is often couched in the individualistic terminology of "autonomy": "I have arrived at my personal moral position and the logical imperative is that I act upon this." However, "Responsibility 3" can also be seen as arising from discursive and linguistic practices, and therefore in one's interactions with others. In particular, one is positioned as a reflexive actor in a "moral" drama which requires certain kinds of action. This would differ from "Responsibility 1" primarily in that for "Responsibility 3," the expectations are *internal*; those people who take risks to intervene to help others, or who compromise their comfort and even their lives, say "I can do no other," or "Anyone would have done this."

The apparent paradox of an internalized commitment (which one would imagine to be the product of autonomous decision-making) arising out of discursive processes (which one would imagine to be social and therefore not autonomous) reflects the paradoxes of agency. Because one is active in engagement with others in the social construction of meaning, and in the interpretation of dialogic activity, the model of agency is consistent with the concept of a social being. The competencies involved are not, therefore, the separation, detachment, and objectifying of the self in resistance to others, but a voluntary connection to others in which meaning is consensual and arrived dialogically. "Responsibility 3," therefore, does not have to be seen only as a "Puzzle Solver" product; it uses cultural stories, and the tools of metaphor and value-language, to provide the role models and the action scripts for taking responsibility.

Conclusion

I have presented a range of competencies and metacompetencies, necessarily superficially and with broad reference to a wide range of research. I regard these as generic; although tied to particular domains, they seem to me to present a rounded picture of the required attributes of effective humanness for the immediate future. Each is a formulation that derives from established psychological research, but is couched in the larger picture – that we are adaptive, social beings and our competencies both derive from these basic attributes and facilitate our effectiveness in meeting the demands of this particular historical period and indeed, geographical location. I have made no attempt to explore non-Western contexts, but my basic theoretical position, that culture is specific but the processes of culture are universal, allows for translation of these principles as appropriate.

I have also explored throughout the paper how the Puzzle Solver, the Story Teller, and the Tool User models illuminate aspects of the development of competencies. In particular, I showed how the stories that we tell in educational contexts and in the wider culture, set the terms of reference not only for what is a proper competence, but how it is to be achieved, and how the stories themselves serve as mechanisms for fostering competencies. Taking a Vygotskian perspective (e.g., Vygotsky, 1978; Van Der Veer & Valsiner, 1994; and Werstch, 1998), I tried to show how the "tools" of culture and language, and the experiences of interaction with the environment through these tools, are the mechanisms by which competence develops, and also, provide the framework through which certain competencies are conceptualized and valorized and others are not.

References

Basalla, G. (1988). *The evolution of technology.* Cambridge: Cambridge University Press.

Bell, D. (1993). *Communitarianism and its critics.* Oxford: Clarendon Press.

Billig, M. (1987). *Arguing and thinking.* New York: Cambridge University Press.

Billig, M. (1992). *Talking of the royal family.* London: Routledge.

Brown, R. (1965). *Social psychology.* New York: Free Press.

Bruner, J. (1996). *The culture of education.* Cambridge, MA: Harvard University Press.

Call, K. T., Mortimer, J. T., & Shanahan, M. J. (1995). Helpfulness and the development of competence in adolescence. *Child Development, 66,* 129–138.

Cohen, J., & Stewart, I. (1994). *The collapse of chaos.* New York: Viking.

Colby, A., & Damon, W. (1992). *Some do care.* New York: Free Press.

Cole, M. (1995). *Cultural psychology.* Cambridge, MA: Harvard University Press.

Csikszentmihalyi, M. (1990). *Flow.* New York: Harper & Row.

Edwards, D., & Mercer, N. M. (1987). *Common knowledge: The development of understanding in the classroom.* London: Methuen.

Ekman, P., & Davidson, R. J. (Eds.). (1994). *The nature of emotion.* New York: Oxford University Press.

Etzioni, A. (1988). *The moral dimension.* New York: Free Press.

Etzioni, A. (1994). *The spirit of community.* New York: Simon & Schuster.

Festinger, L. (1957). *A theory of cognitive dissonance.* Stanford, CA: Stanford University Press.

Fogelman, E. (1994). *Conscience and courage.* New York: Anchor Books.

Frijda, N. (1986). *The emotions.* New York: Cambridge University Press.

Gardner, H. (1999). *The disciplined mind: What all students should understand.* New York: Simon & Schuster.

Gelernter, D. (1994). *The muse in the machine.* New York: Free Press.

Gentner, D., & Stevens, A. L. (1983). *Mental models.* Hillsdale, NJ: Erlbaum.

Gigerenzer, G., & Goldstein, D. G. (1996). Mind as computer: the birth of a metaphor. *Creativity Research Journal, 9*(3), 131–144.

Gilligan, C. (1982). *In a different voice.* Cambridge, MA: Harvard University Press.

Goleman, D. (1996). *Emotional intelligence.* London: Bloomsbury.

Gosling, W. (1994). *Helmsmen and heroes.* London: Weidenfeld and Nicolson.

Hamilton, S. F., & Fenzel, L. M. (1988). The impact of volunteer experience on adolescent social development. *Journal of Adolescent Research, 3*(1), 65–80.

Haraway, D. (1991). *Simians, cyborgs and women.* London: Routledge.

Harré, R., & Gillett, G. (1994). *The discursive mind.* London: Sage.

Harré, R., & Parrott, W. G. (Eds.). (1996). *The emotions: Social, cultural and biological dimensions.* London: Sage.

Harré, R. (1998). *The singular self.* London: Sage.

Hart, D., & Fegley, S. (1995). Prosocial behavior and caring. *Child Development, 66,* 1346–1359.

Haste, H. (1994). *The sexual metaphor.* Cambridge, MA: Harvard University Press.

Haste, H. (1996). Communitarianism and the social construction of morality. *Journal of Moral Education, 25*(1), 47–55.

Haste, H., Helkama, K., & Markoulis, D. (1998). Morality, wisdom and the lifespan. In A. Demetriou, W. Doise, & C. van Lieshout (Eds.), *Life-span developmental psychology* (pp. 317–350). Chichester: John Wiley.

Haste, H. (2000). Are women human? In N. Roughley (Ed.) *Being human: Anthropological universality and particularity in transdisciplinary perspectives* (pp. 175–196). Berlin: De Gruyter.

Heider, F. (1958). *The psychology of interpersonal relations.* New York: Wiley.

Hekman, S. (1995). *Moral voices, moral selves.* Oxford: Polity Press.

Higgins, A. (1991). The just community approach to moral education: Evolution of the idea and recent findings. In W. M. Kurtines & J. L. Gewirtz (Eds.) *Handbook of moral behavior and development* (Vol. 3, pp. 111–141). Hillsdale, NJ: Lawrence Erlbaum.

Lazarus, R. (1966). Psychological stress and the coping process. New York: McGraw Hill.

Lazarus, R. (1991). *Emotion and adaptation.* New York: Oxford University Press.

Lenhart, L. A., & Rabiner, D. L. (1995). Social competence in adolescence. *Development and Psychopathology, 7,* 543–561.

McNeill, D. & Freiberger, P. (1993). *Fuzzy logic.* New York: Simon & Schuster.

Merchant, C. (1980). *The death of nature: Women, ecology and the scientific revolution.* San Francisco, CA: Harper & Row.

Morris, B. (1992). Adolescent leaders. *Adolescence, 27,* 173–181.

National Forum for Values in Education and the Community. (1996). *Consultation on values in education and the community* (COM/96/608) London: School Curriculum Assessment Authority.

Noddings, N. (1984). *Caring.* Berkeley, CA: University of California Press.

Ortony, A., (Ed.). (1993). *Metaphor and thought.* New York: Cambridge University Press.

Paolicchi, P. (1995). Narratives of volunteering. *Journal of moral education, 24*(2), 159–174.

Potter, J., & Wetherell, M. (1987). *Discourse and social psychology.* London: Sage.

Power, C., Higgins, A., & Kohlberg, L. (1989). *Lawrence Kohlberg's approach to moral education.* New York: Columbia University Press.

Rogoff, B. (1990). *Apprenticeship in thinking.* New York: Oxford University Press.

Rosch, E. (1978). Principles of categorization. In E. Rosch & B. Lloyd (Eds.), *Cognition and categorization* (pp. 24–78). Hillsdale, NJ: Erlbaum.

Russell, J. (1996). *Agency*. Hove: Erlbaum Taylor and Francis.

Rutter, M., Maughan, B., Mortimore, P., & Ouston, J. (1979). *Fifteen thousand hours: Secondary schools and their effects on children*. Cambridge, MA: Harvard University Press.

Shotter, J. (1993). Becoming someone: Identity and belonging. In N. Coupland & J. F. Nussbaum (Eds.), *Discourse and lifespan identity* (pp. 5–27). London: Sage.

Stewart, I. (1989). *Does God play dice?* Oxford: Blackwell.

Taylor, C. (1991). *The ethics of authenticity*. Cambridge, MA: Harvard University Press.

Van Der Veer, R., & Valsiner, J. (Eds.). (1994). *The Vygotsky reader*. Oxford: Blackwell.

Vosniadou, S., & Ortony, A. (Eds.). (1989). *Similarity and analogical reasoning*. New York: Cambridge University Press.

Vygotsky, L. (1978). *Mind in society*. Cambridge, MA: Harvard University Press.

Werstch, J. (1998). *Mind as action*. New York: Oxford University Press.

Chapter 6

The Key to Social Fields:
Competencies of an Autonomous Actor

Or How to Avoid Being Abused, Alienated, Dominated or Exploited When One Is Neither Rich Nor Powerful

Philippe Perrenoud

Introduction

Who is qualified to define the *key competencies* everyone needs to live in the 21st century? It is not enough for experts simply to define a conceptual and methodological framework. The question is both ethical and political. No *list* of *key competencies* springs spontaneously from an observation of social practices and trends in societies. What qualifications are needed on the part of those establishing the list, and what are their premises? Will they be able to avoid the temptation to project their own values, will they know how to, and will they want to do so? If there are several of them, will this be enough to ensure that they are representative?

The answers to these questions are vital if the outcome of this work is to influence, even to a very small extent, the orientation of basic education in developed countries. Today, educational systems still invest huge resources in training a highly educated minority, while another minority fails even to acquire basic competencies. If a developed country has a ten percent illiteracy rate and has many more young people with poor language skills, it is failing to consolidate democracy and social justice (Bentolila, 1996). Training a scientific and technological elite so as to maintain their ranking in world economic markets is not all that is at stake for democracies!

What is the point of defining *basic* competencies unless it is to mobilize all the resources required to enable all citizens to acquire them, first and foremost those who are at present failing to acquire them? Those who are rich, well-educated, good-looking, and intelligent do not need any changes to the educational system since they are able, in their family, at school or elsewhere, to acquire all the competencies necessary to guarantee their success and power. Defining basic competencies is not therefore an intellectual game if it could, even to a very small extent, affect educational policy and the purpose of educational systems. That is why such an undertaking cannot be entered into without "questioning the question"!

"Questioning the Question," or How to Resist the Temptation of the "Politically Correct"?

This chapter's sub-title no doubt smacks of the Marxism of the 1950s. It was chosen deliberately to indicate from the outset that the question of key competencies is not ideologically neutral. To reply to it is to defend, implicitly or explicitly, a vision of mankind and of society.

It is also to reply, openly or *de facto*, to the question posed by Howard S. Becker (1966) to social science researchers: *whose side are we on*? He did not mean that research should be at the service of an ideology but that the choice of topics, problems, and approaches could not help reinforce certain visions of the world and weaken others. Social actors need to explain change, power, inequalities, violence, economic crises, unemployment, under-achievement, and drug-abuse, for example. They do not wait for social and human sciences to propose "theories" and when such theories are propounded, they do not hesitate to use them selectively, when it suits them, to confirm their own vision of the world. Knowledge of a society is rarely disinterested. It helps to maintain or change the *status quo*, and to legitimize or challenge public social policies and legislation, as well as the structures and strategies of business, hospitals, political parties, trade unions, administrations, and all the institutions on which citizens depend.

The concept of competence, as defined by psychology, linguistics, and cognitive sociology or anthropology, is no exception to this rule. Depending on how competencies are conceived, certain visions of mankind and society are strengthened or weakened.

Reference can be made to at least three classic controversies:

- Are competencies genetically determined or are they acquired and thus dependent on experience and education? As shown by Weinert (Chapter 3), competencies are often associated with intelligence (cognitive or "emotional"). But representations of intelligence go hand-in-hand with a vision of mankind and social order, notably as regards the inevitability of inequality; something negated by some and asserted by others. Today – as opposed to fifty years ago – there is fairly wide agreement in developed countries that coherent educational policies can greatly help to develop competencies, but not everyone is convinced of this. In the research world, the question remains open, notably because linguistics experts, influenced by Noam Chomsky (1971, 1977), remain attached to the idea of competency as an innate faculty to speak and understand a language.

- Another debate relates to the relationship between knowledge and competencies; upholders of the "culture" school are prone to believe that concentrating on competencies is a threat to culture and the transmission of knowledge. Others, including myself (Perrenoud, 1998b), believe that competencies are not the enemy of knowledge; they are based on it but are more than simply knowledge. This concept emphasizes the mobilization of multiple cognitive resources.

- Lastly, the fashion of identifying competencies in the business world (Ropé & Tanguy, 1994; Stroobants, 1993) is sometimes interpreted as a way of increasing the flexibility of work and job insecurity by taking away from workers the protection constituted by qualification levels negotiated in collective agreements.

Ideological battles of this kind are a constant as soon as the question of competencies is debated. They are aggravated when any attempt is made to define the *essential* competencies in modern societies, and therefore those which should be developed as a priority by educational systems. This takes the debate to a level which it should be said from the outset is political, philosophical, and ethical, as much as it is scientific. Key competencies do not exist in the abstract. They are *constructed* on the basis of a theoretical, but also ideological, *viewpoint*. This therefore gives rise to debate or even conflict.

This is true even in the limited context of a given profession and its corresponding vocational training. In spite of there being a reference to an identified practice, contradictory representations come into conflict as is shown for example by Raisky (1996) in relation to the profession of wine-grower. All occupations that evolve are the subject of discussion that relates notably to their dependence on other occupations, their place in the division of work, and on the real or desirable level of the professionalism or qualification of its practitioners. Adopting any system of reference for competencies is a way of taking a stance on these questions.

Any attempt to do the same thing with regard to life in general and the basic competencies involved renders the question even more explosive since it implies questions of the concept of mankind and of society.

An attempt can be made to reach consensus on the limited basis of what is *politically correct*. In a so-called democratic society, made up of men and women said to be free and equal, united by a supposedly freely agreed social contract designed to give each individual the same responsibilities and the same rights, the question of competencies can be addressed from a doubly optimistic standpoint. It may be readily agreed:

- Every individual needs certain "citizen" competencies in order to participate in the management of this harmonious society.

- Every individual needs other basic competencies in order to live life in accordance with his or her aspirations and projects.

Looking at society through such "rose-colored glasses," it is easy to suggest competencies such as:

- being able to vote and assume one's responsibilities in a democratic political system and in community life, trade unions, etc.;

- in order to survive in a society of free competition, being able to find accommodation, start a family, and conclude and abide by contracts (relating to marriage, work, rental, insurance, etc.);

- being able to invest and spend intelligently one's resources in a free and transparent market, using in a rational manner information about products and services;

- being able to find one's way about in the educational system, receive training, and learn and use available information;

- being able to access culture and the media by making an informed choice of recreational and cultural activities;
- being able to look after one's health by a preventative and responsible use of the medical and hospital system;
- being able to defend one's rights and interests by asking for police protection and making use of legal procedures and the courts.

Conditions for such practices exist to an extent in the most democratic and developed countries, particularly among the upper and part of the middle classes. But that is not to say that this is the "ordinary" human condition. In most countries in the world, such competencies concern a minority of the population only, the privileged classes whose way of life and standard of living are similar to those in developed countries. For most citizens in the Third World, such competencies are irrelevant (given the state of urbanization, the political system, health services, schools, consumption, peace and public order, etc.), while other skills are needed to live and survive when famine, urban poverty, or civil war are the daily lot of the common people. Even in developed countries, there are people without political rights (notably immigrants), unemployed, the poor, members of minorities, and the socially excluded who dream of consumer goods, participation, or integration but who have no way of realizing such dreams. Others, marginal dissidents, do not subscribe to the prevailing conception of a "normal" or "happy" existence.

Declaring some competencies to be "universal" is to favor part of the planet and the lifestyle in privileged societies. Even if we look only at the most developed societies, for example in OECD member countries, two problems arise:

- Some of our contemporaries would very much like to be integrated enough in the consumer society for the competencies listed above to be of use to them; a number of homeless people would be happy to learn how to invest their money wisely, but they do not have any money. Their problem is not to be good consumers but to have access to goods and to survive from day to day; in order to do this, they need skills which are not necessary for those with a comfortable lifestyle.

- Others do not subscribe to the dominant political, economic, social, and moral systems; they need different skills in order to live on the margins of society, outside the norm and sometimes outside the law, not to spend their whole existence working, to survive without fixed accommodation and without starting a family, refusing to be enrolled into the army, or to abide by the most conventional standards of behavior.

Well-integrated citizens living in accord with society usually react differently to these two categories:

- To those excluded from society, they offer assistance, provided that the recipients conform to the rules for assistance, look for work, settle down, educate themselves, look after themselves properly, stop drinking or taking drugs, respect the law, do not waste their meager resources, etc.

- To those on the margins of society and dissidents, they say that in a democracy, people must abide by the law and by the decisions of the majority. If they do not do so, they must accept the risks inherent in their marginality or deviance, including punishment.

From the perspective of society's center, priority competencies are therefore limited to those needed for a "normal social life," recognizing that those who wish to lead such a life but are prevented from doing so (because of their health, education, or economic situation) must be *helped*. Citizens enamoured of normality lose interest in, or are afraid of, those who deliberately choose to live on the margins of society or in conflict with it.

Can an intergovernmental organization whose members are the most developed countries escape this narrow vision of normality? When it asks experts from different countries and disciplines to identify the key competencies needed in developed societies at the beginning of the 21st century, is it, at least implicitly, asking for a "politically correct" point of view? This would not at all be surprising inasmuch as such an organization necessarily expresses the vision of the ruling and middle classes of developed countries, fundamentally in agreement with the political and economic system of its member states. A radically critical sociologist could suggest that under cover of defining key competencies, what is wanted is to reaffirm a vision of *normality*, using modern and apparently non-normative language. He would conclude that it is better not to be associated with a purely ideological enterprise. Perhaps this would be to ignore the convulsions, contradictions, and cultural and technological changes which characterize the world today (Morin, 1977; Dubet & Martucelli, 1998).

Given this complexity, there is perhaps room for *debate* and a chance to define key competencies fairly broadly, taking into account the multiplicity of values and lifestyles and broadening "normality" so as to include all sorts of approaches to work, social order, sexuality, the family, consumption, and culture. Such an approach would take account of the vast majority of conditions, positions, and projects which exist alongside each other in developed societies.

The question is a very difficult one. A democracy cannot allow everything. Competencies are needed to administer a concentration camp, persecute minorities, organize a hold-up, defraud the tax authorities, torture dissidents, organize the sexual exploitation of children, prepare a *coup d'état*, develop new biochemical toxins, or create a fascist party. Such skills are obviously not legitimate competencies that a democratic state could propose developing.

The question is knowing *where to set the limits of pluralism*. Claiming that the Earth orbited the Sun was punishable by death in Galileo's time. Organizing a strike was illegal in the 19th century, carrying out an abortion was prohibited in conservative societies of the 20th century and still is. The limits of legality and psychological normality change in line with cultural evolution. At what point are we today? What degree of dissidence, disorder, difference, resistance, contradiction, or open conflict is tolerated in developed societies? What social practices are defensible? Where is the line beyond which they are not compatible with today's vision of a "normal" life? In short, what concept of the "human condition" should serve as a reference to construct a "universal" system of references for core competencies?

In the face of such difficult questions, it is better, in order to preserve one's innocence, to refrain from replying and simply to analyze the ideological content to be found in all inventories, however neutral they appear to be. I shall risk taking a less comfortable position because, however ambiguous work on basic competencies may be, it does concern also those who, like sociologists, make it their business to question norms and propose considering various approaches to the world and to society as equally worthy of being taken into account and linked to competencies derived from basic school education.

No doubt rare skills are needed in order to be a world leader, manage organizations, or occupy exceptional positions. I have, however, chosen to focus on

- *ordinary* actors, the woman or man in the street, doing their best to survive and live as well as possible, preserving their *autonomy* without infringing on that of others, and

- the competencies they require to avoid being abused, alienated, dominated, exploited, or impotent victims of the world's misery.

It is indeed the woman or man "in the street" who must be the focus of educational policy. Adopting this approach, I certainly do not claim to give an exhaustive list of the competencies needed by ordinary actors. Other voices, coming from other ideological or professional horizons, will make alternative proposals.

Nor am I claiming to present here an objective opinion. It is possible to describe social practices and the competencies they involve objectively. This does not yet define priorities. A statistical approach could not possibly lead to agreement: supposing that a very large number of people were found to lie, cheat, or manage to avoid seeing things that made them uncomfortable, would this mean that the art of lying, cheating, or bad faith should be dignified by the term key competencies? A categorical refusal to address this question is to adopt an idealistic vision of society and power. To accept it fully would be to add the art of stealing, torture, and murder to the list of basic competencies.

The choice I have made here does not circumvent this dilemma. Of course, choosing those who are neither dominant nor privileged can make one feel good, but the poor and exploited do not have a monopoly on virtue. More importantly, how can one defend oneself without resorting to cunning, and at times violence? Who can boast of having solved this dilemma? Better to describe it and live with it than to pretend to have solved the problem.

Another hesitation is as follows: should the argument be limited to developed countries at the risk of coming up with competencies which are only possible because they are based on North-South relations and an economic development pursued at the cost of the Third World? Should the debate be extended to cover the whole planet, succumbing to a type of cultural ethnocentrism and conducting a surrealistic exercise for all those countries which are still very far from living under democracy and which have not reached a decent standard of living?

At the risk of seeming indifferent to the misery of the Third World, I shall limit my discussion here to the so-called developed societies since the task becomes impossible if account has to be taken of a huge diversity of political, cultural, and economic contexts. However, let us not forget that the attempt to define core competencies for the 21st century is the privilege of highly educated societies, rich enough to have the means to formulate and implement a competencies policy, and for whom simply surviving is no longer the essential problem.

Transversal Competencies?

Even if only developed countries are considered, an important question remains: can transversal competencies be identified which are relevant to the different sectors of social life, family, work, health, education, politics, the media, etc.? To answer this question, comparative and interdisciplinary analyses are needed.

Since it has been decided to try to identify a small number of transversal competencies without referring to comparative studies conceived and carried out to this end, only hypotheses are possible.

Clearly, specific practices exist alongside each other in a society, based on theoretical knowledge, expert know-how, and practical knowledge specific to a given social field or organization. Thus, to operate in the world of tax law, health, or real estate, one requires very different competencies. This does not exclude superficial analogies: to look for a way of paying less taxes, medicine to treat illness, or a site on which to build, all require the action of looking, but at a level of abstraction at which the same word masks the diversity of the mental processes and knowledge required.

I believe, however, that the human and social sciences can identify certain "functional invariables" and endeavor to apply to them *transversal* competencies, for at least two reasons:

• Human beings use mental processes, an approach to the world, and relational competencies which retain similarities no matter what framework or activity is being considered.

• They operate like actors in social fields, the functioning of which share certain characteristics.

As an anthropologist and sociologist, I shall concentrate on the second register, i.e., an approach using the theory of social fields. No doubt my colleagues from other disciplines, faced with a similar task, will opt for other transversalities, specific to their discipline in terms of identity, personality, and relational style. This will not necessarily lead to a reference to other social practices. It is rather a case of complementary ways of looking at the same realities.

At the risk of adding to the confusion, I shall use the term transversality here with a particular meaning. In the educational field, transversal competencies (Rey, 1996) are those which *traverse* the various disciplines. In this chapter, transversal competencies are those which *traverse* various sectors of human existence, without reference to scientific or educational disciplines.

I am therefore not claiming to express the viewpoint of *sociology*, but that of an interactionist and constructivist sociologist who specializes in practices and education and whose theoretical references have been dictated by his individual intellectual journey. I will use here in a fairly free way the concept of social field developed by Pierre Bourdieu (1980, 1982, 1993, 1997; Lafaye, 1996; Pinto, 1998), because it seems to me particularly relevant for the identification of one of the interesting transversalities: all actors act in social fields, and the laws of functioning of these fields present important sociological similarities. That is why finding or constructing "*the key to fields*" could constitute a core competency for ordinary social actors.

Acting in a Social Field

No one, even when acting alone, operates in a social vacuum. Common sense and human sciences often speak of a milieu, an *entourage*, or a social or socio-cultural environment. The concept of social field makes it possible to go one step further: this environment is *structured* in multiple social fields characterized by specific *challenges*. Transversality is not to be found in the nature of the challenges but in their very existence and in the practices, interactions, alliances, and struggles to which they give rise.

Lafaye summarizes the concept of field in the sociology of Bourdieu in the following terms:

- A field is a structured – and thus hierarchical – space incorporating positions or posts whose characteristics are relatively independent from their occupants.

- Each field is defined in terms of its specific challenges and interests as compared to those of another field: a scientist is interested in different things than a businessman or an ecclesiastic.

- A field also implies the possession or constitution of a specific capital. Large economic capital is essential in the world of affairs but altogether incongruous in the scientific field, in which the relevant capital is of another nature: a thesis, prestigious publications, international recognition, etc.

- A field requires social agents with appropriate dispositions – which Bourdieu calls "habitus" – to be active in it, which implies knowing the rules of the game of the field in question.

- The structure of a field is the result, at a time *t*, of a balance of power between agents or institutions occupying different positions.

- A field is also a dynamic space in which battles take place to conserve or change the balance of power: to occupy dominant positions, to change from a subservient to a dominant position, to stabilize precarious positions, to gain recognition of positions at the borders of a field, to disqualify others, etc. These battles contribute to the development of a field's structure. Disciplines such as homeopathy or acupuncture, long on the margins of the medical field, have today managed to gain recognition and be included in this field.

- A field is not a closed space. In particular, the borders of a field are constantly the subject of power struggles between the agents or organizations who make it up. The example of the medical field, given above, is a good example of this characteristic.

- Within a given field, the struggle which takes place between the holders of different positions presupposes fundamental agreement on what the battle is about. (Lafaye, 1996).

We can already identify the existence of shared mechanisms, on which competencies transversal to several or all fields are based. However, it is not enough to link a competency to each of the characteristics of a field! We shall therefore have to reconstitute a reference system for competencies in the light of all the functionings thus described.

With advancing years, individuals often participate in several fields:

- the field of parental relationships, in which each individual is and remains the child of his or her parents; over time, he or she may start a new family and become a parent himself or herself;

- the field of culture, values, and social representations, at least from the age at which one is able to communicate and understand;

- the field of sexual and loving relations which, if psychoanalysts are to be believed, is reached at a fairly young age;

- the field of law and justice: even before birth, children become the subjects of rights;

- the field of religion, if one's family are believers or if one becomes so oneself;

- the field of health, as soon as one is taken in charge by medicine and social insurance;

- the field of consumption, first through one's parents and then increasingly on one's own behalf;

- the field of education and training, from birth within one's family and then at school from the age of two or four years;

- the political field, as soon as one is of an age to take part in, or be subject to, decisions;

- the field of work, first at home and then paid work and work relations, sometimes from childhood;

- the field of knowledge, which everyone participates in very early at least as regards to common sense and, as soon as one engages in "theoretical" practice, as a producer of expert or learned knowledge;

- the field of the media and information in a society in which, if nothing else than as a consumer, no one escapes cultural industries and mass communication;

- the community field, as soon as one is of an age to join a club, an association, a trade union, or a party.

It is essential not to close this list. It is presented by way of *illustration* only, and does not claim to be exhaustive. It is limited to those fields in which it is difficult, in a developed society, not to be involved from adulthood, and sometimes from childhood. Many individuals are in addition involved in a given sports or artistic field. Some are actors in the military field, whether by choice or as conscripts. All occupations and specific practices constitute partially autonomous social fields, as does each organization (enterprise, hospital, prison, school, etc.), discipline, denomination, and specific group.

To be an actor in a given field, there must be a kind of familiarity with the knowledge, values, rules, rites, codes, concepts, language, laws, institutions, and objects specific to the field in question. That is why entry into a new field requires a process of *socialization*, varying in length, sometimes highly organized, sometimes not, and usually related to a specific position in the field; different types of socialization are needed to penetrate the hospital field depending on whether one is a patient, visitor, or care-giver.

What I am interested in here are the competencies and knowledge which are transversal, inasmuch as they *traverse* the different social fields and are not specific to any one of them. To prove they exist, comparative research on a vast scale would be needed. On the basis of multiple personal observations as well as social science research, I am suggesting as a *hypothesis* that it is useful, or even indispensable, in all social fields to have the following competencies in order to avoid being at the mercy of strategies and decisions adopted by the other actors:

1. be able to identify, evaluate, and defend one's resources, rights, limits, and needs;

2. be able, individually or in a group, to form and conduct projects and to develop strategies;

3. be able to analyze situations, relationships, and force fields systemically;

4. be able to co-operate, act in synergy, and participate in a collective, and share leadership;

5. be able to build and operate democratic-type organizations and systems of collective action;

6. be able to manage and resolve conflict;

7. be able to play with the rules, using them and elaborating on them;

8. be able to construct negotiated orders over and above cultural differences.

Comparative research based on the observation of social practices and the identification of the competencies they involve would certainly produce a richer and more detailed list making it possible, in each case, to identify better what is transversal and what is specific to each field. Thus, knowing how to *identify, evaluate and defend one's resources, rights, limits, and needs* is necessary for a family member, a pupil, a patient in hospital, a defendant in a court of law, a worker in a firm, or a boxer in the ring. A resemblance between the problems encountered and the solutions applied do not yet, however, mean that the cognitive mechanisms in play are identical. Observing actors who pass from one social field to another shows an element of *transfer*, all the more important when psycho-sociological processes are considered. Prudence requires that we do not rush to form a training strategy on the basis of the identification of similar competencies without considering the fields in which these competencies apply. I shall return to this question in my conclusion.

Defending One's Rights and Interests: A Competency?

To avoid being abused, alienated, dominated, exploited, or the impotent victim of the world's misery, individually or collectively: is this not simply to have rights and the means of making them respected, and to defend one's rights and interests? Why should competencies be required to obtain what should be natural under democracy and the law? Because the law is only a *resource* for actors which modifies the balance of power, but is also a reflection of the following:

- No right is acquired without a fight. If women have the vote today and know increasingly how to use it, it is because other women, not so long ago, had the competencies and courage required to have this right recognized. The same can be said for labor and family law. Victims of sexual harassment, bullying, or discrimination on grounds of health (e.g., AIDS), gender, ethnicity, are far from being protected by law in all developed countries. Law is a product of human action. In this sense, the competencies referred to here do not amount to claiming protection from existing legislation but to making the law evolve into something nearer "human rights" and the principles of justice (Kellerhals, Modak, & Perrenoud, 1997). It should be added that this applies not simply to official legislation and regulations but also to all written and non-written rules and conventions which regulate the family, collective life, various groups, paid work, and the world of education.

- Respect for the law, once adopted, has to be fought for, at least every time its strict application comes into conflict with particular interests or the reason of the state. The texts by themselves have no effect; everything depends on who knows them, interprets them, whether restrictively or loosely, in favor of one individual or another, applies them scrupulously, or cleverly gets round them. Law is a civilized means of channeling power struggles and strategic conflict between social actors. It does not make these disappear but on the contrary, becomes both what is at stake and a tool (Lascoumes, 1997; Robert, Soubiran-Paillet & van de Kerchove, 1997).

My analysis does not relate to legal competencies alone, even though social actors need good knowledge of the law to become or remain autonomous in a developed society. This is only one resource among others.

If the competencies of the autonomous social actor listed above had to be given a label, I would say that they are *tactical* and *strategic* and that, over and above the law, they are based on psychological, sociological, economic, sometimes technical, scientific, computer, or administrative knowledge, whether learned or gained through experience. Each competency also requires abilities such as knowing how to obtain information, reflect, analyze, communicate, anticipate, negotiate, regulate, decide, etc. However, such resources are not enough in themselves to constitute competencies; these competencies are formed through the ability to *mobilize* such resources properly and to *orchestrate* them, at an appropriate time, in a complex situation (Le Boterf, 1994, 1997).

Let us now try to review these competencies one by one in order to specify in which family of situations each is relevant and to describe certain *specific* resources they mobilize.

A Few Competencies Needed for Autonomy

Autonomy requires competencies, though these alone are not enough. No one will become autonomous unless he wishes to do so. This is not a universal value but is indissociable from modernity, democracy, and individualism. It would therefore be wrong to make it a norm for all eras and all societies. In developed societies, however, the value system promotes autonomy as an aspiration and basis for individual identity. My analysis here is placed in this cultural context, therefore diametrically opposed to a vision of the world in which each individual is invited to bury his identity in the collective and the established order. We should, however, remember that the quest for a high degree of personal autonomy is not the only possible source of identity. My analysis in this chapter is only relevant with regard to a type of society that places value on an actor's autonomy, the ability to define *oneself* and fulfill *one's* projects, defend *one's* interests and *one's* rights. The fact that such a model is gradually spreading throughout the planet does not, from an anthropological point of view, make it any less *arbitrary* (Bourdieu & Passeron, 1970).

In this context, we are confronted with a paradox: to devise the project of becoming an autonomous being is already a manifestation of autonomy. Total alienation is to think that one is not a subject capable of autonomy, not to give oneself a high enough value to be able to think and act on one's own. This means that identity cannot be postulated as coming first, and the corresponding competencies as its "logical consequences." It is by mastering the means for an initial autonomy that the beginnings of an identity are forged, and this in turn nourishes the development of new competencies.

Identity and competencies have a *dialectical* relationship and feed each other. That is why developing the competencies analyzed below is only possible if based on an aspiration for autonomy which goes hand-in-hand with identity. At the same time, such a development is going to transform this aspiration and the identity on which it is based, forming a "virtuous" circle, the counterpart of the vicious circle of alienation.

In each of the competencies or families of competencies mentioned, identity components are therefore to be found which spring from relationships to worlds which cannot be reduced to knowledge or know-how, which assume intent and values, which include a side that is lit and shady areas. This is clearer when non-mandatory training is offered: those who choose to take it only do so if they adhere to the practices and postures that support it. When reflecting on core competencies and giving education the task of developing them, a task of socialization is also assigned, which should also be made clear.

Being Able to Identify, Evaluate, and Defend One's Resources, Rights, Limits, and Needs

In social life, as in any living system, nothing is preserved by inertia. There is an ongoing reconstruction process, and no one is sure to keep his place, job, or power if he does not keep sufficient watch or simply stops "looking out for squalls"; a sailor, after all, always sleeps with one eye open. There are organizations or political societies whose leaders do not dare to take holiday or leave on a journey for fear that a palace revolution organized in their absence might lead to their downfall. It is not enough to be there, one must constantly defend one's resources, rights, limits, and needs:

- Defend one's *resources* both to show that the group depends on them and that they are neither inexhaustible nor can they be used without compensation. Grandparents who have reached retirement age possess a resource: time. But they can have this time taken away from them if they do not defend it, when they are made to wait without reason or when, without asking whether it suits them, they are given their grandchildren to look after or other tasks which may seem to others almost like giving them presents since "they have nothing else to do."

- Defend one's *rights*, so that they are not constantly forgotten, underestimated, or trampled on. We live in a society in which we respect the rights of those who have least need for them since they are adults, strong and in good health, have money, are well integrated in the social fabric, well thought of, and not without power. They need make little effort to safeguard their rights because few of their contemporaries take the risk of entering into conflict with those who are in a dominant position. It is usually the rights of the weakest that are abused. But prisoners have rights, as do patients, accused persons, children, immigrants, handicapped persons, the aged, and the unemployed. It is they who need competencies.

- Defend one's *limits* also. When interacting, individuals tend to ignore the limits of others, for example their worries, doubts, ignorance, scruples, or fatigue so as to get them to do "what has to be done." Some parents pretend not to know that their children are terrified of water, some bosses that their employees are at the end of their tether, some officers that the soldiers under their command are disgusted by certain measures against civilians, and some spiritual leaders that their injunctions put their followers in painful dilemmas. There are many examples of a person or group being asked to go beyond their limits either because they do not dare to express them or because they do not know how to say no.

- Lastly, defend one's *needs*. Someone pursuing his or her own project has nothing to gain by considering too concretely the needs of his or her interlocutors and partners. He or she will only take account of such needs if they defend them and oppose them to his or her proposals or expectations. It is possible to ignore the need for rest, silence, security, esteem, or autonomy as long as those concerned do not defend that need.

In all cases, one has to find the *strength to say no*, to require consideration, to assert rights and needs, and put oneself forward as a subject of whom account has to be taken. This requires self-esteem, courage, and also perseverance, since victory is rarely permanent. To say no, to assert oneself, and to claim one's rights also requires competencies, such as:

- knowing the texts and principles on which to base the case so as not to seem as though one is asking for a favor; it is, for example, vital to know the law on labor, the private sphere, freedom of expression, and sexual harassment in order to defend one's rights in an enterprise.

- knowing how to suggest arrangements or alternative solutions to the person who may be willing to recognize one's needs and rights but without sacrificing his or her own interests; thus, anyone wishing to take the leave to which one is entitled at a time which is inconvenient from the employer's point of view has to find an alternative solution, otherwise the request will be refused or one will suffer reprisals, etc.

- finding the right tone and *arguments* in order 1) to have the needs and rights recognized as legitimate; 2) to avoid suffering reprisals worse than the unrecognized right; who wants to exercise one's right to express oneself at the risk of being dismissed or demoted on the slightest pretext?

- ensuring alliances, avenues of recourse, and alternatives so as not to find oneself alone and with no alternative if the request leads to a confrontation.

All this is relevant to some of the competencies described below, in particular "being able to analyze situations, relationships, and force fields systemically" and "being able to negotiate and construct agreement."

Being Able, Individually or in a Group, to Form and Conduct Projects, and to Develop Strategies

In a *société à projets* or project-driven society (Boutinet, 1993, 1995), whoever does not have a project becomes the instrument of the projects of others. Over and above the elementary rights and basic income support which, in the welfare state, are guaranteed to everyone, participation in resources and power presupposes involvement in a collective project or the pursuit of a personal project.

Being able to form and conduct projects does not oblige one to live permanently in this mode. But withdrawal is then a choice rather than the result of a lack of competence. The consequences of this choice are assumed lucidly: without a project the individual or collective actor is sidelined inasmuch as he or she has to submit to the decisions and compromises of those whose projects are in contention. In the business world – save in cases of built-in advantage – living without a project leads fairly quickly to failure. In other, less competitive areas, the effects are less spectacular: one does not cease to exist, but one enters a second circle, that of the onlookers, as it were. This phenomenon can be observed in society, but also in organizations, for individuals and groups alike. It is even to be found in the family.

Being able to form projects is not a minor competency. It is essentially a linkage with life and the world that presupposes a sense of identity, will, energy, and self-esteem, poles apart from shame (De Gaulejac, 1996) and depression. There can be no project without *mobilization* of the individual or group. Necessarily, therefore, project-forming is an exercise which has a *meaning* and which encounters a *force*.

Mobilization, however, is more than an initial impetus. It sustains the inception of the project but also its pursuit. In addition, it has to contend with reality. Everyone is capable of forming unrealistic projects that will be abandoned at the slightest taunt or at the first obstacle.

Being able to form projects is to be on the razor's edge, on the dividing line between inertia and utopia, a path to a future which is possible but which will materialize only if one works for it and gives oneself every chance of success. For the sun to rise, it is not necessary to form a project. To go to the moon, it is. But such a project was utopian until the middle of this century, because the state of science and technology afforded no chance of success. A project has to stay within the realm of the feasible – have an element of dream and optimism, yes, but give the impression that it is not out of reach.

This is where third parties come in. Everyone can, deep down inside, concoct wild schemes which psychoanalysts will class as fantasies. As soon as one shows that one has a project, others notice and judge it. Sometimes it has to be spelled out if one is to have the slightest chance of obtaining the necessary resources, information, cooperation, or authorizations (Amadieu, 1993; Strauss, 1992). A first facet of the necessary competency is therefore to form projects that appear reasonable, which others may judge daring, risky, but not unrealistic. When Alain Bombard set out to cross the ocean on a raft without any means of subsistence, he wanted to prove that one could survive on the nutritive elements in seawater, notably plankton. He was not taken for a madman, because he was a biologist and knew the sea well. When the first yachtsmen set out to circumnavigate the globe solo, the risks were high but they were taken by trained sportsmen who gave themselves every chance of success. When NASA decided that man would walk on the moon, this was a far cry from the musings of Jules Verne.

To form a project that appears reasonable, two resources are therefore necessary:

- an excellent perception of the technical requirements for success and of the ways to overcome or get around obstacles;

- a good psycho-sociological knowledge of the reactions on which the venture will depend, the ability to convince others that one knows what one is doing, that one is taking calculated risks.

These resources are essential to the formation of great collective projects, be they sporting (such as organizing the Olympic Games), artistic (building a cathedral), cultural (creating a museum of civilization), scientific (combating AIDS), technological (developing renewable energy sources), environmental (desertification control), military (declaring and winning the Gulf War), political (reunifying Germany, creating a single currency in Europe) or economic (bringing a region out of underdevelopment, defeating unemployment). Such projects concern an entire society or even the entire world. One finds equivalent ventures, equally ambitious and complex, in certain organizations – for example, when a business, a government department, or a hospital wants to put through decentralization, a change of technology, or a reform; when a party, a trade union, or an association wants to win power, renegotiate a collective agreement, or get more favorable legislation passed. Smaller groups, too, can form bold projects. A football team can plan to win the championship, a rock group to cut its first record, a family to emigrate to warmer climes, a couple to adopt a child.

Collective projects of this sort always rest, in the final analysis, on individuals, those who dream, think, calculate, regulate, decide, negotiate. They generally do so, however, as *members* of groups, organizations, or societies. In that case, it is not essential for every member of a group to possess the competencies needed to form and conduct projects: it is enough if those competencies are present somewhere in the group – in its leaders or its experts, or in some inspired member.

The need for competencies in each individual is more evident in the case of personal projects: plans for travel, career, retraining, education, therapy, saving, investment, creation, search (for a dwelling or for the philosopher's stone, as the case may be). What is important, therefore, is for each individual to be able to form and conduct *personal* projects and take an active part in forming and conducting *collective* projects.

Being able to develop *strategies* is linked here with the project, because one does not need strategy if one lives without a project, from day to day. Strategy is the art of maneuver and calculation, of steering a course towards a medium-term objective while allowing for obstacles, both foreseeable and unforeseeable. A project may aim to change a situation or to maintain it: not all projects are innovative.

Strategic competencies differ partly according to the social field of action and the type of project. But the roots of strategic thought are always the same: to envisage all kinds of possible courses of events – bar the worst – to anticipate the material obstacles and the reactions of partners and opponents, to think up original solutions on the spot, to control the indirect or adverse effects of the action (Boudon, 1977), to gauge minutely the length of time things will take, the resources needed, and the support that can be counted on, to plan everything that can be planned and to depart from the plan advisedly, to take stock continuously, to readjust forecasts and plans of action along the way (Suchman, 1990).

Being Able to Analyze Situations, Relationships, and Force Fields Systemically

Some of the underprivileged remain so because they do not attempt anything. Others because they make disorganized efforts that lead nowhere and sometimes actually make things worse. Dörner (1997) shows that even when there is no conflict, any action that does not correctly allow for systemic interdependence can lead to disaster in the medium term, even though there may be an improvement in the short run. To slow down or divert traffic in a city in order to increase safety and reduce noise is a good thing; but if that paralyzes urban commerce to the benefit of outlying shopping centers, the loss of employment and social life in the city may have very unfortunate effects. Often, the cure is worse than the disease if the organic regulations are not known and only the symptoms are treated.

This example shows that the problem is seldom purely technical, that the groups that think they have something to gain will defend a solution, and those fearing a loss will oppose it. Actors' strategies are part of the force field and the system.

The skills of systemic analysis are obviously necessary for a political or trade union leader, an entrepreneur, or for anyone who wants to mobilize or transform a complex social system, and act on issues like the birth rate, disease prevention, environmental protection, or suffrage.

I maintain that, on their particular level, autonomous actors need the same competencies – not to conduct public policies, but to construct and maintain a coherent line of action. Parents who want to make sure that their children are achievers at school often go about it quite the wrong way because they do not understand the system of action in which they are involved. *The perfect is the enemy of the good* and they would do better to leave well alone; instead they hound their offspring and provoke resistance or escape proportionate to their insistence (Perrenoud, 1998a).

Some victims of injustice or abuse of power make their situation worse by struggling without reason, like animals caught in a trap. Those whom others want to institutionalize on the grounds that they are not in their right mind may react so impulsively that they seem to prove right those who want to put them away and may gain the others the sympathy of witnesses to their actions. Victims of injustices (arbitrary punishment or dismissal from employment) may have such violent reactions that they break the law and change their status of victim to that of aggressor. Such reactions, which go against the tactical interests of the actor, denote first and foremost a lack of composure. Is composure a competency or a manner of living? Probably both. In addition to self-control, the competency to analyze relative strengths, if it is present, may be one of the few assets of the dominated. It alone can make them wait patiently until the moment when their reaction has the best chance of producing an effect, and get them to build more complex strategies, to maneuver until such time as they have found alliances or resources to turn the situation around in their favor.

Leaders/dominators need to master all the "tactics of power" in order to take or retain control of an organization or a bigger system. Ordinary actors do not have such ambitions. They simply need, in order to safeguard their interests or carry out their little projects, to be able to identify determinants, constraints, scope for action, and possible outcomes. For this they have to gain as accurate an idea as possible of how the field functions and of their own position in it. "Sociologically lucid" actors know whether it is in their interests to be virtuously indignant, to make a scene, to formally complain or, on the contrary, to bide their time and keep a low profile. They know if they should honestly disclose their needs, their limitations, their areas of doubt, or inability or, on the contrary, act as though they are in control of the situation (Perrenoud, 1996). They have a mental picture of the system of action and its areas of uncertainty (Friedberg, 1992, 1993), which enables them to anticipate and control the behavior of others and to know what happens if they themselves take this or that initiative.

Training in social sciences can be helpful, but it is not general theory that ordinary actors need, but a conceptual blueprint of the system of action that concerns them *here and now*. Some of the actors who successfully defend their autonomy, or even exercise power, construct this blueprint intuitively, without intellectual concepts, through knowledge born of experience with its share of trial and error, which ties in with good use of experience and careful thinking.

Being Able to Cooperate, Act in Synergy, and Participate in a Collective, Shared Leadership

In a complex society one seldom achieves one's ends alone. Political parties, trade unions, pressure groups, and so on, are bodies that enable those who share the same interests or convictions to join forces.

Defending one's autonomy sometimes means having to limit one's freedom of maneuver and blend into a larger circle of people who champion similar causes or a common cause. This is the principle of any system of collective action. The first competency of autonomous actors is to be able to identify the groups, parties, associations, or other movements already in place which are likely to help them to achieve their ends or defend their interests. The choice is not always easy, for there is competition between coexistent organizations. Furthermore, once one has joined an organization one is subjected to disciplines and a form of orthodoxy that not everybody is ready to endure.

When the actors enter an existing organization, a second competency becomes essential, namely for them to be able to integrate without being used and while remaining true to their principles and their initial project. Militants of trade unions and political organizations learn at their expense that this is not easy, and that they become cogs in a machine of war wherein strategic reason often prevails over personal mindsets and values. Here is one of the permanent dilemmas of the actor: to remain alone and therefore powerless, but free, or to join a collective and be obliged to make compromises so that the collective may achieve its aims. Again, this is not only a question of personality, courage, and determination, but also of competence; to assert one's point of view when a collective is establishing its position and its strategy requires great skill in understanding the dynamics of the debate and the tendencies present, if one is not to find oneself isolated or even reduced to silence. In addition to argumentative and maneuvering skills, there are others just as fundamental, such as being able to detect the limits of solidarity and to construct tactical or more sustainable alliances.

Even in a hyper-organized society, there are systems of collective action that still have to be built, both within the big organizations and outside – for example, in areas where there is no collective actor yet because the problem is a new one, or because a country is emerging from a period of police-state conditions or economic crisis that prevented any collective action. Social life is constantly bringing forth new categories of people with interests in common. Thus, different types of victims (of hostage-taking, acts of terrorism, medical errors, blood transfusions causing AIDS, plane crashes, misfortunes of various kinds) are banding together to defend new rights. Similarly, in the case of diseases, disabilities, organ transplants, or scarce medical equipment, patients or their families are getting themselves organized. One sees unemployed persons forming pressure groups independent of the labor unions and entering into part-conflict with those who still have work. Various humanitarian causes are mobilizing incensed people. Environmental movements are forming in protest against a nuclear power station or nuclear waste, a natural reserve endangered by property developers, the extermination of seals or whales, and so on.

The competencies of the autonomous actor are therefore not confined to choosing an existing organization to join, and in which to play an active role. He or she should also, with others, *be able to construct new collectives* – like user associations, neighborhood committees, environmental movements, etc.

The growing number of social movements suggests that these competencies exist already. The fact that so many of these movements are fragile and plagued by infighting shows that things are still far from perfect, partly because the most current know-how does not readily reconcile efficiency and democracy. One sees democratic associations wearing themselves out in internal wrangling without any grasp of reality, and associations under the thumb of a few tyrants who find themselves isolated once the danger is past. People turn away from them because they disregard their members and simply use the latter's numerical strength and money, without organizing any debate or taking account of members' needs.

Being Able to Build and Operate Democratic Organizations and Systems of Collective Action

This particular ability can be linked with the theme of citizenship, provided it is agreed that education to citizenship is not just a question of values and adherence to the democratic model. Those are preconditions, but without specific and finely honed competencies, all associations will drift towards paralysis or takeover by a few.

Here again, competencies are significant only if they are secured to an identity and democratic convictions. Then they make it possible to work towards such ideals as transparency of decision-making, strict compliance with procedures, equality of opportunity, and justice.

Any urgent cause may mobilize people, even when no democratic process applies. They will obey an authoritarian leader if he appears capable of saving them when the ship is going down. At cruising speed, things are different. Mobilization is maintained only if people feel that they are appreciated and have their say in matters. This is true even in businesses, where various systems of participation are being set up.

Although democracy remains limited – in business, owing to the right of owners to use their assets as they see fit; in government, through the decisions of the government, parliament, and sometimes voters; and in the church, through reference to divine will and to sacred texts as interpreted by the clergy – it has no reason to be similarly limited in the associations of all kinds which one joins, not under a work contract or for a baptism, but as the result of a personal, reasoned, voluntary, and reversible choice.

The spectacle of today's political parties shows that there are still movements, in many cases extremist, under the orders of a charismatic leader or an oligarchy. Most of the big parties retain their militants and voters only by giving them a share of power, often the strict minimum. In the smaller parties, which are less well endowed with resources and competence, democracy is flouted more often, or less subtly. This is probably because those who work hardest and seek office have no intention of meekly following the rank and file. Most party leaders oscillate between unconditional regard for the rank and file and sufficient manipulation to preserve the appearances of democracy. This wavering is due to the ambivalence of the leaders, caught between desire for power and democratic convictions. But it also reflects a dilemma: a democratic decision takes a long time to prepare and often leads to a half-hearted consensus and to a strategy lacking in coherence, which furthermore is unveiled publicly before it even begins to be put into effect. This is why democracy and efficiency are at odds.

To overcome the tension, it is necessary to develop a common culture, methods of work, forms of reversible delegation, and procedures of consultation and decision-making that are realistic as regards timing and tactical constraints. This work falls largely to the leaders, who have to design the structures, regulations, information channels, work methods, and decision-making procedures. However, the more the conception of democratic functioning is widely shared and the more the other members are capable of assuming responsibilities and taking initiatives in the same spirit, and are vigilant and able to prevent authoritarian drift, the more democratic the organization as a whole will be. This is true also in businesses and government departments that want to encourage employee participation.

The corresponding competencies are partly based on knowledge of civil law and democratic principles. Putting them to use, however, depends on numerous know-how instances of a more practical kind such as knowing how to construct a real alternative, moderate a debate, restructure an issue to break a deadlock, or permit the minority to save face, allow dissidents to state their case without allowing them to hold the group to ransom, build compromises that incorporate opposing lines of thought, split decisions so as to avoid hardening of opposition, or get an overall policy adopted from which specific decisions will stem, decentralize advisedly, and set up mechanisms of redress or regulation, etc.

It may be considered that these are political competencies, in the broad sense of the functioning of a community governed by pursuit of the common good. Moreover, it is generally a matter of knowing how to negotiate, build agreements, and make decisions that allow for all shades of opinion.

Being Able to Manage and Resolve Conflict

It is, of course, in a non-membership situation that conflicts develop most legitimately and therefore openly and sometimes violently. Conflicts between nations are not moderated by any strong body, even if the UN tries to play this role. The same is true in the case of civil strife, when justice and institutions are themselves in crisis or torn between warring movements.

Membership in a group does not preclude conflict. The united front is only to be found at the most dramatic moments in the life of a nation or an organization. With easier times it disintegrates. In a democratic society, the state, the law, collective agreements, and a system of shared values provide a legal and moral framework that is widely accepted by adversaries in settling their conflicts. It is the same in organizations where the leadership plays the role of the state. This does not prevent societies and organizations from being the theater of strikes, demonstrations, takeover of premises, and other verbal and sometimes physical clashes between groups or between them and the forces of law and order.

In short, a democratic society does not outlaw conflict: it offers it a legal framework in the broadest sense, including civil, penal, and administrative procedures, but also labor courts, mediatory bodies, collective bargaining structures, and all the institutions which, in one capacity or another, formally or informally, encourage the peaceable expression of differences and the search for equitable compromise. Conflicts can be euphemized as "divergences of views" or "democratic debates" but they can involve interests or opinions as opposed as those between veritable enemies – for example, when the leadership of an organization or the carrying of a decision is the issue at stake.

If matters reach the stage of outright violence – be it in a city, a neighborhood, a tenement building, a prison, or a firm – it is obviously because the mechanisms of peaceful resolution have not sufficed. This does not mean that they are absent or ineffectual. On the contrary, in most cases they prevent things from getting even worse. Unfortunately, their limitations are more eye-catching than their successes.

Today, economic troubles, population movements, multicultural melting pots, urban insecurity and disorganization, rapid technological change, rising unemployment, uncertain job tenure, and inequalities are new sources of conflict. The capacity for peaceful settlement of conflict has no doubt increased over the centuries in absolute terms, but it is probably still insufficient to accommodate the increasing complexity of today's world.

The competencies required are, in part, those of experts: magistrates, mediators, and ombudsmen. They should intervene only at the end of the process, when mediations closer to the parties have failed. Dominique Felder (1985) analyzes the workings of the San Francisco community boards and shows that in disadvantaged areas, where neighborhood conflicts are fierce and numerous, local organizations of voluntary workers and elected councilors can do an excellent job of mediation. At the non-official level, a great deal of informal mediation work is done every day in all kinds of social fields by people not directly involved in the conflicts – persons supporting one party or another but arguing for a negotiated solution – or by the parties themselves when they want to call a halt before matters go too far.

When it comes to identifying competencies that are *necessary*, there is nothing to be gained by maintaining that they are totally lacking. It is rather a question of *reinforcing* them, of enabling more actors to develop them. It is still necessary to use expert mediators in the most difficult cases, but the professionals should constitute a last resort and conflicts should be handled in the first instance by the parties concerned or their kin.

Foremost among the competencies required is a dispassionate recognition of conflict as a *normal*, acceptable, non-evil mode of relationship between human beings, as the quid pro quo for liberty and pluralism. This presupposes a psycho-sociological culture, which does not diabolize conflicts, or try to resolve conflict by repudiating it or stigmatizing it as pathology.

Further, some more specialized know-how is needed:

- analyzing the issues at stake, the origins of the conflict, the reasons of both sides, and the attempts at reconciliation that have failed;

- negotiating and establishing a framework of conditions and ground rules which will permit dialogue, re-examining differences, and developing a solution acceptable to the parties;

- introducing a preventive or monitoring mechanism.

Depending on the nature of the conflict, it is desirable, if a third party performs mediation, that the latter should possess some technical knowledge in order to understand the essence of the difference. But this is not the most important thing. A mediator can understand the issues without substituting for the disputants, less still without being capable of doing their work. The technical issues in dispute often mask considerations of power, territory, precedence, copyright and royalties, merit recognition, freedom and control, division of labor, equity, and so on. The mechanisms concerned are transversal. The mediator's expertise is concerned with their functioning. If the settlement of a conflict necessitates technical solutions, it is not for the mediator to supply them but for him to get the disputants to construct them together

Being Able to Play With the Rules, Use Them, and Elaborate on Them

The introduction of rules can both be of service and of disservice to the autonomy of individuals. In a totalitarian society, or in an authoritarian organization or family, the power imposes rules that deprive actors of autonomy. A democratic society, on the other hand, makes rules that preserve the autonomy of individuals – from the Universal Declaration of Human Rights to the internal regulations of a school, a business, or an apartment building.

To optimize their autonomy, actors therefore need to be able to

- identify and understand the texts that limit or guarantee their autonomy;

- find precedents and possibly a body of case law that might work in their favor;

- gauge the leeway that the rules allow in their ordinary usage;

- ascertain by what procedure they may request and obtain a departure from a rule;

- find out and set in motion the procedures whereby they can propose amendment or repeal of a rule.

These requirements call to mind rules of law in the first instance, but by analogy they also apply to any system of explicit or even implicit norms. A teenager has to fulfil them in order, say, to know how many times a week or month she may stay out late, and how late without causing disagreeable reactions. In the same way a hospital patient has to discover the limits of his autonomy and, in order to push them back, learn to play with the rules of the service he happens to be in.

Where rules of law are involved, knowledge of formal legal language and concepts is obviously required. In this case and in all the others, "psycho-sociological" competencies are needed in order to identify the rule and the leeway it allows, through trial and error: by asking innocuous questions, listening to anecdotes, analyzing the machinery for detection and punishment of deviance, and identifying the vulnerable sides of those who enforce the rules. At an earlier stage, one has to outgrow one's infantile relationship to authority, get rid of some burdensome superego, or stop thinking that the sky will fall on the heads of those who deviate from the norm. This competency of analyzing the human, negotiable, and changeable character of the norm, its arbitrary quality, the interests it serves, the fact that there is nothing sacred about it nor anything automatic or standardized about punishment of deviance, increases individuals' inner freedom and authorizes them to construct a strategic relationship to the rules which limit their freedom.

In return, this presupposes an ethical education which enables one to make good use of the autonomy won through substituting judgment for unconditional compliance with a norm simply because that is the norm.

Being Able to Construct Negotiated Orders Over and Above Cultural Differences

One cannot live in disorder, other than temporarily. Yet in a pluralistic, democratic society in perpetual change, there is no traditional, immutable, or at least stable order that offers a response to each situation and, most importantly, that drastically limits the number of different situations that may arise. The social order is fragile, constantly brought into question or into crisis, regularly revised and renegotiated (Padioleau, 1986). Only those who are able to take part in the negotiation manage to benefit. The others lose what little they have gained when the rules of the game change. Thus the shift to structurally inflationary economies despoiled savers who stood by and watched as a new deal was being constructed.

In our society – with its changing technologies, restructuring of the productive system, reconstruction of whole companies and organizations, amalgamations, population movements from one country or continent to another – an increasing number of people are finding themselves in a new and strange environment, caught up in interactions the rules of which they do not understand or which do not yet have any.

To avoid anarchy *à la Mad Max* and complete withdrawal into oneself or the family circle, it is therefore important that as many individuals as possible know how to construct or reconstruct in a negotiated and essentially practical manner *provisional microsocial orders* which make it possible for people to coexist peacefully. In extreme cases – for example, in certain slum areas, border zones, or deprived neighborhoods – coexistence has to be organized between communities who do not speak the same language, have different cultures, and have to share scarce resources and limited space. For coexistence to be peaceful, the actors need to have the means to invent an order, hence to be able to communicate and express needs and state points of view and interests. What is unlikely to happen in such extreme conditions is a little easier in areas where life is less threatened, disorganized, or insecure. But there too, competencies are needed in order to *organize coexistence*, if not a new community. Even when cultural differences are intrinsic to a society, making concessions so as to construct a livable order is not easy. Nor is it easy even within a homogeneous group, when a number of people who are civilized, educated, and share the same values find themselves adrift in a lifeboat, on a desert island, or in some isolated spot far from help. In Switzerland, civil defense has for years arranged it so that, in the event of nuclear conflict, part of the population will be accommodated in special underground shelters, safe from radiation and isolated from the outside air. To anticipate problems of coexistence in these confined spaces, experiments have been made with volunteer occupants in certain buildings over short periods. They have shown the extreme difficulty experienced by a group brought together by misfortune in devising rules that will permit communal life, notably democratic decision-making procedures and rules of justice for the tasks, living space, and privileges of each according to age, needs, and status.

In less confined spaces or less dramatic circumstances, an absence of competencies does not have such visible effects, but it tends to sap the essence of groups and organizations from within and bring out authoritarian instincts, or it encourages a form of anomie and disorganization of communities whose survival as such depends on negotiation rather than common dependence on a guru or on a dogma powerful enough to compel agreement.

Education in Reflective Practice

These different competencies naturally need to be broken down into their specific components. Similarly, the resources they mobilize need to be identified methodically. Only then can one begin to construct programs for developing the competencies.

It can be assumed that extremely erudite and intelligent subjects will be capable of building these competencies themselves, by learning very quickly from experience. In the case of more ordinary subjects with less impressive resources, competency building goes by way of organized training, from the stage of elementary schooling onwards. Formal schooling does not preclude, indeed it must count on, development of these competencies through life experience and reflective practice. Moreover, a real education will incorporate all these dimensions.

A Restricted Autonomy

As a rule, when actors first enter a defined social field, they do not know much about it and are not very competent. Except, of course, if they have been duly trained, but then the training can be considered to be part of the field: to be a seminary student is already to be part of the ecclesiastical field. Most organized fields have a special status for new arrivals, which allows them to learn what they have to know and gives them the right to error and experimentation, for a period of initiation that is codified to a greater or lesser degree. Socialization, when it is organized, often encourages a sort of conformity. The socialization process is governed by the dominant actors in the field and therefore does not necessarily seek to promote individual autonomy, either because autonomy is not an important value (for example, in an army, a religious order, or certain businesses), or because it clashes with other values (obedience, humility, efficiency, uniformity), or again because it is not associated with the status of newcomer. Becoming an autonomous actor is thus not necessarily "on the program." In many social fields, the competencies and autonomy of an actor are limited to what his or her position allows and requires. To know more would be to threaten the established order.

There are, admittedly, organizations whose work of socialization does seek to promote individual autonomy. If they constituted the rule, there would be no need to worry about developing autonomy and the corresponding competencies during basic education. In fact, socialization in a social field is nearly always a paradoxical exercise which encourages a certain form of autonomy without which the field cannot function, and which at the same time limits it so that it may serve the cause of unity and the aims and interests of the dominant actors in the field, those who control the processes of socialization and, sometimes, admission.

This is evident in an organization, a specific field tightly structured by an organizing power and to which one belongs by virtue of a formal decision and a course of socialization that is provided. In social fields, the processes of socialization are generally not organized so deliberately, but one finds the same tension, with a lower and an upper limit: below the lower limit, lack of autonomy prevents the field from functioning; above the upper limit, autonomy endangers the field's existence or simply the established power structure.

The autonomy of subjects, viewed individually as opposed to collectively, thus has to be developed, at least in part, *counter to the logic of each field*. This is why it is important that the education system should not be wholly dependent on the other organizations and social fields, but should work partly in the interest of the individual, or even the group – irrespective of allegiances – in order to form reflective and critical actors.

Acting as a Reflective Practitioner

The idea of the reflective practitioner has been popularized by the work of Schön (1983, 1987, 1991) in the context of research on professional occupations and education pathways. I am taking it out of that context here because it seems to me closely linked with the question of the development of competencies of autonomous social actors independently of their normalization in this or that organization or social field. More precisely, it is a matter of making actors as independent as possible of the limits which each organization or field sets on their autonomy.

Or again, to put it differently, the object is to make the actor autonomous even in relation to the social norms which govern autonomy in the different fields that make up a modern society. This amounts to saying that actors are not simply the sum of the roles assigned to them in the different fields of which they are willy-nilly a part.

Doubtless this posture is, in some respects, very optimistic concerning democracy and the education system's autonomy relative to social demands. But if such optimism is out of place, all that is needed, in order to give curricula the desired focus, is to ask the authorized spokesmen for each field what they expect from the education system, make a synthesis of these expectations, and build it into the curricula. If, however, the school is not the sum of these demands but part of a project centered on the individual and citizenship, thinking about transversal competencies and autonomy has some meaning.

Reflective practice is then a means of acquiring these competencies and autonomy, preserving and developing them, independently and sometimes in defiance of the socialization and education programs specific to each field or organization. A reflective posture and a reflective approach enable actors to learn from experience and think for themselves, without being prisoners of the exclusive thinking or expectations of their environment. This is an attitude and a metacompetency on which all others depend.

Two Basic Principles

The following are two basic principles for education in autonomy from compulsory schooling onwards:

1. As one learns to walk by walking, so one learns to build one's autonomy by exercising it. Instead of just organizing practical work for students from 2 to 4 p.m. on Fridays, it would obviously be better if the entire education system (formal schooling, adult education, and work too) constituted a *curriculum* for building the competencies linked with autonomy.

2. Each competency necessitates an overall development of critical thinking and reflective practice that has to bear on the sum total of formal and informal knowledge and experiences in life.

This means that taking the development of competencies seriously involves much more than altering or expanding a syllabus or program. Evolution is interdependent with a competency-oriented approach for the curriculum as a whole (Perrenoud, 1998a, 2000a, 2000b, 2001), and a fairly significant shift in the student-teacher relationship and the functioning of educational establishments and classes towards the "self-government" type of education with out-of-classroom learning, active methods, project approaches, learning commitments, and so on.

The field concerned here is education in citizenship, but going far beyond civics. It is a question not only of values and knowledge but of competencies, which implies education, both theoretical and practical, that can be drawn upon in real-life situations – education in and outside school, from childhood throughout life.

No progress is possible here if this project is not embedded in each subject taught. Developing critical thought, debate, and intellectual autonomy is, in principle, the intention in each discipline: mother tongue, mathematics, history, biology, philosophy, etc. In practice, this aim is often set aside in favor of knowledge accumulation. It is also harmed by shortage of time and teachers' fears that they will lose power if they allow debate. To form critical judgment is always to run the risk that it will turn against the school in the first instance. I have developed these arguments elsewhere, notably concerning the connections to be made between citizenship, intellectual debate, and knowledge-relatedness (Perrenoud, 1997, 1998c). Here I shall simply put forth one fundamental postulate: school cannot help to develop autonomy, reflective practice, and critical thought if it prohibits them in its midst. What has to be envisaged, therefore, is a high-risk education, necessitating changes in attitudes and learning/teaching commitments (including student/teacher rating) as much as changes in the prescribed curriculum.

References

Amadieu, J. F. (1993). *Organisations et travail: Coopération, conflit et marchandage.* Paris: Vuibert.

Becker, H. S. (1966). Whose side are we on? *Social Problems, 14*, 239–247.

Bentolila. A. (1996). *De l'illettrisme en général et de l'école en particulier.* Paris: Plon.

Boudon, R. (1977). *Effets pervers et ordre social.* Paris: PUF.

Bourdieu, P. (1980). *Le sens pratique.* Paris: Ed. de Minuit.

Bourdieu, P. (1982). Ce que parler veut dire: L'économie des échanges linguistiques. Paris: Fayard.

Bourdieu, P. (1997). *Méditations pascaliennes.* Paris: Seuil.

Bourdieu, P., (Ed.). (1993). *La misère du monde.* Paris: Seuil.

Bourdieu, P., & Passeron, J. C. (1970). *La reproduction: Eléments pour une théorie du système d'enseignement.* Paris: Ed. de Minuit.

Boutinet, J.-P. (Ed.). (1995). *Le projet, mode ou nécessité?* Paris: L'Harmattan.

Chomsky, N. (1971). *Aspects de la théorie syntaxique.* Paris: Seuil.

Chomsky, N. (1977). *Réflexions sur le langage.* Paris: Maspéro.

Dörner, D. (1997). *La logique de l'échec.* Paris: Flammation.

Dubet, F., & Martucelli, D. (1998). *Dans quelle société vivons-nous?* Paris: Seuil.

Felder, D. (1985). *Les mutants pacifiques: Expériences communautaires du "New Age" en Californie.* Lausanne: Editions d'En Bas.

Friedberg, E. (1992). Les quatre dimensions de l'action organisée. *Revue française de sociologie, XXXIII, 4*, 531–557.

Friedberg, E. (1993). *Le pouvoir et la règle.* Paris: Seuil.

de Gaulejac, V. (1996). *Les sources de la honte.* Paris: Desclée de Brouwer.

Kellerhals, J., Modak, M., & Perrenoud, D. (1997). *Le sentiment de justice dans les relations sociales.* Paris: PUF.

Lafaye, C. (1996). *La sociologie des organisations.* Paris: Nathan.

Lascoumes, P. (1977). *Prévention et contrôle social: Les contradictions du travail social.* Genève et Paris: Médecine et Hygiène et Masson.

Lascoumes, P. (1997). *Élites irrégulières: Essai sur la délinquance d'affaire.* Paris: Gallimard.

Le Boterf, G. (1994). *De la compétence: Essai sur un attracteur étrange.* Paris: Les Editions d'organisation.

Le Boterf, G. (1997). *De la compétence à la navigation professionnelle.* Paris: Les Editions d'organisation.

Morin, E. (1977). *La méthode. 1: La nature de la nature.* Paris: Seuil.

Padioleau, J. G. (1986). *L'ordre social: Principes d'analyse sociologique.* Paris: L'Harmattan.

Perrenoud, P. (1996). *Enseigner: Agir dans l'urgence, décider dans l'incertitude: Savoirs et compétences dans un métier complexe.* Paris: ESF.

Perrenoud, P. (1997). Apprentissage de la citoyenneté…des bonnes intentions au curriculum caché. In J.-C. Gracia (Ed.), *Education, citoyenneté, territoire, Actes du séminaire national de l'enseignement agricole* (pp. 32–54). Toulouse: ENFA.

Perrenoud, P. (1998a). *Construire des compétences dès l'école* (2e éd.). Paris: ESF.

Perrenoud, P. (1998b). Le mieux est l'ennemi du bien! Que conseiller aux parents pour faire face aux éventuelles difficultés scolaires de leurs enfants? *Éducation Enfantine, 3*, 71–76.

Perrenoud, P. (1998c). Le débat et la raison. In *"L'éducation à la citoyenneté,"* Supplément n° 4 des *Cahiers pédagogiques*, octobre-novembre, pp. 4–7.

Perrenoud, P. (2000a). D'une métaphore l'autre: transférer ou mobiliser ses connaissances? In J. Dolz & E. Ollagnier (Eds.), *L'énigme de la compétence en éducation* (pp. 45–60). Bruxelles: De Boeck, Coll. *Raisons Educatives*.

Perrenoud, P. (2000 b). L'école saisie par les compétences. In C. Bosman, F.-M. Gerard, & X. Roegiers (Eds.), *Quel avenir pour les compétences?* (pp. 21–41). Bruxelles: De Boeck.

Perrenoud, P. (2001). Fondements de l'éducation scolaire: enjeux de socialisation et de formation. In C. Gohier & S. Laurin (Eds.), *Entre culture, compétence et contenu: La formation fondamentale, un espace à redéfinir* (pp. 55–84). Montréal: Editions Logiques.

Pinto, L. (1998). *Pierre Bourdieu et la théorie du monde social.* Paris: Albin Michel, Paris.

Raisky, C. (1996). Doit-on en finir avec la transposition didactique? In C. Raisky, & M. Caillot (Eds.), *Au-delà des didactiques, le didactique: Débats autour de concepts fédérateurs* (pp. 37–59). Bruxelles: De Boeck.

Rey, B. (1996). *Les compétences transversales en question.* Paris: ESF.

Robert, P., Soubiran-Paillet, F., & van de Kerchove, M. (Eds.). (1997). *Normes, normes juridiques, normes pénales: Pour une sociologie des frontières.* Deux tomes. Paris: L'Hamattan.

Ropé, F., & Tanguy, L. (1994). *Savoirs et compétences: De l'usage de ces notions dans l'école et l'entreprise.* Paris: L'Harmattan.

Schön, D. (1983). *The reflective practitioner.* Basic Books, New York (trad. française: (1994). *Le praticien réflexif: À la recherche du savoir caché dans l'agir professionnel.* Montreal: Les Editions Logiques.)

Schön, D. (1987). *Educating the reflective practitioner.* San Francisco, CA: Jossey-Bass.

Schön, D. (1991). *Cases in reflective practice.* New York: Teachers College Press.

Strauss, A. (1992). *La trame de la négociation.* Paris: L'Harmattan.

Stroobants, M. (1993). *Savoir-faire et compétences au travail: Une sociologie de la fabrication des aptitudes.* Bruxelles: Editions de l'Université de Bruxelles.

Suchman, L. (1990). Plans d'action: Problèmes de la représentation de la pratique en sciences cognitives. *Raisons Pratiques 1*, 149–170. "Les formes de l'action."

Editors' Note

This chapter was translated into English from the original French.

Chapter 7

Key Competencies Critical to Economic Success

Frank Levy
Richard J. Murnane

An Economics Perspective

In this chapter, two economists identify competencies necessary for individuals to lead a successful and responsible life and for society to face the challenges of the present and the future. We write from the perspective of the discipline we were trained in – a discipline that teaches important lessons about critical competencies, but one with important limitations for defining the good life. Both the strengths and the limitations stem from the discipline's aspirations to conduct itself as a science.

Economics values the development of hypotheses that can be empirically tested, and outcomes that can be measured with available data. As a result, most economic analysis focuses on the economy that exists – not an idealized economy that might exist. It focuses particularly on the operation of markets, important aspects of every Western society. By making restrictive assumptions, most outcomes of interest to economists appear as prices and quantities – well-measured variables. Of particular relevance to this chapter are numbers of people employed, and the distributions of their earnings.

The value of labor market outcomes as a part of the good life for individuals and their families is self-evident. In Western societies, labor market earnings provide the primary source of resources to care for children. The distribution of labor market outcomes is also critical to the future of democracies. Support for democracy depends critically on a general perception among the citizenry that they can share in the country's material wealth and can look forward to a promising future for their children.

In practice, the demand for labor can shift much more rapidly than people can change their competencies. Correspondingly, changes in the distribution of labor market outcomes provide early warnings of changes in the skills required to function well in society. These early warnings are of legitimate concern both to individuals making decisions about education and occupational choices, and to societal institutions including schools that prepare citizens to earn a living.

The economist's focus on markets, while valuable, has two major limitations. First, by restricting most analysis to the existing economy, the analysis implicitly accepts the existing distribution of income. It is this distribution which translates into demands for particular commodities and which, for example, permits good bond traders to earn very high wages compared to good public school teachers.

Second, by focusing on the market economy, the analysis has little to say about those aspects of a good life that occur outside markets: volunteer activities, unpaid work, or leisure time. To take one example, in the standard calculation of a country's gross domestic product, the movement of a woman out of the home and into paid work will be counted as a pure gain; no deduction will be made for the loss of unpaid work or free time within the home.

The discipline's concern with measurable outcomes also puts limits on its theoretical framework. The central economic model of behavior – utility maximization – is, as is well known, a highly individualistic model in which an individual's utility increases monotonically with his or her consumption. There is no satiation and the individual's utility does not depend on the utilities achieved by other individuals. Both assumptions are critical in the creation of testable hypotheses,[1] but neither assumption is a fully accurate description of the existing society, much less the good society. As one example, Easterlin (1974) demonstrates that during the 1950s and 1960s, a period in which the purchasing power of the average U.S. family nearly doubled, the fraction of the U.S. population describing itself as "happy" in national polls remained constant. This work among others suggests increased income does not automatically translate into utility, in part because people judge their situation relative to the situations of others, an interaction most economic models ignore.

Because these limitations are readily apparent, critics sometimes argue that the economist is someone who knows the price of everything and the value of nothing. Unsurprisingly, we believe the criticism goes too far. In the absence of a massive restructuring of society, the ability to earn an income is clearly a legitimate and important goal. If social institutions failed to prepare most young people to work productively – if, for example, many young people could not move out of unemployment – it would be a poor foundation for the other broader goals which a good society encompasses.

With these limitations in mind then, we state the economist's definition of a good life as follows: the maximization of the present discounted value of earned income over a lifetime, subject to limits on hours of work.

In this definition, limited work hours are a crude way to reflect the value of leisure time. The notion of discounting income reflects the idea that a dollar received today can be invested and so is worth more than a dollar received in the future.[2] More subtly, the focus on lifetime income implies the potential value of being able to adapt to

---

[1] If an individual's utility depended on the utility levels of others rather than on the individual's consumption alone, statistical estimation of behavioral responses would be extremely complex. Similarly, utility functions which allowed satiation in consumption would lead to indeterminacies in behavior that would be difficult to analyze. Conversely, the theory can allow utility to depend on leisure time as well as material consumption so that it will not predict total absorption in work.
[2] Discounting may also reflect the fact that at any point in time, an individual's own preferences value a unit of consumption today more than a unit of consumption tomorrow.

shifts in the labor market. That value appears to be of particular importance today when the combination of expanded international trade and technology are rapidly reshaping labor demand in the United States and other industrialized countries (Rodrik, 1997; Levy, 1999).

Writing as spouses, parents, and citizens, we would have a richer, more complex definition of a good life, but this would take us well outside today's mainstream economic perspective.

Following the economics literature, we treat competencies and skills as synonymous. We embrace a broad definition of skills that includes not only cognitive skills, but also non-cognitive skills such as perseverance. Our reading of the economics literature leads us to propose the following lessons:

1. Basic reading and mathematics skills are important in determining long-run labor market outcomes, including the ability to adjust to changing circumstances.

2. The ability to communicate effectively, both orally and in writing, is important in determining long-run labor market outcomes.

3. The organization of work within firms is changing in ways that place increased value on the ability to work productively in groups.

4. Both changes in firms (the emphasis on teamwork) and changes in the economy are placing increased emphasis on elements of "emotional intelligence" including the ability to relate well to other people.

5. Familiarity with computers is of growing importance in the labor market.

6. Formal educational credentials are of growing importance in determining economic success. Yet available evidence does not make clear why employers are willing to pay substantial wage premiums to workers with greater educational attainments.

7. The market forces which value key competencies are modified by a number of institutional arrangements: the organization of work (see 3, above), the links between firms and educational institutions, the extent to which a nation's markets are regulated, and the nation's distribution of income as modified by the welfare state.

At the end of the chapter, we return to these lessons about key competencies, explain the lessons in greater detail, and discuss their implications.

Underlying Theories

Economists rely on several potentially complementary theories to explain why workers' educational attainments are positively related to their earnings. Each of these theories has relevance to identifying key competencies.

Human Capital Theory

Human capital theory treats education as an investment. In this theory, individuals incur costs, including tuition and foregone earnings while in school, to acquire skills that increase their productivity and result in subsequent wages higher than they otherwise would have earned (Willis, 1986). A long tradition of research has focused on the magnitude of the return to educational investments, showing that human capital investments tend to pay off at least as well as investments in physical capital.

This high payoff, in turn, has led many social scientists to ask why employers are willing to pay higher wages to people with greater education. Empirical approaches to answering this question have ranged from statistical studies of existing data sets to ethnographic studies of the workplace. We review the lessons from these approaches in the next section.

Economists also have addressed the earnings-education relationship through the construction of theory. An important example is the work of Theodore Schultz (1975), who argued that education increases individuals' ability to deal with unexpected events, including non-routine problems at work or forced job changes. Support for this theory comes from studies showing that workers with more formal education cope better with unanticipated layoffs than do workers with little formal education (Cyert & Mowery, 1987), and that the wage gains from education are higher in developing countries undergoing economic change than in countries with traditional economies (Jamison, 1982).

Signaling Theory

While Schultz's model lies very much in the tradition of human capital, a quite different explanation for the high payoff to education comes from the market signaling model (Spence, 1974). The heart of signaling lies in asymmetric information in the labor market. A potential job applicant may know his own skills, but he may have difficulty conveying this information directly to employers. In the absence of some way to signal their skills to employers, highly skilled applicants will earn no more than job applicants who lack critical skills. Suppose that regardless of what schools teach, skilled workers have an easier time completing school than unskilled workers. If this were the case, potential job applicants would acquire additional education not to increase their skills, but to signal to employers that they in fact possess skills (Tyler, Murnane, & Willett, 2000). Consequently, employers would prefer workers with more schooling, not because the schooling imparted useful knowledge, but because the completion of schooling was correlated with the skills that employers value.

Of course, the signaling model leaves unanswered the same question that the human capital model does: What are the skills that make highly educated workers of greater value to employers than workers with less education? The signaling model also raises the general problem of how individuals who do possess critical skills can convey this information to employers. This question represents an important step beyond basic economic models in which all persons have access to perfect information.

It suggests that relationships between particular skills and labor market outcomes may depend on institutional arrangements. We return to this point later in the chapter, suggesting that institutional arrangements may play a critical role in determining the incentives for individuals to acquire critical competencies.

Principal-Agent Theory

Over the last 20 years, principal-agent theory, a theory potentially complementary with both human capital and signaling theories, has played a growing role in explaining relationships between employers and employees. The theory assumes that the agent (the worker or potential worker) behaves in a way that maximizes his or her own interests, interests that are not perfectly aligned with those of the employer. For example, the worker may value leisure on the job; the employer would prefer that the employee stick to work. The employer faces the challenge of designing an employment relationship such that the worker will find it in his interest to behave in a manner that furthers the employer's goals. One constraint in the employer's design is that constantly monitoring employee behavior is expensive (Bowles & Gintis, 1998).

From the perspective of principal-agent models, employers' decisions about whom to hire and how many resources to devote to monitoring workers' performances are jointly determined. In this world, employers may be willing to pay premiums for workers with attributes such as perseverance and honesty that reduce the need to monitor.

One implication of this theory is that the value of particular competencies depends on the organization of work. Only in organizations in which monitoring costs are high will employers be willing to pay a premium for attributes such as honesty and perseverance. Surveys conducted by Edward Lawler and his colleagues every three years since 1987 suggest that the percentage of U.S. firms adopting work organizations in which workers are expected to take initiative and work in groups to solve problems – work organizations in which it is very expensive to monitor the performance of individual workers – is growing. This trend suggests a growing importance to firms of competencies such as perseverance and honesty. This theoretical perspective also brings back the question raised by signaling theory: How do potential workers signal to employers that they possess the critical competencies that are needed in a low-monitoring environment?

Most empirical investigations of wage patterns are informed by one or another of these theories. In the next section of the chapter, we describe four research approaches economists use in identifying critical skills. We briefly describe the strengths and limitations of each approach and summarize the lessons the approach has yielded. In the chapter's concluding section, we return to the critical competencies listed above, and elaborate on the key messages.

Research Methodologies and Findings

Studies of Earnings Inequality

Over the past 15 years, one major source of inferences on the changing market value of skills has been studies of earnings inequality. In a world in which all workers were of the same age, gender, race, education, innate ability, etc., simple economic models would predict that all persons' earnings should be equal. Since people in fact differ in these characteristics, earnings inequality can be used to infer how their characteristics are valued by the market. To the extent that these individual characteristics can be linked to specific skills – linkages that are limited by the data (see below) – changes in earnings inequality can provide inferences about changing valuations of skills in the marketplace. In the United States, studies of earnings inequality are most often based on two national household surveys collected periodically by the U.S. Bureau of the Census: the Decennial U.S. Census and the monthly Current Population Report. Together, these data sets offer information on quite large samples of U.S. individuals for the years 1940, 1950, 1960, and annually since 1964. More recently, comparable data sets for selected years have become available for other industrialized countries through the Luxembourg Income Study. In all of these data sets, a large number of individual observations permits the analysis of the distribution of earnings both in the aggregate and for detailed subgroups – for example, men under the age of 30 whose education stopped at secondary school.

The national representativeness of these samples is particularly important for reasons of economic theory. A priori, a price change can come from either the demand or the supply side of the market. Thus, an increase in the relative wage of university graduates vis-à-vis non-graduates[3] can arise because the relative demand for graduates has increased or because the relative supply of graduates has contracted. Because these samples are representative of national populations, they can be used to track changes in the numbers of various kinds of workers over time (labor supply), and so it is possible to divide wage changes into supply responses and demand responses. For simplicity, we will call such divisions "supply-demand analyses."

These census data sets (in both the United States and in other countries) have two important limitations. First, measures of skill are typically confined to two variables: the individual's years of completed schooling, and the individual's age, which, under certain assumptions, serves as an approximate measure of work experience. More refined measures of skill – for example, scores on standardized cognitive tests or measures of interpersonal skills – are absent. Second, these data sets are household surveys that focus on individuals and provide almost no information about place of work. An individual's industry and occupation are identified at a fairly broad level, but the data sets say nothing about the content of the individual's work – i.e., the way

---

[3] To focus on the value of education, such a comparison would be restricted to persons of the same age, gender, etc., so that university education was the only dimension by which such persons differed.

in which the individual uses education that makes him or her valuable to an employer.

To better examine the structure of changing inequality, economists frequently adopt the technique of analysis of variance. In this technique, a sample of workers is divided into apparently homogeneous, mutually exclusive groups: women aged 25–34, with exactly 12 years of schooling; women of the same age who have not completed secondary school; women aged 35–44 with a bachelor's (first university) degree; and so on. Changes in earnings inequality are then decomposed into two sources: changes in average earnings differences between these groups, e.g., between workers of different ages and educational levels; and changes in inequality that occur within these groups of apparently homogeneous workers.

This decomposition, combined with supply-demand analysis (described above) produces a fairly clear historical picture of U.S. wage movements. The sharpest part of the picture involves the demand for better educated workers – part of the "between-group" analysis just described. Beginning after World War II, the relative demand for more educated workers grew steadily through the 1950s, 1960s and 1970s, and then accelerated beginning in the "blue-collar" recession of 1980–82. For much of the 1960s and all of the 1970s, however, the growing demand was more than offset by the rapidly growing supply of college graduates, a reflection of the baby boom cohorts which were both large in size and attended college at high rates.

The net effect of these shifts can be seen in the path of the ratio in equation (1): the premium for men at age 30 of having a bachelor's degree rather than stopping at high school.

$$\frac{\text{Median Annual Earnings of 25- to 34-Year-Old Men with 4 Years of College}}{\text{Median Annual Earnings of 25- to 34-Year-Old Men with 4 Years of High School}} \quad (1)$$

During the 1950s, the ratio stood between 1.25 and 1.30. By the end of the 1970s, the ratio had fallen to 1.17. Most of the falling return to education reflected the increased supply of young college graduates. There was, however, a set of temporary factors which increased the demand for high school graduates: worldwide food and energy shortages which increased the demand for blue-collar labor in agriculture and oil, respectively; a falling international value of the dollar which increased U.S. exports; and the demand for manufacturing workers. By the early 1980s, these temporary factors had reversed, and by 1985 the ratio (1) had surged to 1.48.

In sum, the best developed inequality studies indicate that the labor market has placed an increasing value on well-educated labor, particularly in the last two decades. At this point, the reader may raise a caveat: typically, students who go on to higher education have higher cognitive skills (as measured by standardized tests), and come from more affluent family backgrounds than students who do not. To the extent that a person's years of schooling is a surrogate for innate ability or family background, the inequality studies may have little policy content.

The best evidence that this is not the case comes from a series of studies of the earnings of identical twins who have gone on to receive different levels of schooling. Because the twins are identical, they share the same genetic component of IQ and typically the same family background. These studies suggest that an additional year of schooling now raises earnings by about 6–8 percent, a value in line with estimates based on national census samples (e.g., Miller, Mulvey, & Martin, 1995).

Earlier, we noted that analysis of variance identifies two sources of inequality: earnings inequality between the average wages of homogenous groups (the source of the findings on education), and earnings inequality within such apparently homogenous groups. In contrast to the fluctuations in between-group inequality, this second, within-group inequality has increased fairly steadily since the late 1960s. Explaining this trend, however, has proven quite difficult.

Attempted explanations begin from the proposition that persons of the same age, education, gender, etc., can still differ in other characteristics. It follows that the growth of within-group inequality may reflect the market's changing valuation of these other characteristics – for example, interpersonal skills, a subject we return to below. Since none of these "other" characteristics are measured in the census data, attempts to identify them have, not surprisingly, come up short. If this interpretation is right, however, these other characteristics, whatever they are, must have little or no correlation with education. This follows from the fact that the time path of within-group inequality (steady increase) is quite different from the time path of earnings differences by education (a fall through the end of the 1970s followed by a sharp rise thereafter).

Studies of earnings inequality outside the United States suggest that relative increases in the demand for educated workers have occurred in most developing countries, though countries differ both in the growth of earnings inequality per se, and the extent to which individual earnings inequality translates into family income inequality. The first variation points to the role of national institutions – i.e., government regulation, national wage bargaining – in modifying the workings of the market. The second variation suggests the role of government benefits and the welfare state in translating market earnings outcomes into family living standards (Gottschalk & Smeeding, 1997). We return to these points in the chapter's last section.

In summary, inequality studies have proven valuable in identifying education (and, presumably, the skills learned through education) as an increasingly important determinant of wages across industrialized countries. Similarly, variations in the return to education across countries suggest that the national institutions have some power to shape market outcomes, and thus create demand for various skills. At the same time, the limited nature of the data that underlie these studies leave many questions unanswered – in particular, questions regarding market valuation of skills that are uncorrelated with education (the potential sources of within-group variation), as well as the skills which education itself imparts.

Wage Functions

Wage functions constitute a second, overlapping approach to determining the market's valuation of skills. In this approach, multiple regression techniques are applied to data on a sample of individuals to estimate the direct impacts – in calculus terms, the first derivative – of various factors in determining the hourly or weekly wage. The approach has been applied over 30 years to a variety of data sets (not all of them nationally representative) where, depending on the data set, explanatory variables include the worker's age and education, but also such variables as scores on standardized tests of cognitive skills and, occasionally, measures of non-cognitive traits such as locus of control and self-esteem (Bishop, Blakemore, & Low, 1985; Duncan & Dunifon, 1998; Goldsmith, Veum, & Darity, 1997; Murnane, Willet, Braatz, & Duhaldeborde, in press).

While the results of many studies using the wage function approach are informative, it is important to remain aware of the limitations of studies using this approach. First of all, some types of potentially critical skills do not lend themselves to measurement through pencil-and-paper tests. For example, dimensions of "emotional intelligence," to use the term that Daniel Goleman (1995) has made well known, are not easily measured by the types of instruments included in the surveys that provide the databases for quantitative studies. As a result, there is little quantitative evidence showing that dimensions of emotional intelligence predict labor market performance. However, it would be a mistake to conclude from a survey of quantitative studies that emotional intelligence does not matter in the labor market. The same would be true for several of the seven kinds of intelligence that Howard Gardner identifies (1983). Only some of these lend themselves to valid and reliable measurement by multiple-choice tests.

Some researchers have responded to this measurement problem by including indicators of behavior in wage function studies. For example, Duncan and Dunifon (1998) found that individuals who reported during their early twenties that they kept their homes clean earned considerably more 15 years later than did individuals with the same demographic characteristics who reported that they do not keep their homes clean. This pattern indicates that personal attributes other than cognitive skills matter in the labor market. However, it is not clear what this pattern reveals about the importance of particular competencies.

Even within available data, a second problem occurs because scores on tests of different cognitive skills – math skills, reading skills – are typically quite highly correlated. In this situation, statistical analysis cannot determine which of these skills are the ones which employers value. All one can conclude is that the set of cognitive skills measured by the scores, which include elements of reading comprehension skills as well as math computation and reasoning skills, predict subsequent labor market performance.

A third limitation is that it may not be appropriate to generalize to a wider population the relationship between skill measures and labor market outcomes in particular samples. The reason is that individuals with particular sets of skills make choices about whether to work at all, and if they do work, what sector of the economy to work in or what type of job to accept. As a result, a sample of workers is unlikely to be a random sample of the population (Gronau, 1974).[4] Similarly, a sample of work-

---

[4] Some studies (for example, Tyler, et al., 2000) use earned income as the outcome measure. This has the advantage of assigning a value of zero to the earnings of adults who choose not to work and thereby including them in the analysis sample. The disadvantage of this

ers in the service sector is unlikely to be a random sample of all workers (Heckman & Sedlacek, 1985). In recent years, economists have developed a number of statistical tools to deal with such selection issues. In practice, however, it has proven difficult to apply the tools in a manner that makes it appropriate to interpret the coefficients from wage regressions as estimates of relationships between skills and labor market outcomes for adults in any particular society.

A final limitation of the wage function approach is that correlation need not imply causation. A compelling recent example is a highly publicized study by Alan Krueger (1993). Using data from the U.S. Current Population Survey, Krueger showed that people who use computers in their work earn approximately 15 percent more, on average, than people who do not. It is tempting to interpret this pattern as indicating that skill in using computers earns a wage premium. However, Krueger also found that the largest wage premium was earned by people who used computers to read and send electronic mail. It seems unlikely that this is a difficult skill to acquire. A more likely explanation is that workers who earn high salaries are the first to be given access to computers and to email.

More questions about the interpretation of the Krueger finding came from a study by Dinardo and Pischke (1997) using German data. Like Krueger, they found that workers who use computers in their work earn more than those who do not. However, Dinardo and Pischke also found a similarly sized wage differential between workers who use pencils in their work and those who do not. This raises further questions about the causal interpretation of coefficients in wage functions.

Keeping the limitations of the wage function approach in mind, we turn now to the lessons from this literature about the identification of critical skills.

Many studies show that basic math and reading skills are important predictors of wages. Murnane, Willet, and Levy (1995) show that their importance has increased in recent years. Frederic Pryor and David Schaffer (1997) show that literacy skills are important predictors of wages even among 4-year college graduates in the United States. They define functional literacy as "the ability to use skills in reading, interpreting documents, and carrying out quantitative calculations in real-life situations," (1997, p. 6) They show that in a large sample of college graduates who participated in the 1992 National Adult Literacy Survey, those with weak functional literacy were much more likely to be in relatively low paying jobs than were those with strong functional literacy skills.[5]

The importance of basic reading and math skills in the labor market helps to explain a puzzling recent trend in the relative wages of Black males and White males in the United States. While, on average, Black males in the United States have always earned less than White males, the Black-White wage gap for males declined during the period from the end of World War II to 1975. Improved access for Blacks to edu-

---

choice is that earnings reflect the product of two conceptually different variables: the hourly wage an individual earns and the number of hours the individual works.

[5] The pattern Pryor and Schaffer identify may be unique to the United States, a country in which there is enormous variation in quality among postsecondary educational institutions. In countries in which there is less variation in the quality of colleges and universities, there is probably much less variation in the functional literacy of graduates.

cation explains much of the closing of the gap. However, since 1975 the gap has widened again. For example, Neal and Johnson (1996) report that in the late 1980s and early 1990s, Black males earned 22 percent less, on average, than White males. They show that more than half of this gap can be explained by differences in the average scores of Black and White males on tests of cognitive skills. The explanation is not that the Black-White skills gap increased; it did not. Rather the explanation is that the skills gap mattered more in the economy of the late 1980s and early 1990s than it did in the economy of the 1970s.

In summary, there is a growing body of evidence suggesting that basic cognitive skills, i.e., the ability to understand written material, to do simple mathematics, to reason clearly, are skills that are of growing importance in the labor market. While it would be valuable to identify more clearly just which of these basic skills is of greatest importance, it is difficult to do this from the wage function studies. Several studies show that math scores predict subsequent labor market outcomes somewhat better than reading scores do. However, achieving a good score on a math test requires reading skills. Moreover, the predictive power of a math score may stem from its being a better predictor of skill in following directions than is a score on a reading test.

Students who leave school without mastery of basic cognitive skills are at a significant disadvantage in the labor market. The findings of a great many studies support this message. It is important, however, to put the evidence in perspective. In no study do cognitive skill measures, including information on educational attainments, explain more than one-third of the variation in wages. Nor do trends in cognitive skill measures explain much of the increase in within-group earnings inequality.[6]

Social scientists interpret the evidence from wage function studies in different ways. Some emphasize the enormous variation in wages among individuals with the same observed skill levels. Proponents of this view often argue that public policy aimed at increasing the earnings of low-wage workers should not concentrate on increasing the skills of these workers. Instead, they argue, policies should focus on changing institutional arrangements such as reducing labor market discrimination, enhancing the bargaining power of labor unions, implementing trade policies that reduce imports from low-wage countries, and creating industrial policies that make it more attractive for firms to invest in improving the skills of their workforces than to relocate production facilities in low-wage countries.

Other social scientists argue that the unexplained variation in wages stems primarily from limitations in the measures of skills, especially the lack of good measures of non-cognitive traits that employers value such as honesty and perseverance. Advocates of this position point to studies such as Duncan and Dunifon's (1998), which show that a collection of behavioral indicators such as the cleanliness of the respondent's home explain as large a percentage of the variation in wages as the number of years of completed schooling does. Unfortunately, such studies do not identify which competencies are particularly important in the labor market. They do,

---

[6] For a discussion of alternative interpretations of the evidence relating cognitive skills to subsequent labor market performance, see Murnane, Willet, Duhaldeborde, & Tyler, 2000.

however, suggest that characteristics of individuals other than cognitive skills affect labor market success.

We believe it is a mistake to view as mutually exclusive the two polar interpretations of the wage function studies. The effectiveness of policies aimed at enhancing the skills of the current workforce and the future workforce may depend critically on institutions – a theme we return to later in the chapter.

To learn more about competencies other than cognitive skills that matter in the labor market, we turn to other approaches to identifying critical skills.

Ethnographic Studies of Work

In ethnographic studies of the workplace, trained observers take extensive and detailed notes of employees' on-the-job behavior to determine what employees actually do in the course of their work, and the skills the work requires. These studies are undertaken for a variety of purposes: to understand power and status relationships within the workplace, and to understand patterns of communication among workers. To determine competencies valued by the marketplace, the most valuable subset of these studies are those that focus on the way in which technology – either newly introduced technology or existing technology – helps to shape work (e.g., Zuboff, 1988; Orr, 1996; and Levy & Murnane, 1996).

Zuboff's (1988) study of the introduction of computerized controls in mills making paper pulp illustrates the lessons from this research approach. Prior to the introduction, workers monitored production processes from the factory floor, relying heavily on direct sensory perception – the consistency of the pulp mixture, its taste, its apparent temperature. With the introduction of computerized controls, workers were largely removed from the factory floor and assigned to control rooms where they had to control the process based on digital readouts from electronic gauges. The change required workers to cope with a new level of abstraction in which they had to understand the state of the production process based on numerical readouts rather than through direct, physical observation.

A related example arises in our own work with Anne Beamish on automobile mechanics (in press). Over time, automobile manufacturers have increasingly introduced electronic controls to meet pollutant emission requirements and to implement conveniences (e.g., electronic seat adjustments that "remember" a driver's preferred position) to attract customers. Compared to traditional mechanical problems, most electronic failures cannot be seen or touched. They can be identified only through the mechanic's ability to structure a sequence of computerized diagnostic tests and to combine the resulting numerical information into a mental image of causation.

The major advantage of relevant ethnographic studies is their ability to observe a richer variety of skills than can be obtained from national samples of workers (e.g., the census). As discussed above, those samples typically contain limited skill measures – years of completed schooling and age (which serves as a surrogate for workplace experience). In practice, an automobile mechanic and a sales representative can have very different skills, even though they are of the same age and have the same number of years of completed schooling. The resulting richness of the studies is particularly important when it comes to identifying "soft skills," for example, the ability to interact effectively with coworkers or to inspire trust in customers. As we noted above, analysis of national samples offers inferential evidence that such "soft skills" are increasingly valued by the economy, but fall short of offering hard proof.

In sum, ethnographic studies have the potential to better explain various correlations that exist in available data, such as the increasing positive correlation between education and earnings, the positive correlation between a worker's use of computers and his earnings, and the growth in earnings inequality among workers with the same educational attainments. At the same time, such ethnographic studies are subject to a variety of limitations. The first is the limitation that applies to all case studies: it is never clear whether the case in question represents a significant population or is simply an idiosyncratic example. Thus, one does not know whether the competencies identified in such studies are important outside the workplace being studied.

In most existing ethnographic studies, this problem is compounded because the researcher rarely makes the connection between workplace observations and labor market variables, in particular, wages. In the Zuboff study cited above, the reader gets a good sense of the competencies a worker must have on the redesigned job. There is little mention, however, of what the workers are paid, how this pay compares to other jobs in the existing labor market, or how the introduction of new technology (and the resulting change in skill requirements) changed wages. Without such basic information, the reader has no basis for concluding that particular identified skills are valued in the market.

A final limitation of this method of determining competencies is the extensive time they require. For all but the simplest jobs, ethnographic studies require detailed workplace observation over extended periods. In many jobs, a worker exhibits some of the most valued competencies only episodically. For example, a mechanic's workday usually involves repairing a number of obvious problems using routine procedures (e.g., an engine tune-up). Periodically, however, the mechanic will encounter a very difficult problem not covered in manuals or identified by diagnostic equipment. It is here that the mechanic's own diagnostic capabilities become very important. Observations over several days may not capture such an episode. A similar situation applies to policemen, surgeons, and many other occupations. In each case, extensive observation is required before the full range of skills is revealed.

A second reason for extensive observation comes from the way in which many organizations hire individuals for a career ladder rather than for a specific job. In these cases, workers may appear to need only limited competencies for their current, entry-level jobs; but the workers will require substantially greater skills for the jobs to which the organization expects to promote them.

The Screening Strategies of High-Wage Firms

A final methodology, a variation of ethnographic studies, is the detailed study of screening practices of firms that pay relatively high wages. Such firms have many applicants for each position they want to fill and this allows them to be selective in choosing among applicants. Studying the criteria they use provides another strategy for identifying skills that are important in the labor market.

Because screening is often multi-dimensional – paper-and-pencil cognitive tests, but also structured interviews or simulation exercises – the researcher can look for the importance of "soft skills" that are not captured in the data sets used in the statistical studies above. At the same time, the approach has limits similar to those of case studies. High-wage firms – in particular, high-wage firms that grant access to researchers – may not be representative of the population of employers. In addition, the firms may not know what they are doing – i.e., they may not have tested the economic rationality of their screening strategies. For firms operating in competitive industries, however, it seems unlikely that such behavior would exist for an extended period of time.

Our own work (Murnane & Levy, 1996) provides several examples of this kind of study in high-wage U.S. firms that had histories of profitability and reputations for good management. We focused on firms that historically had hired a significant number of high school graduates. This choice was motivated by the significant decline of high school graduates' wages during the 1980s, a trend that made it particularly important to determine the skills that allowed some high school graduates to fare well in the labor market.

In the firms we studied, six skills proved important. The first two, the ability to read well enough and do basic mathematics well enough to understand training manuals, were not a surprise. High-wage firms invest in training their workers and they want to be sure that new hires can comprehend the manuals that are part of most training programs. The importance of basic reading and math skills to high-wage firms supports the evidence from the quantitative wage function studies.

The third desired skill was the ability to formulate problems and to design solutions to them. For these firms, empowering workers to identify problems and to take initiative in solving them was an effective strategy for improving quality and lowering cost. This cost reduction mechanism required workers who were both interested in and capable of problem-solving – i.e., addressing non-routine situations – and a management strategy committed to encouraging and supporting worker initiative.

While these three skills were expected, the fourth and fifth skills were not. High-wage firms sought workers with good communication skills: the ability to describe a problem in a coherent written description and an articulate oral presentation. They also sought workers who knew how to work productively with people from different backgrounds. The importance firms placed on these skills was evidenced by the expensive screening processes used to determine their presence. Some firms used multiple interviews. Others observed applicants in simulated group tasks. The common thread was that high-wage firms devoted significant resources to learning whether applicants possessed communication and teamwork skills.

A final skill that was important to many, although not all, high-wage firms was familiarity with computers. These firms did not require that applicants have mastery of particular software programs. (They all had training programs to provide these specific skills.) What firms sought was some experience in using computers and the realization that new software programs were not difficult to master.

New work we are conducting on the back office operations of a large bank (Murnane, Levy, & Autor, 2000) helps to put the role of basic computer skills in perspective. In the mid-1990s, this bank invested heavily in new technology that changed a great many jobs associated with check processing, from manually processing masses of paper to processing images of checks on a computer screen. To make this transition, it was necessary for the bank to train a large number of longtime workers to use personal computers. Many older workers initially found the transition difficult, because they were unfamiliar with using a computer mouse and they feared damaging the computers. It took several weeks of training before some workers became comfortable working with computers, but virtually all eventually did so. This suggests that basic computer literacy is a much easier skill to acquire than, for example, the ability to read.

The success of a middle-aged workforce in acquiring basic computer skills from only a few weeks of training could lead some to the conclusion that basic computer literacy does not belong on a list of key competencies critical to economic success. The bank's subsequent hiring policies suggest another perspective, however. Since the training was moderately expensive, the bank has mandated that all future hires must bring to their jobs familiarity with computers. This mandate eliminates access to jobs with career potential for labor market entrants lacking basic computer literacy. A growing number of employers are adopting similar mandates. It is for this reason that we believe computer literacy, even though not a difficult skill to acquire, belongs on a list of key competencies for economic success.

Key Competencies

In this section, we elaborate on the lessons from economics about key competencies for a "successful and responsible life."

1. Basic reading and mathematics skills are important in determining long-run labor market outcomes, including the ability to adjust to changing circumstances.

The payoff to basic reading and math skills increased between the late 1970s and the mid-1980s. A consequence is that students who leave school without these skills are at a much greater disadvantage in the labor market today than they were in the labor market of 25 years ago. One reason for the importance of these basic cognitive skills is that they are critical to following directions. A second reason is that reading and math skills are tools that enable people to acquire job-specific skills. This explains why firms that invest in training are particularly likely to screen job applicants for these basic skills (Cappelli & Wilk, 1997).[7] In fact, the critical competency may

---

[7] It seems plausible that more sophisticated cognitive skills, such as the ability to solve relatively complex problems, may be becoming a basic competency. However, at this time there is no empirical support for this proposition.

not be reading and math skills per se, but rather the ability to continue to learn as one matures and meets new challenges.

The reading and mathematics skills of secondary school graduates in the United States predict their wages a decade after graduation much better than they predict wages in the jobs secondary school students obtain immediately after graduation. The lack of immediate payoff to cognitive skill acquisition in the United States may help to explain the relatively poor performance of American secondary school students on international test score comparisons (Bishop, 1995). In other countries, closer relationships between labor market institutions and secondary schools result in a stronger relationship between skills acquired in school and post-school labor market opportunities. Here as elsewhere, institutional arrangements – in this case, the connections between schools and jobs – may have a marked impact on students' incentives to acquire critical skills.

Much of the payoff to cognitive skills acquired by the end of secondary school comes through the mechanism of postsecondary education. Secondary school students with strong cognitive skills are more likely to earn postsecondary education credentials than are secondary school students with weaker cognitive skills, and postsecondary education credentials pay off in the labor market. An implication of this pattern is that access to postsecondary education may be important in providing secondary school students with the incentives to acquire critical skills. This is another example of the connections between institutions and critical competencies.

2. The ability to communicate effectively, both orally and in writing, is important in determining long-run labor market outcomes.

3. The organization of work within firms is changing in ways that place increased value on the ability to work productively in groups.

4. Both changes in firms (the emphasis on teamwork) and changes in the economy are placing increased emphasis on elements of "emotional intelligence," including the ability to relate well to other people.

While there are still a great many jobs in Organisation for Economic Co-Operation and Development (OECD) countries that consist solely of carrying out routine tasks with little need for significant communication with coworkers or customers, the real wages associated with such jobs have fallen dramatically. One reason is that it is relatively easy to computerize many of these routine jobs such as filing and sorting. Another is that globalization of trade has made it more possible to transfer many routine tasks to lower wage countries. Increasingly, high-wage jobs require not only mastery of cognitive skills, but also distinctly human "soft skills," especially skills related to interacting with other people. Many of the "soft skills" that are in demand are those associated with selling. In particular, a competitive U.S. economy with highly unequal incomes has increased the value of the ability to sell products to high-income consumers, the consumers with the greatest profit potential to firms.

5. Familiarity with computers is of growing importance in the labor market.

In 1997, 51 percent of workers in the United States reported that they used a computer in their jobs, up from 25 percent in 1984.[8]

Our case studies of applicant screening processes indicate that most high-wage firms do not require that candidates for entry-level jobs have mastery of particular software programs. These firms typically have internal training programs to provide these skills. What they do increasingly require of successful applicants, however, are familiarity with the keyboard and a mouse, recognition that most software programs are put together the same way and have on-line help systems, and an openness to learning new programs.

6. Formal educational credentials are of growing importance in determining economic success. Yet available evidence does not make clear why employers are willing to pay substantial wage premiums to workers with greater educational attainments.

Undoubtedly, some employers pay college graduates more than they pay high school graduates because they value skills that students learned in colleges and universities. Yet it is not clear what these skills are. Differences in measured cognitive skills explain only a small part of the differences in wages. The case study evidence suggests that critical skills that college graduates are more likely to possess than high school graduates include communication skills and teamwork skills, but there is no quantitative evidence to support this hypothesis.

Particularly puzzling is the practice of many firms that hire college graduates almost independent of their disciplinary field and then place them in intensive, months-long training programs aimed at teaching them technical skills. The explanation may be that completion of college is a signal of the ability to learn new things efficiently or a signal of perseverance. Understanding more about what college graduates can do better than high school graduates would be extremely helpful in identifying key competencies. It might turn out that many of the critical skills are not skills learned in college, but rather skills that some secondary school students possessed before going to college, but could only signal by acquiring a college degree. If this is true, it would be useful to explore whether less expensive signals of key competencies could be devised.

7. The market forces which value key competencies are modified by a number of institutional arrangements: the organization of work (see 3, above), the links between firms and educational institutions, the extent to which a nation's markets are regulated, and the nation's distribution of income as modified by the welfare state.

The central theme of an economic perspective is the market's valuation of various skills. Throughout the chapter, however, we have warned that market forces should not be equated with purely natural forces, totally immune to any intervention. The distribution of earnings will be determined by market forces, of course, but also by

---

[8] We thank MIT Professor David Autor for calculating these computer-use statistics for us from Current Population Survey files.

institutions, including the strength of unions and the presence of national bargaining agreements. Various kinds of regulation can determine the speed at which technology can reshape an industry or an employer's ability to send work offshore. Wages are also determined by the supplies of workers with various skills. These supplies reflect both the responsiveness of educational distributions and the ease with which workers can signal their skills to prospective employers.

In a similar way, household incomes rest on individual earnings and so are determined by market forces as well. But the household income distribution is also modified by the workings of the welfare state. This income distribution, in turn, affects demands for different products and ultimately the demand for various worker skills.

As mentioned above, the extent to which academic performance in secondary school influences immediate job prospects – something that varies across countries – influences students' incentives to do the hard work needed to acquire critical skills. Students' perceptions of the accessibility of postsecondary educational opportunities also influence incentives to study in high school. Similarly, labor market discrimination, which reduces job opportunities for particular groups, may reduce incentives to acquire skills.

Firms that expect workers to demonstrate initiative, work in teams to solve problems, and continually upgrade their skills place a high value on the key competencies defined above and are willing to pay wage premiums to workers with these skills. Such firms, which are sometimes called high-performance firms, tend to rely on the ideas of their workers to improve the products and services they produce. At the other extreme, firms that require workers to complete narrowly defined tasks and to do exactly what supervisors tell them to do tend not to pay wage premiums for the key competencies defined above. Such firms typically concentrate on making standardized products at low cost. In any given country, the demand for the competencies defined above will depend on the percentage of firms that fit the "high-performance" profile. There is some evidence from the United States that the percentage of firms organized in this fashion is growing (Lawler et al., 1995).

An important question is the extent to which government policies and regulations influence firms' incentives to adopt a high-performance mode of organization. One type of policy that may make a difference is the tax treatments of firms' expenditures on training. The reason is that when firms that invest heavily in training workers, they tend to be selective in hiring them (Cappelli & Wilk, 1997). To the extent that government policies influence firms' decisions about whether to adopt characteristics of a high-performance mode of organization, such as providing workers with opportunities to upgrade their skills, these policies will affect the demand for worker competencies.

Implicit in the theme of this chapter is that well-functioning markets are valuable institutions in OECD countries. They promote economic growth, which is a necessary condition for improvements in standard of living. Markets do not automatically flourish, however. Widespread respect for the rule of law, including mechanisms to settle property disputes without violence, are necessary for firms to be willing to engage in long-term contracts.

While respect for property rights is a necessary condition for markets to flourish, it is not the only condition. In a dynamic economy, especially one deeply involved in international trade, there are both winners and losers. Among workers, winners are those employed in industries that are flourishing; losers are those employed in industries that are dying. For example, in the United States, pharmaceutical and computer industries are growing; textile industries are declining. As a result, many workers employed in textile-producing firms lose their jobs. Especially for older workers, acquiring the skills for employment in other industries is often difficult.

As the economist Dani Rodrik (1997) has explained, democratic countries such as Denmark and Sweden have been able to maintain public support for open international trade because they have national policies in place that provide extensive retraining benefits to the losers from such trade. In democratic countries that lack such benefits for the losers, it is often difficult to maintain legislative and public support for international trade, even though such trade is an engine of growth.

One lesson we want to emphasize is that in considering human resource policies aimed at providing present and future workers with key competencies, policymakers need to pay attention to the ways in which national and local institutions affect workers' incentives to acquire critical skills, firms' incentives to pay premiums to workers with critical skills, and national support for international trade. A related lesson is that respect for the rule of law and an appreciation of society's obligation to soften the blows that fall on some workers as a result of global trade are key competencies in democratic societies.

We conclude this chapter by addressing generic questions about the role of key competencies.

Does each competency have an independent impact on life outcomes or should the competencies be viewed as interdependent?

The economic evidence bearing on this question is limited. In our research, high-wage firms searched for applicants who had strong basic cognitive skills *and* "soft skills" *and* basic familiarity with computers. All of these skills were critical to work in organizations that wanted workers to learn from each other, to work together to identify and solve problems, and to continually acquire new skills. Bresnehan (1999) argues that organizations that make extensive use of computers search for workers with both mastery of cognitive skills and "soft skills" (or "people skills"). The logic is that computers handle routine tasks effectively, leaving to humans the solving of exceptional problems. Doing this effectively requires not only problem-solving skills, but often the ability to successfully obtain information and help from others.

Are there levels of skill within each competency?

Again, the empirical evidence provides little guidance on the answer to this question. For example, tests of reading skills included in large-scale surveys typically assess the extent to which respondents can find factual information in paragraphs and know the meanings of particular words. These tests typically do not assess respondents' ability to draw nuanced inferences from the paragraphs. Yet, it is reasonable that this more advanced reading skill is valued in a variety of jobs. Similarly, the task simulations some firms use in evaluating job applicants assess whether they are able to communicate with other applicants and to work productively with applicants from different backgrounds. The simulations typically do not assess the extent to which applicants' communication skills include the ability to persuade reluctant colleagues to participate in team efforts. Yet this communication skill is likely to be valued in a variety of workplaces, as well as in other social settings. The essential point here is that most quantitative studies of the skills valued in the labor market include measures of only quite low levels of skills. It would be a mistake to infer from these studies that higher levels of skills are not important in labor markets.

Are the same competencies needed throughout the life cycle?

We have no direct evidence bearing on this question. However, it seems logical that the ability to continue to learn and to interact successfully with a range of different people would be as important in promoting a rich and fulfilling retirement as it would a successful work life.

Can critical competencies be learned?

In the wake of the controversy surrounding Herrenstein and Murray's book, *The Bell Curve* (1994), a number of studies have addressed this question. They have shown that formal schooling has a strong impact on a range of cognitive skills. The large investments many private sector firms make in training programs to teach communication skills and how to deal effectively with coworkers and customers suggests that many "soft skills" can also be learned. There is abundant evidence that computer skills can be learned.

Are the same competencies critical in different societies?

The globalization of trade and the international spread of technology are strong forces pushing toward a global set of key competencies. These are forces likely to be even stronger in the years ahead. At the same time, cultural differences among countries undoubtedly play a role in defining the meaning of certain competencies. For example, the particular behaviors that enable one to work effectively with others may vary across cultures. These differences, as well as others, are likely to be particularly pronounced in contrasting the economies of industrial countries with the economies of countries that are still primarily agricultural. For this reason, it seems prudent to restrict this project to searching for key competencies in industrial societies.

One difference among countries that may play a role in determining the importance of particular competencies is the degree of diversity in the population. In countries with relatively homogeneous populations, communication skills and the ability to work productively with coworkers may not be considered critical skills because workers have so much in common. In relatively heterogeneous societies, these same "soft skills" may be of greater importance because workers need to communicate and work with individuals who come from very different backgrounds, have different cultures, and often speak different languages.

Are the skills critical to an economically successful life relevant to being a responsible citizen in a democracy?

Some competencies critical to leading a responsible and fulfilling life have no value in most labor markets. Compassion and empathy are two examples. Yet these competencies may be critical to the survival of democratic societies. The reason is that technological changes and the globalization of trade create not only economic winners, but also economic losers. Compassion and empathy may be critical prerequisites to developing and sustaining social institutions that support economic losers and retain the commitment of all elements of society to democratic processes.

We do not argue that the competencies we identify are the only ones critical to living a responsible and fulfilling life in a democracy. However, we do believe that the competencies we have identified are important not only to earning a living, but also to living a responsible and fulfilling life in a democratic society. For example, the ability to communicate well and to work productively with people from different backgrounds are skills relevant to creating social capital (networks of mutually re-enforcing obligations and expectations and information channels) that are valuable in raising children as well as finding jobs (Coleman, 1988). Basic computer skills are valuable outside of workplaces, as a growing number of people, including the elderly, use electronic mail and the Internet to collect information and keep in touch with friends.

In summary, the skills we have identified are critically important to earning a living. However, even if earning a living were not necessary, the skills we have identified would be important competencies for citizens in democracies.

References

Beamish, A., & Levy, F. (in press). *Selling cars, fixing cars, and information technology.* Cambridge: Department of Urban Studies and Planning, Massachusetts Institute of Technology.

Bishop, J. H. (1995). *Expertise and excellence* (Working Paper 95–13). Center for Advanced Human Resource Studies, New York State School of Industrial and Labor Relations, Cornell University, Ithaca, NY.

Bishop, J. H., Blakemore, A., & Low, S. (1985). *High school graduates in the labor market: A comparison of the class of 1972 and 1980.* Columbus, OH: National Center for Research in Vocational Education.

Bowles, S., & Gintis, H. (1998). The determinants of earnings: Skills, preferences, and schooling. Working Paper, Economics Department, University of Massachusetts at Amherst.

Bresnehan, T. F. (1999). Computerization and wage dispersion: An analytical reinterpretation. *Economic Journal, 109*, 390–415.

Cappelli, P., & Wilk, S. L. (1997). *Understanding selection processes: Organization determinants and performance outcomes.* Philadelphia: Management Department, Wharton School of the University of Pennsylvania.

Coleman, J. (1988). Social capital in the creation of human capital. *American Journal of Sociology, 94,* 95–120.

Cyert, R. M., & Mowery, D. C. (Eds.). (1987). *Technology and employment: Innovation and growth in the U.S. economy.* Washington, DC: National Academy Press.

DiNardo, J., & Pischke, J. S. (1997). The returns to computer use revisited: Have pencils changed the wage structure too? *Quarterly Journal of Economics, 112,* 291–303.

Duncan, G. J., & Dunifon, R. (1998). *"Soft-skills" and long-run labor market success.* Evanston, IL: Institute for Policy Research, Northwestern University.

Easterlin, R. (1974). Does economic growth improve the human lot? Some empirical evidence. In P. David & M. Reder (Eds.), *Nations and households in economic growth: Essays in Honor of Moses Abramovitz* (pp. 89–125). New York: Academic Press.

Gardner, H. (1983). *Frames of mind: The theory of multiple intelligences.* New York: Basic Books.

Goldsmith, A. H., Veum, J. R., & Darity, W., Jr. (1997). The impact of psychological and human capital on wages. *Economic Inquiry, 25,* 815–829.

Goleman, D. (1995). *Emotional Intelligence: Why it can matter more than IQ for character, health and lifelong achievement.* New York: Bantam Books.

Gottschalk, P., & Smeeding, T. (1997). Cross-national comparisons of earnings and income inequality. *Journal of Economic Literature, 35,* 633–87.

Gronau, R. (1974). Wage comparisons: A selectivity bias. *Journal of Political Economy, 82,* 1119–43.

Heckman, J. J., & Sedlacek, G. L. (1985). Heterogeneity, aggregation and market wage functions: An empirical model of self-selection in the labor market. *Journal of Political Economy, 93,* 1077–1125.

Herrnstein, R. J., & Murray, C. (1994). *The bell curve: Intelligence and class structure in American life.* New York: Free Press.

Jamison, D. (1982). *Farmer education and farm efficiency.* Baltimore, MD: Johns Hopkins University Press.

Krueger, A. B. (1993). How computers have changed the wage structure: Evidence from microdata, 1984–1989. *Quarterly Journal of Economics, 108,* 33–60.

Lawler, E. E., III., Mohrman, S. A., & Ledford, G. E. Jr. (1995). *Creating high performance organizations.* San Francisco: Jossey-Bass.

Levy, F. (1999). *The new dollars and dreams: American incomes and economic change.* New York: The Russell Sage Foundation.

Levy, F., & Murnane, R. J. (1996). With what skills are computers a complement? *American Economic Review, 86,* 258–262.

Miller, P., Mulvey, C., & Martin, N. (1995). What do twins studies reveal about the economic return to education? A comparison of Australian and U.S. findings. *American Economic Review, 85,* 586–599.

Murnane, R. J., & Levy, F. (1996). *Teaching the new basic skills.* New York: Free Press.

Murnane, R. J., Willett, J. B., Braatz, M. J., & Duhaldeborde, Y. (in press). Do different dimensions of male high school students' skills predict labor market success a decade later? Evidence from the NLSY. *Economics of Education Review.*

Murnane, R. J., Willett, J. B., Duhaldeborde, Y. & Tyler, J. H. (2000). How important are the cognitive skills of teenagers in predicting subsequent earnings? *Journal of Policy Analysis and Management 19*(4), Fall 2000, 547–568.

Murnane, R. J., Levy, L., & Autor, D. (2000). *Upstairs, downstairs: Computer-skill complementarity and computer-labor substitution on two floors of a large bank.* Paper presented at the National Bureau of Economic Research Summer Labor Economics Workshop (NBER Working Paper No. W7890).

Murnane, R. J., Willett, J. B., & Levy, F. (1995). The growing importance of cognitive skills in wage determination. *Review of Economics and Statistics, 77,* 251–266.

Neal, D., & Johnson, W. (1996). The role of pre-market factors in Black-White wage differences. *The Journal of Political Economy, 104,* 869–95.

Orr, J. E. (1996). *Talking about machines, an ethnography of a modern job.* Ithaca, NY: Cornell University Press.

Pryor, F. L., & Schaffer, D. (1997). Wages and the university educated: A paradox resolved. *Monthly Labor Review, 120,* 3–18.

Rodrik, D. (1997). *Has globalization gone too far?* Washington, DC: Institute for International Economics.

Schultz, T. W. (1975). The value of the ability to deal with disequilibria. *Journal of Economic Literature, 13,* 827–46.

Spence, M. (1974). *Market signaling.* Cambridge, MA: Harvard University Press.

Tyler, J. H., Murnane, R. J., & Willett, J. B. (2000). Estimating the labor market signaling value of the GED. *Quarterly Journal of Economics, 115,* 431–468.

Willis, R. J. (1986). Wage determinants: A survey and reinterpretation of human capital earnings functions. In O. Ashenfelter & R. Layard (Eds.), *Handbook of Labor Economics* (Vol. 1, pp. 525–602). London: Elsevier Science Publishers.

Zuboff, S. (1988). *In the age of the smart machine: The future of work and power.* New York: Basic Books.

Chapter 8

Competencies and Education: Contextual Diversity

Jack Goody

Introduction

The general aim of the DeSeCo Project is to identify, in an international context, a set of competencies necessary for individuals to lead a successful and responsible life and for society to face the challenges of the present and the future. The long-term goal is to develop measures of these skills and competencies as they emerge within a school environment, in such a way as to influence educational policy. The approach of addressing both the general question about competencies and the long-term goal of developing measures coincides with my orientation, which attempts to combine theoretical with practical (policy) considerations. I see little profit in discussing problems at an unrealistically abstract level that fails to take into account the societal context or the aims of the project.

Let us for convenience set some arbitrary parameters to the terms which are being used. Education will refer to school (and scholastic) activities; the wider process of bringing up the young is called socialization. Abilities refer to inherited potentialities; capacities refer to cultural endowments; skills to more specific achievements. How do all these relate to competencies? The problem of defining and assessing competencies is well laid out by Weinert when he writes that most general cognitive approaches to competencies aim at defining context-free abilities, like earlier intelligence tests, for example. The problem he recognizes is that the more general a competency (i.e., the greater the range of different types of situations to which it applies), the smaller the contribution this competency offers to the solution of demanding problems (Chapter 3). In other words, the attempt to define highly generalized competencies (even within the limited educational framework being pursued) has minimal practical applications. That surely must qualify our enquiry and suggest a possible case of the misapplication of theory, or the search for inappropriate theory.

One concept of competence that has become important for a certain section of anthropology is that used by Noam Chomsky in his work on linguistics (Chomsky, 1980). There he distinguishes between competence and performance. The former has to do with built-in abilities to learn a language, which he regards as a human universal. Performance on the other hand is how people develop the use and practice of language. Clearly this concept of competence has no relation to specific natural languages, since these are certainly not built-in – it has to do with what I have called abilities, in contrast to capacities or even skills.

The Chomskian notion of built-in abilities and capabilities has been of considerable importance in those anthropological circles that are close to cognitive science, especially in the work of Dan Sperber and his colleagues (Sperber, 1985; Bloch, 1991; Boyer, 1994). However, the idea of built-in competencies can have little significance for the search for individual and social differences, as it specifically excludes the relevance of cultural considerations ("learned behavior"). And what I want to say has more to do with internal differentiation and broad cultural differences than it does with supposed constants.

I want to try and approach this problem that has been posed at a general level, asking three questions: whether there can be any overall measurements of competencies at an international level or even a national one; whether the educational process (schooling) is the only or the main focus for developing life skills (what are the family or friends for?); and how the situation differs in the developing world. Regarding the first, by measurement here I refer not only to measures of a statistical kind but any overall assessment of competencies as envisaged in the general aims where reference is made to the construction of future measures. If there has to be some overall assessment, there seems to be little point in specifying, for example, flexibility, as a key competency unless one has some form of assessment in mind, since without it the concept can have little empirical utility; to consider the theoretical underpinning for such indicators can only be done by taking account of both what and how one is measuring. I discuss this problem in more detail in the section on measurements and indices below.

With regard to the second question, schools are clearly not the only context in which life skills are developed. If we are considering the development of competencies, we have (again as pragmatic actors) to think very carefully about the context in which they can be developed in or out of school, and how that would be done. Otherwise, one may find oneself engaged in a sterile exercise.

It may seem irrelevant to raise the third question of developing countries when the project focuses on Organisation for Economic Co-operation and Development (OECD) countries. The limitation to OECD countries, however, seems unrealistic given firstly the numbers of immigrants from the Third World in OECD countries and given that any specification or assessment of competencies is bound to be used in a broader context, as was the case with intelligence tests. In addition, what is appropriate for "advanced" nations will be thought to point the way forward for others. The Third World is in all these senses part of our world, since the West has provided the models for contemporary schools and universities in those areas, has given much aid to keep them going, and is concerned generally with economic and other competencies in these countries in relation to "development." As a consequence, the approach must clearly be global and cross-cultural.

It should be recognized more openly than it is that the competencies required to survive, let alone to prosper, in "advanced" countries are very different than for the bulk of the population in the "Third World," in much of which formal schooling is relatively recent. Moreover, in such countries the relation of these new schools to the social system is very different than in the contemporary West, as indeed it was in Europe's past.

From the outset, I took very seriously the idea that we were looking for competencies that could be developed in practice through socialization, education, or through general cultural experience. My orientation is therefore somewhat different from that of those who have chosen a more abstract approach. Partly this reflects the approach of most anthropologists which is essentially ethnographic, that is, based on the collection and analysis of observed data, largely forgoing the decontextualized discussions of many other social scientists – not neglecting theory but considering it always in the context of concrete social life. Given that orientation, I want to make some general remarks on the development of competencies in societies with and without schools.

Competencies in Societies Without Schools

Until recently, most anthropologists dealt with societies in which competencies were either in-built (for example motor skills) or had to be acquired in the absence of schools, that is, within the household, in interactions with peers and from the wider society. As far as livelihood skills were concerned, these were gained through participating in production activities as soon as one's competence or strength allowed. In Ghana, little girls took small pots to the pools at an early age to bring back water for the house as well as engaging in other domestic tasks; young boys looked after livestock and later accompanied their fathers to the fields. There was no question of children not working, or having "to find a job." All participated automatically; there was no other route to survival, indeed existence, for there were no "social services" to sustain them, only kin. Upbringing led directly to maintaining oneself, to occupying one's post in life. There may have been under-employment, or there may have been over-employment (both seasonal), but there was no unemployment. Lack of "employment" on economic tasks gave an opportunity to perform other social tasks, rituals such as funerals, sacrifices to the Earth, or initiation rites. There was no question of having to match educational competencies to later life (though socialization may have revealed different potentialities among individuals) since all had to make their way in agriculture or fishing or hunting for food, whatever else they did. Cognitive, emotional, together with moral competencies, were learned, acquired, as part and parcel of living, of participating within the culture.

Competencies in Societies With Schools

The situation changed dramatically with the introduction of schools. These institutions first appeared in Mesopotamia (I exclude the existence of so-called "bush-schools" associated with initiation rituals) and were specifically set up to teach a limited number of individuals, not necessarily from the highest social groups, to read and write (Goody, 1977). Especially with logographic scripts, which represented each word or morpheme by a sign, that was a long process, there being as many signs as words. Furthermore, it was considered necessary to learn to read all the existing written corpus, the "literature." The pupils had therefore to be segregated from their families, from "natural" participation in daily living, and taught in special locations, some frequently walled off in schools. These institutions were often run by temples or other religious bodies, and their organization was conceived in partly "familial" terms: for example, in Mesopotamia the headmaster was known as "big brother." They obviously had to be supported out of the surplus primary production of others, to which this educational training may or may not have indirectly contributed. When the pupils had finished, they had to be found specialist employment, probably as scribes attached to this or that national organization. That situation gave rise to the problem of matching competencies to work; schooling did not lead to automatic employment (as did farming) and those who had been "educated" in this way may no longer have had the competencies for employment in activities that did not demand literacy but instead, like agriculture, required practical involvement.

For the next five thousand years, a minority of any society that possessed writing were literate; the rest were illiterate rather than non-literate (or oral, a term which I use for cultures that lack writing). The result was a vast cleavage in all such societies between high and low, between elite and popular cultures, between those who could read (and probably write) and those who could not. These two groups had unmediated access to quite different cultural material (Goody, 1989).

The great shift in education in this last hundred or so years has been the move to a universal system whereby we try to provide schooling (of a formal kind) for the whole range of society's children, thus teaching them to read and write and modifying, if not getting rid of, the cultural divide. The contemporary schooled population includes all social classes, all ability ranges, and all motivational regimes (whether on the part of parents or children). The task of dealing with this "mass" is enormous and made more so because of democratic ideologies which claim not only that all children need schooling to participate but that they need a schooling that produces similar outcomes, similar competencies; everybody should be able to read and write and perform a set of literacy-dependent tasks.

The aim was revolutionary. I do not quarrel with that for "advanced" countries; I only question their ability to achieve it. All previous societies, ever since the invention of writing, made such acquisitions optional, taking into account individual talents and abilities. The result was that all had been culturally divided in a radical way, a division that controlled people's capacity to contribute to major cultural activities, that distinguished the teller of tales from the writer of novels, the singer of songs from the composer of poems, the masquerade or folk play from the theatre, folk music from the classical tradition.

The new dispensation did something to overcome the cultural divide, by way of universal schooling and the mass media. But at the same time it raised the question of matching school training to jobs in the community. The accompanying ideology dictated that schooling had to be democratic, egalitarian, and the same for all. But abilities differed (a question I touch upon later) and so did outcomes, especially with regard to the filling of jobs in a highly differentiated role structure. The political economy now demanded not a single way of making a livelihood, as in earlier pre-Bronze Age, pre-written, oral cultures, but a wide variety of tasks, from financial managers to window cleaners. How can a democratic system of schooling ever hope to cope with this great diversity, let alone with the need under the present capitalist world system, to take account of rates of unemployment ranging from 3 to 18 percent of the adult population, a figure that includes a proportion who, because of their disposition, do not want any particular category of jobs (for example, "manual") and a few who do not want any formal employment at all but who prefer to remain "free" on the dole, supported by the community at large ("the state")? Are there any conceivable competencies that cover all these possible outcomes?

What is certain is that the competencies for living in society are not always best taught in schools. A large number of essential skills are learned in the family, not in the school. That applies to speech itself, to basic motor skills, to practices to do with washing and eating, with sleeping and dressing. Some, such as dressing and accent, get modified by participation in a peer group. And it is there by and large that competency in sport develops, although parents too may successfully encourage such activities.

Schools do successfully teach competencies in reading, writing, and mathematics, which for many are valuable later on. But are they the best environment for preparing the young for working in or running an enterprise, for employment in administration or in a service industry, selling by telephone, operating a computer, managing money, or supervising staff (or being supervised) (Goody, 1975)?

Competencies for the Western World

Competencies for living in the contemporary world must include the ability to cope with unemployment, not necessarily permanent, but as a recurrent possibility even for the middle class, the managers and executives. But it also requires the ability or capacity (and this is not necessarily a question of individual flexibility) to provide for a whole range of occupations. The alternative is for the society to rely even in part on an immigrant class of workers to make up the shortages in certain occupations – in Israel, the Palestinian building workers; in Germany, the Turks; in France, the Arabs and West Africans; or in England, the Caribbean transport workers and Iberian hotel employees. In practice, the interrelationship between educational skills and the workplace is subverted by the introduction of immigrants from the Third World, who are required by below-replacement birth rates and undertake the more lowly, least well-paid jobs in the community. Can there be a system of evaluation of competencies in schools and for life itself that can take care of this disparity? For in making any assessment of the success of any system for developing competencies (for living), it is important to consider what it fails to do. It provides scant training for unemployment nor does it train or anyhow inspire workers for the many essential jobs in society which are not highly prestigious nor well-paid, and that in developed countries are only too frequently filled by "disadvantaged" immigrants from the developing world who are prepared to take those (or any) positions in order to escape the comparative poverty or lack of opportunities in their native lands. That is to say, any assessment of "life skills" at an international level has to take into account not only the range of internal cultural variations, not only the great spread of the division of labor in advanced countries, but also the areas of work activity for which schools make no attempt to train citizens but leave to non-citizens, either at home or abroad, to carry out. We must recognize that such political economies depend if not upon slave labor, since the choice of work is in a sense self-imposed, at least on the exploitation (or the employment, to be less slanted) of the globally underprivileged.

Setting aside the question of immigrant labor, is the matching of skills and capacities with work opportunities sufficiently close, even in OECD countries, to justify the establishment of overall notions of competence, let alone a single measure? That seems doubtful. I am at present looking out on the Etang de Thau in the Hérault, France. There, an interesting community of "fisherfolk" make their living cultivating mussels and oysters in complex ways, gathering the adults and either packing them off to urban restaurants or selling them locally, raw or prepared. The men spend much of their time in open motor-powered boats; the women stay in the village dealing with consumption.

These are people who spend their leisure watching national television, reading the *Midi-Libre*, playing at petanque, patronizing the café, eating and sleeping very much like those in developed areas. Yet the competencies needed to pursue their lives are very different: an easy relationship to the water, the ability to tinker with engines and to arrange oyster parks, some knowledge of the life cycle of sea creatures. Neither for work nor for leisure is anything learned at school of very much use, except in a totally general way. Their competencies in these areas have been learned in the family (these are family occupations) or in the community ("on the street"). Formal education has played little part except in teaching the basic skills of literacy and numeracy. People read some magazines; the men read few books; both men and women write some letters and make some calculations. It can of course be argued that school education and the inculcation of its competencies has enriched the lives of those who have attended, even if it has made little difference to specific socio-economic skills or competencies. In this way they have acquired certain capacities for living a "fuller life." That may well have been especially true for women, leading them to expand their horizons and to join the burgeoning reading public for novels and women's journals. Reading in turn, together with the cinema, radio, and television, has understandably resulted in a greater awareness of national and international issues than ever before, in a broader understanding of the situation of the rest of the world. But does this add up to improving competencies for leading a more successful and responsible life, especially in view of the increase in crime (particularly theft by the young), possibly in public and private violence (including, it would seem, in child abuse by the old), increases that cannot be simply attributed to increased awareness of what always went on? In certain areas of living, the process of taking socialization outside the family and into school has led to a weakening of the role of kin, especially in the moral and emotional domains, which the school has succeeded in doing relatively little to replace, particularly with increased secularization and the loosening of supernatural sanctions on social action. With respect to developing some of those types of moral competency, most schools have not been at all successful. Attempts have of course been made to fill the gap with Boy Scouts, Young Pioneers, Youth Clubs, and other forms of association but their influence overall has been marginal.

With the possible exception of sport, it is difficult to see how schools can help encourage competencies across the total range of "non-academic" outcomes, given that teachers themselves often lack these competencies. There is one aspect of the introduction of a wider range of more practical competencies into schools that has been broached in some quarters but not pursued systematically and which is particularly important given the extent of early retirement (or adult unemployment) of personnel with just such skills. I refer here to the proposed use of older members of the community in schools as auxiliaries or in some comparable role. Recruitment could be on a voluntary or on a paid basis but older citizens with skills in the wider world could be used to supplement the more academic work of teachers (even in return for their state pensions). In that way, competencies and experience could be communicated that are outside the abilities of teachers to teach and that are more closely associated with the process of living and working within a community. That possibility would encourage the practical competencies desiderated by the other contributors to this discussion.

Optimally, such a program would be integrated with the opportunity for children to work in the community, under supervision. The educational world has tried consistently to incorporate all the learning of skills and competencies into the school environment, even to the extent of excluding those with practical experience who did not possess a teacher's diploma and of insisting that pottery, for example, should be learned on the school premises rather than in the town workshop.

One understands why teachers should insist on hegemonic control but it is something that should be resisted and reversed by the public. Equally the introduction into schools of those with non-academic competencies will always be challenged by the teaching profession, but that too should be challenged by the community. For such a possibility would certainly be preferable to the attempt to provide training in wider competencies to the teaching profession who have, as in the case of other professionals, insulated themselves from the outside world by trying to remove their activities from more public control and responsibility.

Competencies for the Third World

We are here faced with the question of the effect of globalization (or McDonaldization) of the world in contrast to local socio-cultural diversity. Both considerations are relevant but diversity calls for different competencies than those associated with globalization, particularly when modes of livelihood are at stake. The competencies required by a hoe farmer in West Africa or a pastoralist on the borders of the Sahara are very different from those needed for any rural workers in Europe, let alone for someone engaged in factory work or in a service industry. In the first place, the former "owns," or has direct access to, the means of production and has to take decisions and organize his or her life on that basis. In the second, the necessary competencies do not include the ability to read and write, except possibly in order to participate in the new political processes. National politicians are keen to promote those literate skills that have brought them to the top and that will help to make their message heard by all. For that purpose, competencies of a literate kind have been forcefully advocated by politicians and parties throughout the developing world ever since the advent of independence. But, setting aside long-term and somewhat utopian goals, how necessary is this question of educational competencies viewed in a wider frame?

After gaining independence, primary school education in African countries became widespread throughout the continent. It was expanded very rapidly and hence the teachers were inevitably less well trained than previously; those who had just learned to read were instructing their immediate juniors. The result was a lower level of competence among staff and students than in developed countries. Moreover, the program became confused between learning to read and learning to read in a language of major circulation, usually English, French, Portuguese, or Spanish, which is what most people wanted to know. It is not difficult to teach a willing pupil to learn to read something written in his own natural language. The problem in Africa, as elsewhere in the developing world, is that learning to do so brought few immediate benefits since there was little or nothing to read except a handful of folktales transcribed by teachers which were already well known orally to the pupils from their childhood. People were taught to read and expected to have access to "the book," finding at the end of their efforts that the book was published in English or in Arabic and that before they could effectively "read," they had to learn another language. That is quite a different proposition, requiring different competencies, and is a problem faced by thousands of the children of immigrants in Europe today, not to speak of the many "native" children who do not speak the standard dialect incorporated in the written versions of the language (Goody, 1973).

One great lacuna is that nowhere in Africa is there a concerted effort to publish what has occasionally been laboriously written in the local languages by local scholars, partly because there are so many of these languages and hence relatively few speakers of any given one (there are in effect more than 4,000 languages spoken in the world). A similar difficulty exists even for manuscripts written in the language of major circulation, English, or French, especially by local authors. People have been taught to read and write, but publication remains a discouraging problem for those local authors and hence for local readers who find little local material to read.

Learning to read and write, especially to the minimum extent pupils often do, means that this learning has little or no significance for general life and as a consequence many have gone back to living in the traditional non-literate way, as a hoe-farmer or a housewife. Some of those who continued with education fared better and took posts in the newly expanding administration. But the economy did not expand *pari passu* in a parallel manner and the number of bureaucratic jobs was limited (since they all had to be paid for). There was relatively little feedback on the economy so that the children who did not make it into the few available jobs had to return to the traditional tasks in which they had had little training and which in many cases education had taught them to look down on. As a result, there was a great incentive for the educated to find jobs abroad, as legal or illegal immigrants, or possibly as "refugees." There, they could not usually find work commensurate with their training since "natives" were often better trained, had better linguistic and other competencies, better contacts, so they had to take the more menial jobs, e.g., driving taxis in the United States.

What has happened is that training in competencies in literacy has been promoted for political and ideological reasons which have little to do with the existing social situation. That situation cannot absorb the number of people produced by universal education which has trained them out of jobs in the traditional, largely agricultural, economy. The result is a discrepancy between training and the socio-economic system, between competence and performance, a relationship that always has to be context-specific. As I have noted, for the first five thousand years of written cultures, only a minority were taught to read and write. The remainder were technically illiterate but had their own popular culture which did not necessarily bow down to the educated who might well be pilloried not only by the populace but even by critical writers such as Shakespeare, Molière, and others. In other words, different competencies were required by different segments of the population. Only recently in advanced societies, after the Second Industrial Revolution of the later nineteenth century, has the insistence on universal schooling become an ideal, let alone an actuality. Only then did reading and writing become universally required competencies, creating not equality but another ladder of achievement, another way to distinguish some people from others. To transfer these requirements of universal literacy to the developing countries with very different socio-economic situations is to pose enormous problems for those cultures and to distort the whole emphasis of their training in other functionally necessary competencies, leading to internal dissatisfaction and external migration that empties those countries of personnel on whom so much has been spent to educate.

A recent meeting in Tokyo of the UN Committee concerned with development in Africa had as a primary aim the elimination or at least reduction of non-literacy. That aim, in a continent already spending a large proportion of its budget on school education, is one example of the possibly adverse effects of applying aims and measures of competency (literacy in this case) appropriate to one set of societies to another in which quite different situations obtain. In a system where hoe agriculture predominates, little is served by insisting on the capacity to read, unless one can develop *pari passu* a more advanced agriculture and a range of alternative employment. Otherwise, one is educating not for development and success, but for dissatisfaction and hence for political instability and increased emigration. One is training for a measure of disintegration of the present culture without offering anything effective as a local substitute.

School education in itself is no sign of successful development. In fact, schooling has been very successful in Africa and the view was widely held that this achievement would automatically result in overall long-term development. That has been the case for a minority of individuals but not for the society at large, which as a result has lost a great deal and made few gains. Rather, what is required for this inevitably non-homogeneous social situation is more recognition of differentiation in its education and training, not more homogenization. Such "globalization" is to be avoided, not simply on the grounds of encouraging cultural diversity but of pursuing the aims suggested in the OECD project. In the Third World, the valuable competencies to be cultivated have to be diverse and diversified, and that caveat remains true in Europe.

Problems in Defining Key Competencies

The major competencies must be how best to spend one's work and leisure-time within the framework of the society in which one lives. If that society rewards musicians in a manner that enables them to earn a living (even by busking), then clearly musical ability becomes an important competency for a number of individuals. The same goes for sports. The problem becomes where do you encourage the development of these competencies, in the home, in the school, in the community? The school does not always seem the best option. Whether or not that is the case, are there useful existing performance criteria that can be established? In the case of sports, they clearly exist for various age-groups, either informally or formally.

The notion that there should be any general competency for living in one country let alone across nations seems open to serious question, not only questionable, but dangerous. It is questionable because different countries have different life courses. And within countries there are clearly different expectations in terms of the lives that people are likely to lead and that are required to fill their social, cultural, and economic needs.

The problem with laying down generalized core skills is that one is bound to be left with some individuals who for one reason or another cannot attain them. So one has to encourage alternative skills for them. Take literacy and numeracy, which are obviously core skills for many people's future in developed societies. But as we have seen, some people have severe problems with learning to read, either for physical, psychological, or social reasons. The same is true of numeracy. In these cases, one obviously needs to try and develop non-core skills, to encourage diversity rather than establishing uniformity.

Another problem is that for each skill chosen as a core skill, one finds that there are circumstances in which quite the opposite competency is required. It is not difficult to lay down certain broad parameters for the "good life" such as flexibility and sociability (cooperation) which may appear as universal goods, but each of these "virtues" has to be strictly contextualized. Take for instance flexibility, which seems an obvious candidate for a generally useful competency in our changing world. Flexibility is at odds with perseverance, with constancy, with not giving up, which is undoubtedly relevant in many circumstances, including notably the sporting arena (a subset of the increasingly significant leisure area) as well as in many spheres of work. Sociability, cooperation, is of less value where one is up against the "bad" or the "enemy," when direct opposition may be called for. The feud is often an instrument of social control; hostility may have its uses. Indeed, many relations contain a mixture of opposites, demanding different competencies on the part of actors. Meyer Fortes has written of kinship as being governed by the "axiom of amity" (Fortes, 1969, p. 26). True, but it is also the case that most murders, most violence, most abuse, occur within the family.

So which does one specify as a core skill, flexibility or perseverance? Obviously the choice depends upon context, and the actor himself has to make a contingent selection and beware of the acceptance or inculcation of a single strategy.

Measurements and Indices

While we have not been asked to elaborate indices, considerations related to this topic are relevant in view of the long-term goal of the DeSeCo Project. The indices and the statistics which form the basis of much national and international planning are utilized mainly by economists who work with money, and with relatively abstract units of exchange and account. Although indices of national income (such as GNP) can be produced, it is well known that including non-market transactions, not to mention considerations of quality, is a difficult and contentious task. Even national income figures have been subject to a good deal of criticism and revision, for example by the Boskin Committee in the United States (Boskin, Dulberger, Gordon, Griliches, & Jorgenson, 1996).

Other important statistics have run into similar problems, for example, the rate of unemployment that purports to summarize the national situation. Great difficulty has been experienced in establishing comparable figures in Europe owing to the different bases of calculation adopted by different countries, depending partly on whether account is taken of government measures to assist the unemployed into work or of the numbers of people encouraged to take early retirement. A consideration of these facts leads to a variation in the calculation of such rates in France, for example, between 12.4 and 23.0 percent and in the UK between 8.2 and 12.0 percent (Larouche, 1998).

How much more difficult it is then to establish an index for cognitive or emotional competency when these vary so much between individuals and depend so greatly on cultural context. Competence has to be "competence for what?" Have we not seen some of the problems with intelligence tests which were originally supposed to be international but which were later acknowledged to be much more context-bound? Even when set up on a national or perhaps European basis, they turned out to have a limited use despite all the immense worry, time, and effort devoted to their administration. Are we in danger of trying to establish indices for yet more problematic qualities?

It is often noted that there is no statistic without a purpose. Likewise, there is no competency without an end. The end cannot be competence for "an individually and socially valuable life" in the abstract since such lives differ enormously both within and between cultures. An index at such a level of generality would have little or no practical purpose, except that involved in its formulation, gathering, and distribution; indeed, it could have negative feedback in that it would tend to homogenize what needs to be differentiated.

That is not to deny the possibility of making useful assessments, especially concerning the outcome of the educational process in schools. Indeed, we need to carry out such exercises if we are to monitor or improve performance in what is an area of fundamental social concern and of immense public expenditure. But, we have to do so bearing in mind the societal need for a gamut of competencies to correspond to the many roles that individuals are called upon to fill, roles that differ in different parts of the world. What we have to do is to make assessments that are based on much more modest calculations, that are capable of taking into account such differences, in other words which are not "reductive" in the manner suggested.

Let us take a very basic competency in a literate society, the capacity to read and write itself, which remains the central orientation of schools, at least of primary schools – at other levels, it is a competency assumed to have been acquired. As is well known, there are different rhythms of learning to read and write, though it is not always clear how these influence later achievements. What does undoubtedly have an effect in this sphere is the existence of books (and of literate activity) in the home environment. Those brought up with books are more likely to develop this competency in that direction. Bernard Lahire (1997) has shown the extent to which the motivation and practice of reading and writing depend upon the family milieu and upon gender differences. Men in upper families are more likely to dictate than write; women are the dominant ones in domestic literacy. In lower families, writing itself may be seen as a gendered activity, leading to a lack of interest among boys. This highly significant influence of the family, well known to educators, is a factor behind school achievement and competencies; it is not something that can be wished away and has to be reckoned with as an aspect of education but even more so of socialization.

Inherited abilities as well as cultural capacities affect this process, especially in alphabetic cultures where the intervention of a physiological (others maintain social) condition of dyslexia delays, sometimes very considerably, a child's reading age. Dyslexia does not occur with logographic scripts like Chinese or Japanese for technical reasons concerned with the lesser need to impose direction on script in order to communicate. Another important consequence is associated with these logographic scripts. Firstly, the assessment of literacy, basic to all educational attainment, becomes much more problematic, because there is not a single code to break (as with the alphabet) but a large number of visual signs to learn; in the case of Japan, the knowledge of some 6,000 signs or characters has to be acquired before pursuing higher studies at university. In other words the basic process of reading requires very different skills, competencies, depending upon the script. Logographic scripts require the lengthy development of visual memory in order to store the wide range of signs for future use and recognition.

Despite the efforts of teachers, not everyone has equal ability to be able to read and write alphabetic scripts. These abilities have little to do with any general measure of intelligence. As Neo-Piagetians have amply demonstrated, abilities are frequently very specific and success in one domain does not predict, let alone guarantee, success in another. Skills are highly differentiated, both inherited and acquired. For example, people who score very highly on verbal tests may do badly on spatial organization. For women in particular the results may display a bimodal distribution. Both are useful life skills or competencies but in some, one is highly developed, in others not. Testing also has to be very specific, gender specific in this case, but also culturally specific in matters like color-recognition.

Equally, failure in one area does not mean failure in another. As we have seen, schools have always been centered on the acquisition of literate skills. Those who cannot succeed in these tasks tend to be seen as failures. Often enough, little is done to encourage them in other directions. A limited training is given in sports, sometimes some in music, both spheres in which individuals may excel in later life. But those are activities based on competencies in which the environment of the home (and in the first case of the street) makes a fundamental contribution. Consider the number of tennis stars who attribute their success to parental interest and help. Think of families who manage to instill a musical ability in the classics in their children. The educational system itself is often notably deficient in providing such help, with the exception of a few specialist schools. Yet these are areas, especially in popular music and sport, which present many openings for the talented. Such competencies can certainly be encouraged among a minority to provide them with a satisfying life. But it means that we should not only concentrate on a narrow range of competencies and their measurement, particularly those promoted by schools and their teachers in written cultures.

Are there any competencies which cut across different modes of life, at least in Europe, to warrant a description? It can be argued that contemporary life requires some general types of adjustment, such as flexibility in the work place as well as the home (since both are likely to change in the course of a lifetime), an ability to communicate with people, tolerance towards people different from oneself, participation in the democratic process, the avoidance of extremes of either right or left (the adoption of the "third way") – though sizeable groups will disagree with many of these attributes. In any case, they seem too vague to make the basis of any useful set of measurements.

Conclusion

At the heart of the undertaking is the assumption that the construction of a set of competencies and skills indispensable in a conflictual world is possible. However, if one takes the notion of "world" seriously, I think such an outcome is only possible at a very general level, which I regard as rather useless. Even if one restricts the "world" to that of the OECD, the same seems to be almost as true. Every possible candidate (for example, flexibility) is complicated by its opposite (in the case of flexibility, perseverance). Occupational and class differences, employment status, these factors are such as to render any general statement subject to challenge. That is even more true among the immigrant communities who are allowed, by and large, to fill the unwanted jobs.

Admittedly, if one limits the arena to upper groups in OECD countries, one can specify some more specific skills and competencies such as literacy and numeracy, but one has to make provision for those unable to achieve these standards. Except in a very general way, a small or limited set of key competencies cannot be determined. For example, even the competency of sociability cannot be a universal desideratum: we have to allow for the non-sociable artist or academic. Further, unless one is working at a very abstract level, competencies will differ according to cultural context. Beyond that, age and the developmental cycle must change the nature of desired competencies, such as are involved in being a child, a parent, or a grandparent – or a person taking up his or her first job, a mature worker, a retired person. Finally, while specific competencies such as literacy and numeracy can certainly be learned, they are conditioned by individual dispositions. And although formal settings are very important for instruction in writing and mathematics, family background is significant in encouraging achievement. One cannot afford to neglect any social context, and more abstract competencies beyond literacy and numeracy are often part of the whole human experience.

The basic problem is that the questions have been posed about competencies that are *necessary* for a successful life. But all competencies are contingent and have only a contextual relevance, both within and across societies. Treating them as necessary underestimates the capabilities of the non-achievers (in this respect) who may make important contributions in many areas of social life.

References

Bloch, M. (1991). Language, anthropology and cognitive science. *Man (New Series), 26*, 183–198.

Boskin, M. J., Dulberger, E. R., Gordon, R. J., Griliches, Z., & Jorgenson, D. (1996). *Toward a more accurate measure of the cost of living*. Final Report to U. S. Senate Finance Committee from Advisory Commission to Study the Consumer Price Index.

Boyer, P. (1994). Cognitive constraints on cultural representations: Natural ontologies and religious ideas. In L.A. Hirshfeld & S. A. Gelman (Eds.), *Mapping the mind: Domain specificity in cognition and culture.* New York: Cambridge University Press.

Chomsky, N. (1980). Rules and representations. *The Behavioral and Brain Sciences, 3*, 1–61.

Fortes, M. (1969). *Kinship and the social order.* Chicago: Aldine.

Goody, J. (1973). Literacy and the non-literate in Ghana. In R. Disch (Ed.), *The future of literacy*. Hillsdale, NJ: Prentice-Hall.

Goody, J. (1975). Schools, education and the social system: Some utopian suggestions. *Interchange, 6,* 1–5.

Goody, J. (1977). *The domestication of the savage mind.* Cambridge: Cambridge University Press.

Goody, J. (1989). *The interface between the written and the oral.* Cambridge: Cambridge University Press.

Lahire, B. (1997). Masculin-féminin: L'écriture domestique. In D. Fabre (Ed.), *Par écrit.* Paris: Maison des Sciences de l'Homme.

Larouche, M. (1998). Des statistiques imparfaites. *Le Monde* (29 Sept. 1998).

Sperber, D. (1985). *On anthropological knowledge: Three essays.* Cambridge: Cambridge University Press.

Chapter 9

Scholarly Comments: Common Ground

The five preceding chapters are comprised of essays written by scholars in various disciplines, in which they define what they consider to be key competencies. Though these contributions initially appear to be quite different, a close reading will reveal that despite the divergent disciplinary contexts, there are common threads between them. These essays were submitted to two other academics whose task it was to draw out linkages among the proposed key competencies. Robert Kegan, a psychologist in the Graduate School of Education at Harvard University, and Cecilia Ridgeway, a sociology professor at Stanford University, comment on and react to the these contributions, focusing on conceptual and theoretical elements that are useful, from their viewpoint, for building a common understanding of the most relevant competencies.

In his comment, Kegan discusses the level of mental complexity associated with responding to the demands of modern life. He sees the "self-authoring" order of mental capacity as a central component of some of the key competencies identified by the philosophers, the psychologist, the sociologist, and the economists. Ridgeway outlines two broad areas of common ground among the essays: the ability to join and function in groups, and the ability to develop a concept of self that allows for the management of emotions. She also comments on the desirability of large-scale assessments and the importance of computer literacy.

These two commentaries bring to light some of the common threads, as well as some of the differences, between the essays, thereby providing a better understanding of the issues surrounding the definition and selection of key competencies.

Competencies as Working Epistemologies: Ways We Want Adults to Know

Robert Kegan

Introduction

Since receiving the OECD materials describing the DeSeCo Project, and since having read the essays, I have felt two kinds of selfish excitement. The first is akin to discovering relatives one never knew one had! Here were people gathering around a topic I have been pondering from my own partial perspective, more or less by myself, for more that fifteen years! The idea that the DeSeCo Project might, among other things, inspire an interdisciplinary community to address the subject over a certain period is enormously appealing. The second is that it seemed to me the project might amount to a kind of free-of-charge naturalistic "test" of one of the central propositions I advanced in my book *In Over Our Heads: The Mental Demands of Modern Life* (Kegan, 1994). As a developmental psychologist studying the complexity of individuals' meaning-making systems and their evolution throughout their life span, I undertook over several years an analysis of the "hidden curriculum" of modern democratic society. Though admittedly more grandiose, my basic stance was not very different from the one cognitive developmental psychologists have long taken toward any school curriculum (e.g., that of an elementary social studies class). Three kinds of questions are routinely asked: (1) What demands does the curriculum make on the minds of its students in order for them to succeed? (2) What do we know about the minds of the students of this age? (3) What is the fit between the *demands* of the curriculum and the *mental capacities* of the students?

Conceiving of Competence as a Way of Knowing: Its Logical Priority

A great benefit to a concept like "competence" is that it directs our attention beneath the observable behavioral surface of "skills" to inquire into the mental capacity that creates the behavior. And it directs our attention beyond the acquisition of "knowledge" as storable contents (what we know) to inquire into processes by which we create knowledge (how we know). This is not to say that our skills and our fund of knowledge are unimportant. But it is to remind us what every teacher or manager knows: teaching skills or knowledge contents without developing the underlying mental capacities that create the skill or the knowledge leads to very brittle results. Engineered behavior and rote learning seldom travel well beyond the narrow contexts in which they were taught. And all the authors of the essays agree that the adult of the 21st century will need to be able to travel across a wide variety of contexts.

So when I suggest that the several essays are best read conceiving "competence" as first a question of how we know, I do not mean this to exclude the question of how we behave or what we know. I just mean that the first question is prior to the other two. Let us consider an example from a slightly simpler world than the world of adulthood – namely, the world of adolescence. We adults have a host of expectations of teenagers that amount to our working definition of a competent adolescent. Just to name a few, we want adolescents to be law-abiding, personally trustworthy, employable, possessed of common sense, able to think abstractly, able to reflect on their internal psychological processes, to have good values, and to feel a part of some community or group beyond themselves (Kegan, 1994). On the surface, there are a host of social skills and knowledge contents that would have to be mastered to meet these expectations for competence, but I want to make a number of generalizations about these competencies:

1. All of these competencies are first of all about ways we want adolescents to know (not ways we want them to act or contents we want them to know).

2. The order of mental complexity required to meet each of these competencies is, surprisingly, identical.

3. This order of complexity rarely exists in childhood and usually only gradually develops during the teen years; thus many teens will not automatically be able to meet these expectations.

4. The existence or non-existence of the mental complexity needed to demonstrate the competencies can be reliably assessed empirically.

Quickly elaborating on these assertions will serve as a useful foundation for addressing the essays and the more complex questions of adult competencies. Why are the expectations for teens more a matter of how they know than how they behave or what they know? Consider as an example the parents' wish that their child be trustworthy and hold up his or her end of family agreements, such as abiding by a curfew on Saturday night. What appears to be a call for a specific behavior ("Be home by midnight or phone us") or the acquisition of a specific knowledge ("Know that it is important to us that you do what you say you will") actually turns out to be something else if you interview parents with an orientation to their individual meaning-making, as my colleagues and I do. Parents do not simply want their kids to get themselves home by midnight on Saturday night; they want them to do it for a specific reason. If their kids abide by curfew, but only did so because the parents have an effective monitoring system to detect if they do not, and a sufficiently noxious set of consequences to impose when they do not, the parents turn out to be disappointed even though the kids behave correctly. Parents of teens want to resign from the role of "parent police." They want their kids to hold up their end of the agreement, not simply because they can frighten them into doing so; they want their kids to do so out of their own intrinsic prioritizing of the importance of being trustworthy. This is not first of all a claim on their kids' behavior; it is a claim on their minds. Nor will the mere acquisition of the knowledge content, "it is important to my parents that I do what I say I will" be sufficient to bring the child home by midnight. Many non-behaving teens know precisely what their parents value. They just do not themselves hold these values as their parents do! They hold them extrinsically, as landmines they need to take account of, to maneuver around so they do not explode.

In order for teens really to be "competent" vis-à-vis this parental expectation, they need to grow mentally beyond the self-interested, short-term, others-as-supplies-to-the-self orientation they ordinarily develop in late childhood. They need literally to relativize or subordinate their own immediate interests on behalf of the interests of a social relationship, the continued participation in which they value more highly than the gratification of an immediate need. When they make this epistemological shift, then sustaining a mutual bond of trust with their parents becomes more important than staying out all night. Interestingly, though not intuitively obvious, the mental complexity entailed in this shift toward a more intrinsically relational or mutually trustworthy social epistemology is identical to that entailed in the shift from a concrete to an abstract cognitive epistemology, or from an unreflective to a self-reflective intrapersonal epistemology. In all cases, the adolescent, before making this shift, is relying upon an order of mental complexity limited to the "durable category" or class. This enables one, for example, to create the concrete world of later childhood "actuality," as opposed to the highly labile world of early childhood "fantasy," but it constrains one from subordinating "actuality" to the bigger world of "possibility" which is at the heart of abstract thinking and the creating of "ideals." This same reliance upon "durable categories" enables one to take other people's points of view as distinct from one's own (which egocentric young children cannot do), but constrains one from subordinating one's own short-term interests and personal preferences to the welfare of a sustainable interpersonal relationship.

An Evolutionary Model of the Complexification of Mind

As these brief descriptions of developing mental complexity suggest, the basic underlying principle of "complexification" of mind is not the mere addition of new capacities (an "aggregation model") nor the substitution of a new capacity for an old one (a "replacement model"), but the subordination of once-ruling capacities to the dominion of more complex capacities. The old capacities are not lost but come under the governance of the new capacities. As the geometrist's point comes under the "governance" of the line, and the line comes under the governance of the plane, the earlier structure always remains; it just gets re-dimensionalized. Put more epistemologically, what was "subject" in our knowing (that with which we are identified, and the principle by which we construct our knowing) becomes "object" in our knowing (that which we can reflect on, take responsibility for, integrate with some other aspect of our knowing, exercise control over). In contrast to an "aggregation model" or a "replacement model," this is an "evolutionary model" of complexification. Figure 1 presents a rough schema of five distinct epistemologies which a variety of research conducted over twenty years suggests people have the potential to gradually grow through over their life span (Kegan, 1982, 1994).

This same and related research (Selman, 1980; Kohlberg, 1984; Piaget, 1954) suggests that adolescence is a period of only gradually growing from what figure 1

	SUBJECT	OBJECT	UNDERLYING STRUCTURE	
1	PERCEPTIONS *Fantasy* SOCIAL PERCEPTIONS IMPULSES	Movement Sensation	Single Point/ Immediate/ Atomistic ●	**LINES OF DEVELOPMENT** **K** COGNITIVE **E** INTERPERSONAL **Y** INTRAPERSONAL
2	CONCRETE *Actuality* Data, Cause-and-Effect POINT OF VIEW Role-Concept Simple Reciprocity (tit-for-tat) ENDURING DISPOSITIONS Needs, Preferences Self Concept	Perceptions Social Perceptions Impulses	Durable Category	
3 (TRADITIONALISM)	ABSTRACTIONS *Ideality* Inference, Generalization Hypothesis, Proposition Ideals, Values MUTUALITY/INTERPERSONALISM Role Consciousness Mutual Reciprocity INNER STATES Subjectivity, Self-Consciousness	Concrete Point of View Enduring Dispositions Needs, Preferences	Cross-Categorical Trans-Categorical	
4 (MODERNISM)	ABSTRACT SYSTEMS *Ideology* Formulation, Authorization Relations between Abstractions INSTITUTION Relationship-Regulating Forms Multiple-Role Consciousness SELF-AUTHORSHIP Self-Regulation, Self-Formation Identity, Autonomy, Individuation	Abstractions Mutuality Interpersonalism Inner States Subjectivity Self-Consciousness	System/Complex	

Figure 1. Four Orders of Consciousness (from Kegan, 1994)

depicts as the second to the third orders of mental complexity. (A variety of inter-view-oriented and task-oriented measures have been developed by this research para-digm for the longitudinal and cross-sectional study of the gradual development of this mental complexity).[1] But sometime during the second decade of life most people do develop an order of mental complexity characterized by the third level in figure 1. This order of complexity permits one to think abstractly, identify a complex internal psychological life, orient the welfare of a human relationship, construct values and ideals self-consciously known as such, and subordinate one's own interests on behalf of one's greater loyalty to maintaining bonds of friendship, or team or group partici-pation.

As extraordinary as this mental capacity may be, the question now arises, "Would this 'third order' equip one to meet the demands of adult life in modern democratic societies?" There is no reason why, in and of itself, this order of mental complexity should prove insufficient to meet the demands of any of several perfectly reasonable

---

[1] See Lahey, et al., 1988; and Loevinger & Wessler, 1970.

ways cultures could construct and have constructed adult life. It is a dignified, so-phisticated, and socially responsive way of organizing experience. It is the culmina-tion of "adolescence" (etymologically, "becoming grown up"), and so, by rights, it should constitute a respectable form of adulthood. The third order of mental com-plexity amounts to the psychological threshold for what sociologists call "socializa-tion": we become truly part of society (rather than its ward or charge) when society has become truly a part of us. Our capacity to internalize, and identify with, the val-ues and beliefs of our social "surround" – as these may be communicated by family, peer group, state, religion, ethnic clan, geographic region, or social position – makes us inducible into the commonweal.

But the question before us is whether the third order would equip us to meet the actual demands of adult life as these do exist in present-day democratic industrial and post-industrial societies. I am not questioning the soundness of the third order mental complexity or the adults who organize their experience according to this principle. I am considering, rather, whether the third order of mental complexity is adequate to enable adults to meet the mental demands of modern life. In the book, *In Over Our Heads*, I surveyed literatures on parenting, intimate partnering, working, living in an increasingly diverse world, and adult learning (in school and in psychotherapy) – highly frequented arenas of private and public adult life – subjecting the implicit and explicit expectations and directives for success that run through these literatures to an epistemological analysis. By bringing these non-communicating discourses of exper-tise and expectation together, and by subjecting them to a single gradually building analysis of their demands on our minds, I hoped to generate sufficient thrust to move us temporarily beyond our own "gravitational field." Attempting to achieve some distance may help us to understand better the different roles we play and the different demands being made within them throughout our lives. Figure 2 presents a summary of some 38 frequently demanded competencies in the literatures concerning these six common roles and venues of adult life. What is notable about these expected com-petencies – and, as we shall see, about most of the competencies hoped for by the authors of the essays – is that they tend *not* to be satisfactorily accomplishable by the third order of mental complexity ordinarily reached after two decades of life. We have tended to yoke our conceptions of full mental development with our concep-tions of full physical development – i.e. that in both cases we reach our full stature sometime in late adolescence, but of course, that is not the case, and though we may stop growing in our late teenage years, it is imperative that we continue to grow mentally.

The remainder of this comment addresses the following questions:

1. What order of mental complexity is required to handle expected competencies such as those in figure 2, or in the discipline-oriented essays?

2. What, if anything, do we already know empirically about the distribution of men-tal complexity in the adult population of modern democratic societies?

3. What are the implications of this line of argument for the DeSeCo Project?

The Consistent Demand for a "Self-Authoring" Order of Mental Complexity

My survey of expected competencies across highly frequented arenas of adult living led to an unexpected finding when they were subjected to the first question of developmental curricular analysis: What mental demands does the curriculum make if the student is to succeed? By far, the overwhelming majority of expected competencies require us to be (1) well socialized, (2) self-reflective, (3) abstract-thinking, and (4) value-bearing persons. However, these competencies alone are not sufficient. We are also required: (1) to gain some distance from the socializing press so that we can look at and make judgments about the expectations and claims that bombard us from all directions – whether it be as personal, blunt, and close-at-hand as our children telling us "everyone else's parents let them," or as public and subtle as the messages of male-entitlement (or other arbitrarily advantaged in-groups) that still saturate most democratic societies; (2) to be able not only to identify an inner life of feelings and thoughts but to take responsibility for the fact that we are the creators (not merely the locus) of those feelings and thoughts – i.e., it is not enough to reflectively identify the origins of our dysfunctional behaviors, thoughts, and feelings in our early family experience, as if we could only become more astute audience members viewing the drama of our inner psychologies; rather we are expected as mature adults to become more like playwrights who can jump on stage and re-author the scripts of the dramas themselves; (3) and (4) to create a more complex system of abstractions or values – a whole framework, theory, or ideology – which generates distinct abstractions or values, prioritizes them, and internally resolves conflicts among them.

The expected competencies that I identified in my survey outstrip the third order capacities of "the socialized mind" and call for a qualitatively even more complex "self-authoring mind" which, as figure 1 describes and depicts, retains but subordinates the mental structures of the third order on behalf of an internally generated authority – which gives the self distance from both its own mental productions and the reality-framing tendencies of society.

A few examples will perhaps make clear that a whole different mental world from that of adolescence is implied if we are to succeed in the curriculum of modern adulthood. To return for a moment to our "curfewed" teens, recall that when adolescents begin to genuinely internalize the expectations and values of their parents, such that it matters intrinsically to them if they violate these expectations or lose their parents' approval, we call this becoming responsible on the part of the adolescent. Note that a widely agreed upon necessary competency of parents is the ability to set limits on their children, quite literally to defy them; that in a family with an eight-year-old someone needs to be in charge and it had better not be the eight-year-old. Now, note that if an *adult* were to be as shaped by the expectations of others – as intrinsically oriented to others' approval – as we want "responsible" teenagers to be, that identical behavior would be called, in an adult, *irresponsible*! Clearly, although we do not fully realize it, we have quite different definitions of what being responsible means in

As Parents

Take charge of the family; establish rules and roles
Institute a vision and induct family members into it
Support the development of the young within and away from the family
Manage boundaries between the generations
Set limits on children, ourselves, and those outside the family

As intimate partners

Be psychologically independent of our partners
Have a well-differentiated and clearly defined sense of self
Transcend an idealized, romanticized approach to love and closeness
Set limits on children, selves, extrafamily involvements to preserve couple
Support our partner's development
Listen emphatically and nondefensively
Communicate feelings directly and responsibly
Have an awareness of how our psychological history inclines or directs us

At work

Be the inventor or owner of our work (rather than see it as owned and created by the employer); distinguish our work from our job
Be self-initiating, self-correcting, self-evaluating (rather than dependent on others to frame the problems, initiate adjustments, or determine whether things are going acceptably well)
Be guided by our own visions at work (rather than be without a vision or captive of the authority's agenda
Take responsibility for what happens to us at work externally and internally (rather than see our present internal circumstances and future external possibilities as caused by someone else)
Be accomplished masters of our particular work roles, jobs, or careers (rather than have an apprenticing or imitating relationship to what we do)
Conceive of the organization from the "outside in," as a whole; see our relation to the whole; see the relation of the parts to the whole (rather than see the rest of the organization and its parts only from the perspective of our own part, from the "inside out")

As citizens of a diverse society

Resist our tendencies to make "right" or "true" that which is merely familiar, and "wrong" or "false" that which is only strange (contravene our tendencies toward ethnocentrism, gendercentrism)
Be able to *look at* and evaluate the values and beliefs of our psychological and cultural inheritance rather than be captive of those values and beliefs

Be able to recognize our *styles* (how we prefer to receive stimulation and energy, prefer to gather data, prefer to make decisions, and how spontaneously or structured we prefer to orient to our lives; our orientation to separateness or connection) *as preferences* (rather than as superior apprehensions)

In psychotherapy

Perceive our standards as based on our own experience (rather than upon the attitudes or desires of others)
Perceive ourselves as the evaluators of experience (rather than regard ourselves as existing in a world where the values are inherent in and attached to the object of our perception)
Place the basis of standards within ourselves, recognizing that the goodness or badness of any experience or perceptual object is not something inherent in that object, but is a value placed on it by ourselves
Transform our energies from manipulating the environment for support into developing greater and greater self-support
Learn to stand on our own feet emotionally, intellectually, economically
Learn to stop reindoctrinating ourselves with the unwholesome philosophies of life, or values, we imbibed and taught ourselves in youth
Learn to challenge and question our own basic values, our own thinking, so that we really think for ourselves
Take responsibility for our lives
Learn the psychological myths or scripts that govern our behavior *and reauthor them* (rather than just use insight for better understanding of why the script is as it is)

In school

Exercise critical thinking
Examine ourselves, our culture, and our milieu in order to understand how to separate what we feel from what we should feel, what we value from what we should value, and what we want from what we should want
Be a self-directed learner (take initiative: set our own goals and standards; use experts, institutions, and other resources to pursue these goals; take responsibility for our direction and productivity in learning)
See ourselves as the co-creators of the culture (rather than only shaped by culture)
Read actively (rather than only receptively) with our own purpose in mind
Write to ourselves and bring our teachers into our self-reflection (rather than write mainly to our teachers and for our teachers)
Take charge of the concepts and theories of a course or discipline, marshalling on behalf of our independently chosen topic its internal procedures for formulating and validating knowledge

Figure 2. Role-Based Competency Expectations of Contemporary Adults (from Kegan, 1994)

adolescence and adulthood. The order of mental complexity that would enable an adolescent to succeed in being one kind of "responsible" will cause him or her to fail in satisfying the adult form of "responsibility."

Equally, we are required in adulthood to win some distance from ourselves, from our own internal reactions. For example, adults will only continue to live amidst increasing diversity, sharing a democratic society with people who are unlike them ethnically, racially, economically, sexually, and so on. Underlying the hidden curriculum of "respect for diversity" is an expectation that we have the competency to overcome our own "centrism," be this ethnocentrism, heterosexual-centrism, or whatever. And what would it take to overcome our centrisms? Centrism is a tendency to make right and true that which is merely familiar and comfortable. Our capacity not to unfairly exclude and make others wrong will not derive from our purging ourselves of all centric reactions of offense and discomfort when our powerfully ingrained (and often culturally arbitrary) notions of how things should be are transgressed. My reactions of offense and discontent are inevitable if you eat differently, make love differently, use time, and take space differently than the way I was raised. This is why culture is so powerful. Our level of competence with the "diversity curriculum" does not require our purging ourselves of all such reactions. Rather, it requires us not to unwarrantedly privilege these reactions, to have the capacity to be discerning about them, even to discount our own reactions. The purpose of this kind of "distance" is not to "become remote from," but actually the opposite – to be able to *be in relation to,* rather than *fused with.* The "diversity curriculum" requires us to have a relationship to our own reactions, rather than to be captive of them. This, again, requires a qualitatively different order of mental complexity, "the self-authoring mind" versus "the socialized mind."

This central finding – a preponderant call for the so-called "fourth order of mental complexity" – is precisely the one that receives a kind of free-of-charge "test" of inter-rater reliability from the interdisciplinary DeSeCo essays. The central thread that runs through these is a call for a kind of mental agency or autonomy which allows us to detach or distance ourselves (Canto-Sperber & Dupuy, Chapter 4) from both the socializing press of the surround and from our own internal productions, albeit in such a way that does not prevent us from connecting and joining in community and personal relationships (Haste, Chapter 5). Haste, Perrenoud, Canto-Sperber and Dupuy, and Levy and Murnane all present us a picture of socializing processes, but they all ask the "competent adult" to be simultaneously mindful of them (thus not a sociopath or irresponsible ward of society) without being captive of them (thus not merely a faithful, loyal, obedient part of an unquestioned set of arrangements).

At the heart of Perrenoud's sociological reflection is the alert concession that processes of socialization, whatever their merits, are not great promoters of the key competency he values, "autonomy" (Chapter 6). This central competency that he proposes is clearly another form of a call for more "fourth order complexity," since there is no way to perform the competency without developing a complex enough system to take the socializing press "as object," something that can be reflected upon, decided about, not only refused, at times, but reframed.

From the perspective of philosophy, Canto-Sperber and Dupuy not only invoke the same metaphors of making what was once subject into object but the particular subject-object epistemology they call for in their proposed competencies also sounds very much like the fourth one in figure 1, the "self-authoring" order of complexity. This is especially clear in their "normative competence" when they ask adults to take a reflective overview as well as gain a distancing of the judgment from the context. But, note that the same order of complexity is implicitly demanded in other competencies such as their "narrative competence." The capacity to "tell a story" can be handled by a variety of working epistemologies, beginning in later childhood when the "if-then" constructions are created. But Canto-Sperber and Dupuy make clear they are calling for a much more complex form of narrative capacity, one which allows us to "detach ourselves from what happens, to distance ourselves from the continuous flow of events in order to understand their meaning" (Chapter 4).

Haste also attends to the narrative dimension and cautions against valorizing a form of autonomy and self-agency that neglects the importance of the relational world of the collective and the interpersonal. At the same time, she too, wants adults, cognitively and ethically, to be able to distinguish their thinking and moral meaning-making from the available givens. She is not pressing for a kind of connection-orientation that leaves one "made-up-by" the surround; she wants adults to be "originators of their own perspectives." Her competencies call for the fourth order as clearly as do the others, but she reminds us that the development of self-authoring capacities need not entail a move toward fractionating, hyper-individualistic, or atomistic glorifications of the self. The "distance," "stepping back," and "detachment," of which many of the authors speak, involve separations from previously ruling mental structures; they need not represent separations from persons or communities. Indeed, the capacity for self-authoring may thicken my connection to communities and relationships now more freely chosen by me and may enable me to contribute more fully to my connection through my capacity to raise questions about existing arrangements.

Nor even do the economists escape participating in this wider discourse of unwitting epistemological demand. While Levy and Murnane concede the economists' vantage point is a highly circumscribed one, nonetheless, their perspective is not the one common to all economists (Chapter 7). Their "new basic skills" take us into the world of complex psychological functioning. Their picture of workers who will find themselves increasingly in "high performance" settings is a picture of adults who will be overtaxed by the mental demands of these settings if they are to remain subject to the third order complexity of the socialized mind. The third order will equip one to take out loyalty to the organization; to pick up on, and identify with, the expectations of the boss; to access and operationalize an available supply of prescribed responses for the finite, predictable, low-novelty routines of a traditional work setting. But it may be that these were more valuable assets yesterday than they will be tomorrow. Prized as such conscientiousness and loyalty may be, what Levy and Murnane are saying is that modern work settings will be filled with unpredictable, non-routine situations, and an even higher premium may be placed on employees' capacities to consult their own internal authority in order to take initiative and create value by their original decisions. This distinction is identical to the different ways of "being responsible" discussed earlier.

A Preliminary Empirical Indication: The Available Supply May Not Meet the Increasing Demand

A fast answer, thus, to the first question the developmental analyst asks of any "curriculum" – what is the nature of the mental demand? – might be that "the fourth order of mental complexity" (the self-authoring mind) is generally what is required in our notion of needed adult competency – and that some corroboration of this answer can be found in the DeSeCo essays. The second question the developmental analysts asks is: what is the mental capacity of the students?

I do not pretend we have anything more than a suggestion of an empirical answer to this question, when it comes to the distribution of mental complexity in the adult population of complex democratic societies. But the data we do have are quite consistent and are perhaps surprising: even among highly educated, resource-rich, middle-class, professional samples, while the fourth order of mental complexity is certainly present, a majority of subjects in various studies do not appear to have fully developed this level of complexity, as assessed by the two measures that may be most appropriate for identifying the complexity of a person's working "epistemology." These two measures are the Subject-Object Interview (SOI) (Lahey et al., 1988) and the Loevinger Sentence Completion Test (SCT) (Loevinger & Wessler, 1970). The SOI is an hour-long structured interview procedure in the Piagetian tradition in which the subject's construction of real life contents is actively probed until the most complex epistemologies available to the subject have been clarified. The SCT is a written test in which the subject completes 36 sentence stems; each completion is separately analyzed and scored, leading to an assessment of the level of complexity of the subject's overall frame of reference.

Figures 3 and 4 indicate distributions of mental complexity among different segments of the U.S. population as assessed by the SOI and the SCT respectively. When all the studies in figure 3 are taken as a composite (N=342), 58 percent of the sample does not reach the fourth order of complexity. When all the studies in figure 4 are taken as a composite (N=500) – completely different subjects using a completely different measure than figure 3 – again, exactly 58 percent of that sample does not reach the fourth order of complexity. Figure 3 also looks at a comparison among studies in which all subjects are highly educated professionals with studies in which subjects are from a wide range of socio-economic backgrounds. The professional, highly educated group has 52 percent who do not reach the fourth order; the composite with a wide range of backgrounds has 79 percent who do not.

Order of Conscious-ness	Original Dissertation Composite (Studies 1-12) N=282		"Full SES" Composite (Studies 1, 5, 11) N=75		"Professional Highly Education" Composite (All but 1, 5, 11) N=207		Bar-Yam Study (a highly edu-cated sample) N=60	
5	0	0%	0	0%	0	0%	0	0%
4-5	17	6%	2	3%	15	7%	6	10%
4	97	34%	14	18%	83	40%	25	42%
3-4	91	32%	23	31%	68	33%	22	37%
3	40	14%	9	12%	31	15%	7	11%
2-3	22	8%	17	23%	5	2.5%	0	0%
2	15	5%	10	13%	5	2.5%	0	0%

Total N= 342

NOTE: Total less complex than Level 4 = 58% (197/342)

Figure 3. Distributions of Mental Complexity From Studies Using the SOI (from Kegan, 1994)

Order of Com-plexity	Study 1 (First-Line Supervisors) N=37		Study 2 (Junior and Middle Managers) N=177		Study 3 (Senior Managers) N=66		Study 4 (Nurses) N=100		Study 5 (Executives) N=104		Study 6 (Entrepre-neurial Pro-fessionals) N=13	
5	0	0%	0	0%	0	0%	0	0%	0	0%	0	0%
4-5	0	0%	4	2.5%	9	14%	4	4%	15	14%	5	39%
4	3	8%	71	40%	22	33%	31	31%	41	39.5%	5	39%
3-4	25	68%	77	43.5%	31	47%	54	54%	45	43.5%	3	22%
3	9	24%	16	9%	4	6%	9	9%	3	3%	0	0%
2-3	0	0%	9	5%	0	0%	2	2%	0	0%	0	0%
2	0	0%	0	0%	0	0%	0	0%	0	0%	0	0%

Total N= 497

NOTE: Total less complex than Level 4 = 58% (287/497)

Figure 4. Distributions of Mental Complexity From Studies Using the SCT (from Torbert, 1987)

If these preliminary explorations of mental complexity have any merit, they could be taken to suggest the following:

1. The underlying order of mental complexity necessary to enact successfully the kinds of competencies suggested in the DeSeCo essays is certainly in evidence; it may already exist among a large number of persons.

2. It may be more available to more highly educated and socio-economically more affluent, professional persons.

3. However, more than half of even advantaged adults may *not* yet possess the level of mental complexity that would equip them to enact successfully the competen-cies we suggest are necessary for adults in the 21st century.

Two Brief Implications

Finally, if the preceding line of argument has any merit, two broad implications follow:

1. A general underlying commonality runs through suggested adult competencies when those competencies are analyzed with respect to their implicit mental demand. This so-called fourth order of mental complexity, the self-authoring mind, is the epistemological underpinning of modernism. The third order, the socialized mind, is an adequate order of complexity to meet the demands of a traditionalist world, in which a fairly homogeneous set of definitions of how one should live is consistently promulgated by the cohesive arrangements, models, and external regulations of the community or tribe. Modern society is characterized by ever-expanding pluralism, multiplicity, and competition for loyalty to a given way of living. It requires the development of an internal authority which can "write upon" existing social and psychological productions rather than be "written by" them. Postmodern society, which would require the fifth order of consciousness, asks us to gain distance not only from the socializing press, but from our own internal authorities, our favored ideologies, or ruling theories. Postmodernism asks us to deconstruct the primacy of existing social and psychological identities, in favor of loyalty to the transformative process that brings such organizations into being, and reconstructs them. Fifth order complexity is obviously in even shorter supply than fourth order complexity. In spite of current fascinations with postmodernism among American and European intellectuals, it may be entirely appropriate that *our suggested competencies for adults in the next century amount to a call, not for a capability with postmodernism, but a capability for modernism.* The hidden curriculum of modernism may be far tougher than we have realized. It is likely we are yet far from mastering it.

2. If one accepts the metaphor of "culture as school," then how should we regard the possibility that our suggested competencies may comprise a very challenging curriculum, one in which many of us are unprepared to succeed? One answer to this question might be that we should reconsider our list and revise our expectations downward. We should, perhaps in sympathy, consider our suggested competencies to be the elitist favorites of advantaged intellectuals, and comprise a less complex set of expectations. But since the world is not going to become less demanding simply because we might wish it would, I suggest another kind of answer: No good school presents its students with a curriculum they can master immediately. A challenging curriculum – one that is even at the moment beyond our grasp – is actually one of two key ingredients for an excellent school. The other is that *the school must provide its students the support to master the challenging curriculum over time.* The gap between the mental demands implicit in our suggested competencies and the mental capacities of the "student" actually provides a heretofore missing intellectual foundation for the purposes of adult or lifelong education that is as strong as the foundation which exists for the education of the young – namely, education not merely for the acquisition of skills or an increase in one's fund of knowledge, but education for development, education for transformation.

References

Kegan, R. (1982). *The evolving self.* Cambridge, MA: Harvard University Press.

Kegan, R. (1994). *In over our heads: The mental demands of modern life.* Cambridge, MA: Harvard University Press.

Kohlberg, L. (1984). *The psychology of moral development.* New York: Harper and Row.

Lahey, L., Souvaine, E., Kegan, R., Goodman, R., & Felix, S. (1988). *A guide to the Subject-Object Interview.* Cambridge: Subject-Object Workshop.

Loevinger, J., & Wessler, R. (1970). *Measuring ego development.* San Francisco: Jossey-Bass.

Piaget, J. (1954). *The construction of reality in the child.* New York: Basic Books.

Selman, R. (1980). *The growth of interpersonal understanding.* New York: Academic Press.

Torbert, W. (1987). *Managing the corporate dream.* Homewood, IL: Dow-Jones Irwin.

Joining and Functioning in Groups, Self-Concept and Emotion Management

Cecilia Ridgeway

The essays representing philosophical, sociological, economic, and psychological perspectives show substantial common ground despite highly divergent approaches to the problem of defining key competencies necessary for successful, responsible lives that provide appropriate human and social capital for modern, democratic societies. The anthropological contribution is the exception to the general agreement. Since that essay largely rejects the task as impossible, I have set it aside in framing these comments. My comments are based on the contributions offering philosophical, sociological, economic, and psychological perspectives. Two general comments frame my specific observations about what is useful and problematic in these four essays.

In different ways, each of the essays considers broadly what the task of defining key competencies for a good and useful life in modern democracies entails. The writers implicitly or explicitly recognize that defining, institutionalizing, and measuring some competencies rather than others as necessary in society will, in itself, transform the rules according to which a society operates and relates to its citizens. The psychological essay is especially explicit about this point. In recognition of this fact, each of the writers shows his or her own democratic commitments in seeking to define key competencies in ways that will contribute to egalitarianism in society rather than simply foster the interests of an elite. This commitment is illustrated by the focus on learned skills rather than innate abilities and on competencies necessary for an adequate, meaningful life that could be available to all rather than one that will be inherently confined to an elite. I consider this democratic commitment in the delineation of competencies not only useful but essential to the future development of democratic societies. As the process of defining and selecting competencies proceeds, we must keep the social impact of our choices firmly in mind and evaluate decisions in terms of it as well as other factors.

My second general comment points to a slightly problematic aspect of the essays. The generally broad frame brought to the task of defining and selecting competencies in each of the contributions is highly valuable. The manner in which key competencies derived from these broad frames are conceptualized is potentially problematic, however. Many of the recommended competencies are general composites that are framed to represent desirable outcomes. Yet these composites, in my view, often appear to involve multiple, divergent, specific competencies. As a consequence, I often found it difficult to imagine how these composites could be reliably measured, even though I endorsed the value of the outcome that the composite represented. A valuable next step in the project might be to balance a broad conceptual focus with a brief consideration of what that focus yields in terms of specific competencies to be taught and measured. The philosophers, for instance, specifically suggest that they know of appropriate measures of the general competencies they list. It would be useful to learn about these measures.

The need to balance a broad conceptual focus with a concern for the advisability and feasibility of measurement will serve as a frame for my more specific comments and observations. I will combine my analyses of what I found useful and problematic in the disciplines-oriented contributions with additional insights from my perspective as a sociologist who studies interpersonal and group processes. I outline two broad areas of common ground among the essays, delineate some of the measurable skills they entail, and raise questions about the feasibility or value of measuring other component competencies. I comment briefly as well on a third area of competence raised by some of the authors.

Joining and Functioning in Groups

Given the content-specific nature of competence, all the writers recognize the difficulties and tensions involved in extracting a set of general competencies that are common to the entire set of modern, democratic, Western societies. The writers are largely skeptical about the further possibility of defining competencies that are universally necessary to the good life in any type of society. I generally agree with this skeptical assessment. Most of the competencies that can be appropriately defined as necessary for a successful, responsible life in modern democracies are only meaningful within that context.

There is one obvious exception to this assessment, however. The one truly universal key competency is the ability to join, form, and function effectively in social groups. For material and psychological survival, for a sense of self, identity, and social meaning, human beings are dependent on ties to others throughout their lives. Interestingly, this one universal core skill area is not currently assessed in a systematic manner in modern, democratic societies.

Each of the four writers singles out the ability to cooperate and form ties as a key competency. Other competencies noted by several writers, such as the ability to evaluate actions according to shared social norms or to act responsibly in regard to a social order, are also part of the process of joining and functioning in groups. Thus, this is an area in which there is broad common ground among the diverse perspectives. It is clear that skills required to join and operate in groups form prime candidates for inclusion in a list of key competencies.

Several of the authors point out that in modern, democratic societies there is a distinctive version of the ability to join and function in groups which is especially important for both the individual and the society. The sociologist makes two useful observations about what the ability to join and operate in groups entails in the modern, democratic context. First, it involves the skills to understand complex social fields and to act in several such fields at once. Social fields are understood in the Bourdieuian sense as a structured set of social positions dynamically organized around a given set of social interests. Second, the necessary competency entails the skills to operate within groups in a manner that fosters shared opportunities and responsibilities for participation and leadership within the group. In other words, it entails the skills to operate democratically in social groups and fields. Most of the authors add a third useful observation as well. In modern, democratic societies, it is important for people to have the skills to form and act effectively in groups and social orders whose members are from diverse cultural backgrounds.

In the context of modern, democratic societies, then, it is important for people to be able to join and form multiple, complex, and socially heterogeneous groups and social orders, and to operate democratically within them. Stated in this manner, this representation of competence delineates a set of desirable outcomes that are fostered by a diverse composite of social skills. How can we break this composite down into key competencies that can both be taught and measured?

First, as the philosophers comment, an essential skill for joining and operating in groups is the *ability to take the role of the other*. As symbolic interactionists from C. H. Cooley and G. H. Mead to the present (e.g., Stryker, 1980) have demonstrated, an ability to imagine the situation of action from the perspective of the other, at least to some minimal degree, is necessary to coordinate interaction and engage in joint, cooperative behavior. Since it is essential for social interaction, people routinely acquire some basic skills in taking the role of the other. However, people generally acquire these skills in the context of interaction within the family and other intimate groups where members tend to be socially and culturally similar.

The task for modern, democratic societies is to teach people to expand their skills to learn to take the role of diverse, socially different others. This involves teaching people to recognize that their own taken-for-granted perspective on a situation of action will not necessarily be shared by others. (It seems redundant to say "different others" because "others," in my mind, signifies "different" by definition.) Thus they must actively seek cues to the distinctive perspective of the other. People whose occupations require them to analyze the perspective of diverse others, such as anthropologists or international businessmen, sometimes develop enhanced skills in this regard and even receive formal training to do so. Therefore, skills in taking the role of diverse others should be teachable and measurable.

A second skill that is important for acting effectively in diverse groups is the *ability to negotiate in the face of conflicting interests in order to find mutually acceptable solutions*. Several writers delineate the ability to deal with conflict as an essential key competency. Acquiring competency in dealing with conflicts of interest involves learnable skills in the analysis of interests, negotiation, and the design of solutions (see, for example, Lawler, 1995). Importantly, however, it also involves the acquisition of a normative value for seeking mutually acceptable resolutions for conflict.

The third set of competencies entailed in joining and acting in groups in a modern, democratic context are those associated with *operating democratically in groups*. Defining the specific skills necessary to achieve this vital outcome raises a host of complex issues that are mentioned by nearly all the essays. These issues involve learning to balance commitment to the group and its norms with the capacity for autonomous action. Also involved is the related problem of balancing responsibility for active participation in the collective with the willingness to share leadership.

It is not clear to me how best to conceptualize these trade-offs as competencies that could be taught and measured. It is straightforward, for instance, to teach either independence from the opinions of others or conformity with the rules of the social order. However, both of these extremes are socially problematic. The difficulty is in conceptualizing the skills required to balance between these extremes in an appropriate manner. The authors, while affirming the importance of the question, are similarly uncertain about how to usefully conceptualize these skills. This is an area where it would be helpful to have the writers develop their arguments in greater detail.

At a minimum, however, we can recognize that operating democratically and effectively in multiple, complex, and heterogeneous social groups requires *cognitive complexity and ideational flexibility*. This is a well researched set of cognitive skills that involves the ability to hold complex, partially conflicting sets of information in mind in order to examine a situation from multiple perspectives at once and to abstract higher order commonalities from the information. It is a set of skills that also helps people switch frames to approach topics from very different points of view.

As a well-known aspect of "cognitive style," there are several measures for cognitive complexity and ideational flexibility. In their extensive studies of occupation and mental style, Melvin Kohn and colleagues (1983, 1990) have shown that when people move to jobs that require greater autonomy and complex judgments, they tend to learn from the demands placed on them and develop greater cognitive complexity and ideational flexibility. This work has three important implications for our considerations here. First, it indicates that cognitive complexity and ideational flexibility are a learned set of skills that can be taught and measured. Second, it provides empirical evidence that this set of skills is indeed related to successful functioning in complex jobs that require more autonomy, initiative, and judgment. As the economists make clear, high-wage jobs in advanced capitalist societies are increasingly of this nature. To moderate economic inequality, it is important that citizens have broad access to the skills necessary to succeed in high-wage jobs. Third, the association of this set of skills with the ability to function autonomously on the job suggests that they will increase people's ability to balance commitment to group norms with the capacity to act independently. Thus these skills will increase people's capacity to operate democratically in heterogeneous groups. As purely cognitive skills, however, cognitive complexity and ideational flexibility do not ensure that individuals are *motivated* to act democratically.

In addition to their importance for managing complex, heterogeneous social fields, the skills involved in cognitive complexity and ideational flexibility are also those behind another composite competence mentioned by several writers. They argue that the ability to adapt to and manage change and ambiguity in the social world, on the job, and in technology is an essential competence in modern, democratic societies. Cognitive complexity and ideational flexibility provide the cognitive skills to analyze and respond to a complex, changing situation.

Again, however, cognitive skills are not all that is required to manage change and ambiguity successfully. A number of emotional and motivational skills are involved as well. As Haste argues, responsiveness to change must be balanced with a commitment to continuity and tradition. A commitment to continuity depends on people maintaining strong ties to social groups and, through them, to social norms and coherent, socially acceptable identities. As most of the authors recognize, modern, democratic societies need people who adjust well to change while remaining committed to social groups. Enhancing people's abilities to take the role of diverse others should assist people in forming and maintaining ties to social groups despite change and ambiguity, but it does not ensure that outcome.

Self-Concept and Emotion Management

A second area where there is substantial common ground among the diverse essays is in the importance of a group of related personality attributes. Most writers argue that these personality attributes are necessary for individuals to live a full, successful life in a complex, changing social world. These attributes are also important contributors to the ability to engage in autonomous yet responsible action.

The attributes fall into two related sets. The first attribute is a strong, positive self-concept that allows the individual to act confidently. The second set of attributes involves the ability to manage motivation and emotion to deal adaptively with frustration, disappointment, and failure, to delay gratification when necessary, and to avoid destructive conflicts with others.

I agree with the writers that these personality attributes are important for a satisfying life that contributes to a complex, democratic society. Important questions remain, however, about how (and whether) to conceptualize these attributes as competencies that would be valuable and feasible to measure. Let us consider in this regard the attributes associated with a positive self-concept. As Weinert (Chapter 3) indicates in his essay, research has shown that global self-esteem is not, by itself, closely related to effective action and agency in any particular context. The aspect of self-concept that is most closely associated with the capacity for effective action is a context-based sense of mastery and competence. Since it is rooted in specific contexts and varies across contexts, an effective self-concept for action is difficult to teach or measure as a general competence. Instead, it may be more useful to view an effective self-concept for action as an outcome of the acquisition of a reasonable level of other basic and socially valued competencies such as the ability to successfully operate in groups or the mastery of a particular skill or knowledge area.

Perhaps schools can help children develop contextual senses of mastery and confidence by reinforcing the value of each child and seeking to value some special talents in each. Beyond such diffuse techniques, however, schools may not be able to directly teach an effective self-concept for action. Instead, they should help students master skills in valued social contexts which will indirectly foster in the students a positive sense of mastery and confidence. Although context-based senses of mastery and confidence are theoretically measurable, the fact they vary across contexts poses problems for the development of a general measuring device. Therefore, although I agree that a positive self-concept is an important asset for a good life, I do not consider it a good candidate for a key competency that should be directly taught and measured in schools.

The management of emotion and motivation is a set of personal skills that, in my view, are best taught as part of the process of teaching other key competencies. As

Weinert comments, the teaching of any key competency involves imparting a set of emotional and motivational approaches to a situation as well as a specific cognitive or other skill. The appropriate management of emotion and motivation could be taught both in the process of teaching classic skill mastery (i.e., in language or mathematics) and in teaching conflict resolution skills. The development of reliable, quantifiable measures of emotion and motivational management skills is feasible but complex. While I believe that it is important to train children in such skills while teaching other competencies, I am not convinced that much would be gained by developing and employing systematic measures of emotion and motivational skills.

Computer Literacy

The economists and the psychologist comment on the importance of computer skills for a successful life at this juncture in time in modern, democratic societies. It is clear that computers will play an increasingly important role in modern life although it is equally clear that the nature of this role and the nature of computers themselves will continue to evolve at a very rapid rate. In this context, I agree with the economic writers that what matters for a successful life is not a specific set of computer skills but a basic familiarity with computers and an associated confidence that one can learn new specific skills as needed. I also agree with those authors that such a basic level of computer literacy is easily acquired. Although a relatively simple competency, computer literacy is important because it functions as a "gateway" skill that can include or exclude people from valued social positions in society. Therefore, in the interests of moderating inequality, OECD countries should ensure that *all* citizens have the opportunity to acquire basic computer literacy through the schools. Since only a baseline level of computer familiarity is important, however, there is little value in developing and administering systematic measures of the levels of computer skills that children acquire. Instead, it might be reasonable to compare countries on the percentages of their populations that have a basic familiarity with computers.

Conclusion

In sum, there is broad agreement about the importance of two general areas of competence beyond those routinely measured at present. The first is the ability to join and form multiple, complex, and socially heterogeneous groups and to operate effectively and democratically within them. The abilities to take the role of diverse others, to negotiate conflicting interests to achieve mutually acceptable outcomes, and enhanced cognitive complexity and ideational flexibility are teachable and measurable skills that would contribute to an improved ability to join and act democratically in heterogeneous groups. Questions remain, however, about the best way to foster skills for appropriately balancing commitments to groups and social norms with the capacity for autonomous action.

The second area of broad agreement is in regard to the importance of a positive self-concept that facilitates confident action and the ability to manage emotion and motivation to overcome challenges and avoid destructive conflict. In my view, these important personal attributes are best acquired as concomitant to the mastery of other skill areas. As such, they are not best defined as separate new competencies that should be taught and measured in schools.

In the interests of moderating inequality, the opportunity to acquire a basic familiarity with computers should be made available to all in a society. There is little value, however, in defining and measuring levels of computer skills as a key competence.

References

Kohn, M. L., Naoi, A., Schoenbach, C., Schooler, C., & Slomczynski, K. M. (1990). Position in the class structure and psychological functioning in the United States, Japan, and Poland. *American Journal of Sociology, 95,* 964-1008.

Kohn, M. L., & Schooler, C. (1983). *Work and personality: An inquiry into the impact of social stratification.* Norwood, NJ: Ablex.

Lawler, E. J., & Ford, R. (1995). Bargaining and influence in conflict situations. In K. Cook, G. Fine & J. House (Eds.), *Sociological perspectives on social psychology* (pp. 236–256). Boston: Allyn and Bacon.

Stryker, S. (1980). *Symbolic interactionism.* Menlo Park, CA: Benjamin/Cummings.

Chapter 10

Key Competencies From the Viewpoint of Practice and Policy

In the first part of this volume, academics from different disciplines were asked to identify and justify theoretically a limited set of key competencies. In keeping with DeSeCo's commitment to pursuing a dialogue between academic research and the world of practice and policy, a different perspective is adopted in this chapter, one in which representatives of different sectors of society examine the concept of key competence as it relates to their field. They were invited to read the academics' chapters and to contribute short commentaries, exploring the ideas presented about competencies and discussing any concrete actions being taken in their field of activity regarding acquiring and measuring competencies. A few questions were suggested to the authors to guide their reflections: Is the issue of defining and selecting key competencies addressed in your field? How? What conclusions or recommendations have been reached? How do the theoretical approaches reflect the views held by your organization or field of activity? Are any of the points made in these reports particularly relevant to your field? What questions or concerns need to be addressed in your view? What place is given, in your field, to reflection on the concept of competence or on key competencies? Representatives were not asked to answer these questions one by one but rather to take them into consideration while formulating their commentaries.

This chapter includes comments from the perspective of UNESCO (Delors and Draxler) and from education (Harris), as well as the viewpoint of business and employers (Callieri, Farrugia) and labor (Ritchie). It concludes with a set of scenarios related to social changes in the future that are relevant for setting the goals of education (Trier). The discussions raise important points related to the practical aspects of defining and selecting key competencies for professional life as well as for other aspects of life, deciding how to teach or promote them, and measuring them using appropriate methods. They also provide a sense of the practical implications that may be involved should the proposed key competencies proposed be selected and assessed.

Though strengthening the theoretical foundations of the concept of key competence is a prime objective of DeSeCo, the theory cannot be developed in a vacuum, neglecting considerations of the practical world. Though these commentaries do not presume to reflect all the possible applications of competencies in the field, they do spark further reflection on the practical aspects of competencies and give some clue as to the complexity of the issues involved. Since the commentaries are briefer than the academics' reports, they are compiled into one chapter.

From Unity of Purpose to Diversity of Expression and Needs: A Perspective from UNESCO

Jacques Delors
Alexandra Draxler

This attempt to bring together elements from an explicit vision of society and humanity on the one hand and from empirical observation on the other is a welcome initiative. It is, we believe, very timely to extend the ambitions of education and educational policy-making to the competencies needed throughout life. Indeed, it was this ambition that guided the drafting of the report of the International Commission on Education for the Twenty-first Century, *Learning: The Treasure Within,* which was presented to the Director-General of UNESCO a few years ago (UNESCO, 1996). It is also in the light of the findings of this Commission that the following remarks are made.

The DeSeCo Project's undertaking is vast, and success will not be achieved in a short period of time. Irrefutable indicators of the outcomes of social intervention, including education, are difficult, if not impossible, to come by. Yet, such a project goes far towards acknowledging the complexity of the acquisition of competencies, the various actors and factors that come into play, and the need to expand our examination of these issues. If the chapters in this volume only partially meet the ambitious goal that has been set for them, this is not a negative reflection on the quality of the undertaking but a sign of the size of the task. We think many more questions have been raised than answered at this stage, but believe this to be a good thing.

All collective human endeavor is based on the assumption that there are things that unite us, that is to say, universals or constants. These can be situational and temporal, but they can also be relatively long-standing, even timeless. While clearly, there can be a persuasive case made that the notion of universality is too idealistic, ideological, or simply unproven to be workable, such an assumption would render most kinds of cooperation meaningless. The United Nations system and democratic governments, to give only two examples, function on the assumption that there are certain ideas, values, and notions that we can agree upon and use to found collective enterprises.[1]

When it comes to competencies, the same kinds of assumptions apply. The definition of a successful life mentioned in the description of the DeSeCo Project will vary according to individual beliefs and ideologies. Even the notion of a successful life in a modern democratic society, although narrower, is subject to wide interpretations. Yet, we firmly believe the descriptive task is possible. The difficult part is to operationalize this description in ways that are empirically sound, subject to analysis

---

[1] "Education shall be directed to the full development of the human personality and to the strengthening of respect for human rights and fundamental freedoms. It shall promote understanding, tolerance and friendship among all nations, racial or religious groups, and shall further the activities of the United Nations for the maintenance of peace," (Article 26.2 of the Universal Declaration of Human Rights).

and testing, and reproducible in other settings. This difficulty is not the main issue at this stage for two reasons. First, the project is an attempt to make a conceptual advance that goes far beyond output-oriented information about education. We are well aware that the tools available to make that advance are imperfect to say the least. But, one should be able to carry out this exercise in sequence, looking at the big picture first. Second, looking at competencies in this far-reaching way will shed light on the difficulties that have arisen from focusing on what is measurable, that is, devising tests and certification in the light of the available tools and the management needs.

Unity of Purpose and Values

During its three years of work, the International Commission on Education for the Twenty-first Century discovered a much greater agreement about the nature of competencies than one would assume. The ability to make moral judgments and apply them, to describe the world and our own real and desirable place in it, the ability to marshal our own skills to construct a future that involves living in society (with its freedoms and constraints), and so on, are universally recognized as competencies for a successful life.

There are, of course, many individuals who do not value, possess, or use these competencies. There are governments and other institutions that tread with gay abandon on the principles that underlie them. That does not negate their existence: one obvious example is the debate that took place a few years ago about human rights, when they were criticized as being a Western invention and thus not appropriate to all regions of the world. This debate has largely died out, and although the practice of human rights is far from universal, those who try to reject it on ideological grounds no longer get a serious hearing.

One caveat is in order in this portrait of agreement emerging from the work of the International Commission on Education for the Twenty-first Century. During its sessions, a significant difference emerged in the ways in which members of the Commission described and analyzed challenges and issues. Those from Western industrialized countries leaned towards the isolation and description of discrete phenomena, in units, as it were. The Asian members often reminded us that their vision of the world was, if not more complex, at least more nuanced. They tended to be uncomfortable with dichotomies, or a Manichean way of describing phenomena. They preferred description and analysis based on equilibrium, on finding the correct balance between what can seem to be opposing phenomena. Such a view, which integrates the relational notion of phenomena, could be a helpful addition to our reflection on constant features: competencies are very broad sets of aptitudes, but the means one needs to exercise them and give evidence of them can be very different according to circumstances. In this specific context, we think one could describe this seeming difficulty as unity of aspiration and diversity of application.

Then there is a contradiction, which we see as only apparent, between the utilitarian, that is to say economically useful view of competencies on the one hand, and on the other, the view of competencies as being liberating forces enabling individuals to take charge of their own lives. That is where, it seems to us, it is more a question of time frames than of real conflict. Mere training for tasks can produce short-term results in terms of productivity, but the evidence shows that, in the long-run, economies are better served by a broadly educated population.

The Role of Tradition

Tradition and history underlie all educational systems and every method for describing them. It is not because we do not scientifically discuss attitudes towards success, happiness, and the competencies for achieving them that they do not exist in society and are not aimed at and rewarded by education systems. In fact, we all know that schools do on the whole admirably reproduce the status quo, or even reinforce the existing social hierarchies, without clear instructions and even in spite of many attempts to change things. Our attempt to classify and describe "competencies" for a good life has the felicitous outcome of bringing this debate again into the open, and will perhaps enable us to do a better job of reinforcing equity and social cohesion against social reproduction and inequality.

Most of the authors in this volume recognize that, whether we like it or not, economic considerations currently dominate the debate about competencies for a successful life. This is also true in contemporary education systems on the whole. Perhaps one of the principal merits of this project will be to try to discover whether this state of affairs is truly the one that the majority aspires to, as Perrenoud points out (Chapter 6). For the moment we live in a paradox: stated goals for education involve a broad number of humanistic and ethical characteristics that are not reflected, or at least not adequately, either in what is taught, how teaching takes place, or how educational establishments are organized. We want young people to learn to live together, to be cooperative and caring individuals, yet what element about teaching math or science or even literature incorporates and rewards learning along these lines?

Diversity of Expression and Needs

Seriously taking into account individual and cultural variability is a direct, even mortal, challenge to comparability as we know it, and thus to some extent a scientist's nightmare. But, even though we constantly acknowledge, in words, the uniqueness of each individual, each learner, each child, this acknowledgment goes little further when we come to measurement. Finding an equilibrium between the normative, the universal, and the diversity of paths and expressions of normative principles is a challenge we must meet.

A new balance must be found between the empirical and the descriptive, which enables us to take into account the different expressions of human behavior and actions, to introduce the notions of context, equilibrium, differentiation in space and time. A truly creative approach to diversity would surely begin with the individual, with a look at her or his qualities, aspirations, and needs and continue with an attempt to ensure that she or he can possess or craft the tools for a successful life. This is a way of turning the notion of deficits on its head, and thus truly making a virtue and an asset of diversity.

Getting the Big Picture Right

At the risk of sounding philistine, it is perhaps not as problematic as one might think for the project to be putting forward some unproven assumptions: the reality is that most decisions about the organization of education are based not on research but on tradition, democratic agreement, politics, instinct, common sense, and a whole range of other unscientific but often valid criteria. Recognizing and working with that reality is essential. Finally, and very pragmatically, focusing on our differences is easy: they are based on culture, discipline, and ideology, and they can be combined infinitely. Focusing on what is common and then trying to describe these elements in a language that can be widely understood if diversely interpreted, can serve a variety of extremely valuable functions. It can help clarify the debate at a time when the relationship of economic development to human development is the subject of heated argument; it can shed precious light on the whys and hows of formal and continuing education – what we expect from it and how we try to achieve the desired results; and it can contribute to clarifying how we can strive to help each human being realize her or his full potential, individually and as a contributing member of society.

Can We Define Competencies for Life?

Several general themes that we find particularly interesting emerge from the essays. They are promising in terms of policy options, and challenging in the face of current educational practice. The first is that, however one defines a "successful" life, all individuals need solid, basic abilities in reading and mathematics in order to understand, describe, and participate in the mainstream contemporary world. (There were some caveats about whether or not all people need to be prepared to participate in the mainstream. We do not share these views, for both ethical and practical reasons.) Secondly, beyond these basics, to which computer literacy is rapidly being added as essential, most competencies are described in non-cognitive terms and bring together various combinations of human skills that are based on both cognitive and intuitive abilities. Interestingly enough, Levy and Murnane point out that the competencies they define as necessary for economic success are also important to living a responsible and fulfilling life in a democratic society (Chapter 7). Third, all the authors make it clear that we know much less than we wish we did about how competencies are acquired, and even less about how they can be taught. Fourth, they hinted at the difficulty inherent in describing competencies over the wide spectrum of human cultures, societies, and thought or belief systems. Lastly, it is clear that if one is to de-

fine and then try to ensure acquisition of competencies, many more actors are involved than schools and universities.

The concept of learning throughout life has emerged as a major organizing feature
for discussions about educational change. It is clear that no initial education, however
well conceived, can prepare people for a lifetime. With rapid change as the most salient feature of today's society, learning new skills and incorporating them into new
competencies is essential. Looking at what tools people need for life and then thinking about how we can build on what is already available in terms of learning opportunities is an excellent way to respond to these changes.

What Are the Challenges for Education?

Throughout history, thinkers on education have always included what we might call
"life skills" or "tacit knowledge" in the aims of a complete education. Work-related
skills have always been only part of the picture of a complete education, and generally a relatively minor part. Wilhelm von Humboldt, founder of Berlin University,
felt that, "The commonest jobbing worker and the finest graduate must at the outset
be given the same mental training, unless human dignity is to be disregarded in the
former and the latter allowed to fall victim to unworthy sentimentality and chimera,"
(cited in Hohendorf, 1993, p. 673). And before him, Condorcet defined the aims of
the school thus:

> To offer all individuals of the human race the means to provide for their needs and
> well-being; to know and exercise their rights and understand and fulfil their duties;
> to have the opportunity to perfect their skills, make themselves capable of per-
> forming the social functions to which they have a right to be called and develop
> the full range of talents given them by nature; and in so doing to establish between
> citizens an authentic equality to make real the political equality recognized by the
> law (cited in Jolibert, 1995, p. 200).

Thus, the linking of the cognitive with other human skills on the one hand, and
conceiving education as something to be carried out throughout life on the other,
have both a practical contemporary legitimacy and an historical one. No great teacher
has ever been content with imparting knowledge alone; it is the capacity to use
knowledge creatively and wisely in the interests of the individuals and society which
has been the ambition of educators throughout until today.

The difficulty, of course, lies in devising a system of universal education that can
address these needs, from the jobbing worker to the highest graduate. However, one
can build on some general principles. The ones that we suggest here as germane to
the subject at hand are neither simple to apply nor to spell out in practice. They are
challenges we must meet nonetheless.

We must reaffirm the importance of the foundations, and put the energy and resources into compulsory schooling that will ensure the acquisition of the capacity to
read, write, communicate, and compute for all. There is agreement on the importance
of basic education, but we are still far from realizing this goal, and perhaps too com-
placent in accepting a high percentage of failure.

We must recognize that most of the social competencies discussed by the authors that are not cognitive, are interpersonal competencies or are at least exercised in an interpersonal setting. Thus, compulsory schooling must focus much more on the development of group skills, and conceive testing and certification accordingly.

It is necessary to reflect on the challenges posed by the awareness that various competencies are needed at various times of life. Surely this must lead us to vary the paths through formal education and to build more bridges between formal and non-formal learning experiences throughout life.

We must think very hard about how to reach those people, young and old, who have been left out or who have opted out of formal education, to offer them meaningful opportunities to learn, to acquire skills, and to possess the five categories of competencies suggested by Canto-Sperber and Dupuy (Chapter 4).

Unanswered Questions

It is normal – indeed essential – that at this stage most of the questions posed by the DeSeCo Project remain unanswered. We shall attempt to point to some of them which we feel have particular relevance for education.

We shall begin by expressing disagreement with elements of both Goody's and Perrenoud's chapters. Perrenoud sets forth an important philosophical question, concerning the existence or not of "normality" in human competencies (Chapter 6). Goody is even more radical, claiming that "training in competencies in literacy has been promoted for political and ideological reasons which have little to do with the existing social situation" (Chapter 8). There is no difficulty in understanding the philosophical legitimacy of Perrenoud's question or the frustration that lies behind Goody's view that literacy without the other tools for creating a better life is sadly inadequate. Yet, all societies, and the entire system of international cooperation, are built on the postulate that there are some agreed-upon norms (both rights and responsibilities) on which societies and relations between societies must be based. These are enshrined in international conventions, agreements, and legal systems. More specifically, basic education has been recognized as a human right, and it is a near-universal aspiration, in spite of the frustrations experienced by many with the reality. It would be unfortunate to throw out the baby with the bathwater by incriminating all formal education either because it does not bring with it solutions to other problems or because it is overly standardized. We firmly believe that some key competencies do exist, based on standards of human behavior, which enable both the individual freedoms our societies cherish and the social behavior that Perrenoud quite rightly calls "citizen" competencies.

All the authors show an awareness of what we feel is a central question: if one identifies some core competencies (universal literacy has been inscribed as such a competency through a number of international declarations and agreements), then what can be done to ensure their acquisition if not by all then most? The issue of how to reach the two-thirds of the global population living on less than three dollars a day is an urgent one, and not just for humanitarian reasons: core competencies for all should enable better capacities to create wealth, to limit the tensions among different regions of the world and different groups, in other words to build social cohesion.

Another issue is the role of learning after the completion of initial education. If skills and competencies are needed at different times in life, and if various skills are combined in different ways to meet each new phase of life, then clearly much more needs to be understood about non-formal learning, learning styles at different ages, and the best ways to bring out in people the ability to change and adapt to new circumstances. Furthermore, it may be necessary to consider the possibility of returning to formal learning at intervals throughout life.

Then, there are cultural issues to be explored, as pointed out in several of the chapters. During the work of the International Commission on Education for the Twenty-first Century, several members pointed out with emphasis exactly what Perrenoud explains, that the quest for a high degree of personal autonomy is not the only possible source of identity. The same members took pains to emphasize that it is not universal to view the world in terms of dichotomies or oppositions but rather in a seamlessly connected way, in which human existence is made up of a continuum of features. And yet, societies that have this vision, which is not a purely individualistic or Manichean one, very successfully devise and carry out collective projects. It would be useful to spend some time on understanding what competencies are required in that context.

To return to the non-cognitive nature of many of the competencies described, we think this is the most striking, although perhaps not the most surprising, feature to emerge from the contributions. These non-cognitive competencies are enhanced by cognitive skills but are not directly related to them in many instances. This means that we need to learn more about how contemporary education influences the acquisition of life skills, how their acquisition is related to various types and levels of education, and, of course, what might be done to make personal and interpersonal skills more explicitly central to learning outcomes of compulsory and post-compulsory education.

Goody raises the question of learning to cope with unemployment. This is an important question, but could perhaps better be subsumed under both the ability to manage stress and conflict and to make plans and carry them out. While the ability to work to overcome adversity of all kinds is certainly one that is essential, and even the ability to endure things that are tragic or difficult but inevitable, there is an implied resignation in the way it is stated that is perhaps not helpful. The ability to live through difficult and dramatic situations surely includes the ability to analyze them, to take charge, and to use the energy emerging from dissatisfaction to try to change things. The value of education has been very closely identified with employment and levels of income; using this as a principal yardstick is to use a narrow vision of learning and education that will not even serve these narrow goals best in the long-run, we believe. It can produce the perverse effect of discouraging some segments of the population from seeking more education and, therefore, adding to their disadvantage, as Levy and Murnane pointed out (Chapter 7). But again, one returns to the notion of equality: when education is very unevenly distributed among populations, it is good neither for the economy as a whole nor for social cohesion. More needs to be known about what skills or abilities are needed for groups to learn together and progress together. Thus, what competencies are useful for group learning and what competencies emerge or are improved by it?

Although socio-economic status is one of the most important factors in successful progress through education, and indeed in the acquisition of mainstream competencies, we do not know how to compensate for "low" socio-economic status to create truly equal opportunities. This is another unanswered question, which will probably never be satisfactorily answered, but which we must continue to address nonetheless.

And lastly, we need to try to monitor how the dramatic changes in information technology will shift emphasis towards certain types of competencies as being important and valued. There is a lot of discussion at the moment about the importance of tacit knowledge in situations of information overload. Will knowledge-based skills diminish in importance even further as more and more knowledge-based tasks are turned over to computers, or will the type of knowledge simply change? What will the consequences be for learning? What will the consequences be for interpersonal relationships, for work, and for the skills and competencies needed for them?

Each technological revolution engenders heated arguments about the societal changes it will bring about; the current one is no exception. What we know already is that the hallmark of the coming years is rapid change, and that education must incorporate change and prepare people for it in ways it has never aimed to do in the past. The collection of data will be an important element in the research that needs to be carried out to operationalize some of the notions that will be considered. Beyond the empirical analysis, however, must lie a vision of how we can continue to strive for a better and more just society, a vision that is to a large extent both descriptive and interdisciplinary.

References

UNESCO. (1996). *Learning: The treasure within.* Report to UNESCO of the International Commission on Education for the Twenty-first Century. Paris: UNESCO.

Hohendorf, G. (1994). Wilhelm Von Humboldt. In Z. Morsey (Ed.), *Thinkers on education, 2* (pp. 665–676). Paris: UNESCO.

Jolibert, B. (1994). Condorcet. In Z. Morsey (Ed.), *Thinkers on education, 1* (pp. 197–209). Paris: UNESCO.

Are All Key Competencies Measurable? An Education Perspective

Bob Harris

I have to confess that I began the task of reviewing the chapters in a very skeptical frame of mind. How on earth could the OECD think of developing internationally comparable indicators of competencies for preparation for life? Agreement on so-called key competencies is difficult enough in any one national society; how could agreement be reached across the OECD membership? Even if a definitional consensus were possible, it would be so general that it would be impossible to operationalize it. How could indicators be developed with credibility, especially credibility beyond circles of specialists?

Reassurance comes from the review, for some authors clearly share my skepticism, while others articulate the dilemmas that must inevitably confront such a project. Overall, there is a strong sense of scaling down the ambition – dare one say the fantasy – of the project as initially presented. For the question of competencies for preparation for life requires no less than pursuit of the ongoing debate over the purposes of education. Today that debate is more passionate and vital than ever. It should not be reduced to a lowest common denominator in a misguided quest for OECD-wide consensus.

Moreover, out of the chapters, one can glimpse the beginning of some ideas for the OCED to develop this project in ways that will respond to the very real need for new approaches to education in the 21st century. I will return to these ideas at the end of this brief commentary.

Viewpoints of Educators

To suggest that there is a homogenous perspective among educators would be both pretentious and inaccurate. In fact, there is tremendous debate within the profession over the very issues addressed in this set of chapters. Much of that debate occurs within education unions and is pursued when national representatives meet each other at the international level. From these exchanges, however, it is possible to make a number of general observations:

- Educators generally recognize that the development of competencies for life in society cannot be separated from questions of values.

- Education is an investment in economic terms both for individuals and societies, but must not be limited to an economic function – competencies developed through education must also prepare people for other roles, including that of citizens in democratic societies, aware of their own rights and respectful of the rights of others.

- Education should help people to develop competencies that enable them to become actors able to influence the course of their own lives and to exercise responsibility.

- Equity remains a major concern – education should provide access to the development of a full range of competencies irrespective of gender, socio-economic status or ethnic origin.

- Education should encompass the development of competencies that have to do with community as well as individual advantage.

- Lifelong learning is fast becoming a necessity and a reality, but nobody knows how the concomitant changes in institutions, policies, mentalities, and resources will work out in practice.

- As the debates over competencies (and purposes of education) continue, teachers have to continue teaching, evaluating, interacting with parents, and responding to so-called reforms that often are really cost-cutting exercises in disguise; there are real problems of overload and burnout.

This list of observations – far from exhaustive – establishes the relevance of many points made in the chapters to the people represented by Education International[2], the several million in OECD countries who have taken up the vocation of teaching. Following are some reflections on where this project seems to be taking us.

Why a DeSeCo Project?

It is not hard to imagine the combination of factors underlying the DeSeCo undertaking. National authorities place their emphasis on outcomes rather than inputs. The OECD has gained credibility in education policy making with its INES (Education Indicators Programme) and related projects, and with the publication of the *Education at a glance* volumes (see, for example, OECD, 2000). But everyone – education unions included – agrees that indicators limited to curriculum-based competencies do not capture the full range of outcomes expected of education. Employers state that competencies related to productive work entail more than literacy and numeracy – they also involve the ability to work with others, to solve problems, to communicate. Educators point out that these same competencies are required to function effectively as citizens in democratic societies. In other words, there is a nice consensus in favor of extending the INES work in an attempt to obtain hard data enabling education systems to compare their relative success in attaining the goals of education, defined broadly, rather than narrowly.

But it is precisely at this point that we run into a dilemma. It is a genuine dilemma, for it is not a reflection of one set of interests or another. Simply put, the endeavor to arrive at consensus on the definition of competencies is directed, inelucta-

---

[2] Education International is a world-wide trade union organization of educational personnel, representing all sectors of education from pre-school to university. It includes 304 national trade unions and associations in 155 countries and territories.

bly, towards the search for a common basis for evaluation. This is one of DeSeCo Project's explicit goals. So we are setting out to evaluate *all* outcomes of education, including the least tangible outcomes. But we determine, almost in the next breath, that we cannot evaluate *all* competencies, that we have to *select* the ones that are most important. Furthermore, attention will be directed, inevitably, to that which can be measured. We cannot escape the reality that as valuable as indicators may be, they do have their limits, and we can neither describe nor compare everything that happens in or beyond education simply by using them.

Secrets of Survival and Success

The DeSeCo Project starts with a number of laudable and eminently understandable notions. Competencies are the result of both formal and non-formal education (and the genetic predisposition of individuals). We need to look beyond school outcomes to education outcomes. While cognitive competencies may be related to content, more general competencies for life are not bound by curricula. Moreover, previous use of indicators has been largely restricted to those competencies that were more obviously measurable.

From these beginnings emerges the entirely logical suggestion that it is time to develop a "theoretical and conceptual framework" in order to understand and define the competencies required for life – encompassing all its dimensions: personal, social, economic, political, cultural. The next logical question is whether to develop this framework around a minimal or an optimal set of competencies.

We really are hankering after the optimal set, aren't we? The DeSeCo Project, like much of the OECD work on indicators, is driven forward by the search for the "secrets," not just of survival, but of success! Whether academic or policy-maker, teacher or student, employer or employee, we really want to unlock the mysteries that would explain the success of individuals, institutions, enterprises, and nations. It seems reasonable to state that "success" is largely, but not entirely, assessed in economic terms.

We know, intuitively, that these "secrets" are not entirely tangible. At the individual level, we know that motivation plays a major role (Weinert, Chapter 3; Haste, Chapter 5). At the level of groups – institutions, enterprises, nations – we place much emphasis on leadership, the capacity to motivate in a social context. Can we define, then measure, the essential components of motivation and leadership? That seems to be a long-term goal of the project.

Motivation, like problem-solving skills, learning habits, communication skills, ability to work with others, flexibility, and perseverance, enhances the capacity to exercise other more instrumental competencies. Weinert (Chapter 3) uses the term "metacompetencies" to describe such phenomena. That terminology may find favor in academic circles, but it is too jargonish for most of us – perhaps a term like "generic" would be better suited to our purposes to describe these competencies. And let us remain cautious even about the use of the term "competency," for these phenomena do involve, quite simply, human qualities, inclinations, desires, and will.

Furthermore, as both the philosophers (Canto-Sperber & Dupuy, Chapter 4) and the sociologist (Perrenoud, Chapter 6) rightly remind us, we cannot escape the normative question of equity. If we penetrate even tentatively the secrets of success, we are bound to confront the question of equity of access to the conditions for realizing that success.

Creativity and Courage

How many books have been written about the role of creativity and innovation in economic success? The renowned case-study approach of the Harvard Master's Degree in Business Administration leads students to understand the primary place of these intangibles in business success. Creativity is a word that crops up in descriptions of every kind of human activity. A business approach is creative, as is a technological advance. A creative play wins the match; an innovative political campaign overturns the pundits' predictions. A writer creatively captures the imagination; a teacher's creativity opens young minds to wondrous discoveries. A work of music or art uplifts or stimulates reflection. How much do social scientists understand about the many facets of creativity? Chances are a poet understands, and communicates that understanding, much better.

How much has been said and written about courage in the broad sweep of human existence? Courage is the stuff of legends, of tales passed on sometimes over millennia. Within groups of every kind, trade unions, enterprises, sports teams, political movements, religions, and nations, there are contemporary legends, stories told of exemplary courage and success. Courage may require altruism through a willingness to sacrifice or egoism that drives one on to success against the odds, or it may even require a mixture of both! Can courage be defined as a metacompetence?

Creativity and courage are both associated with inspiration. It may be inspiration from within: the insight, the creative flash that leads to a breakthrough, or the source of extraordinary willpower. It may be inspiration from without: a speech, a film, a song, a news item, an example. The ability to inspire is a quality of leadership. Can we measure inspiration? Can we compare it between nations?

Culture and Context

Much has been written about the influence of culture on the measurement of competencies. Cross-cultural comparability was an issue in the development of the International Adult Literacy Study (United States Department of Education, 1998). It seems reasonable to suggest that the more competencies are defined in a generic way, as distinct from an instrumental way, the more cultural factors may exert an influence. Take the ability to communicate. There are significant cultural differences in forms of communication between people from different languages, ethnic groups, or socioeconomic backgrounds. The question is how to compare the *ability* to communicate among groups using different *forms* of communication. The same can be said for the ability to solve problems or to work with others. In each of these cases the notion of comparability of competence across cultures or sub-cultures raises fascinating challenges. The case for the determinant role of culture is made by Goody (Chapter 8).

Similarly, generic competencies may function in different ways according to the context. The assumption that lessons about teamwork learned on the playing field are transferred to the workplace is questionable. There is also the context of the study of comparability. A study conducted in the context of political pressures to improve the cost-effectiveness of education systems is unlikely to take the same approach as an independent study of human behavior. As the economists (Levy & Murnane, Chapter 7) make clear, each discipline also creates a context for such studies.

Conclusions

This commentary has argued that many of the key factors in individual or societal success are intangible, neither measurable nor easily comparable. Moreover their evaluation is subject to cultural and contextual factors which require that they be handled with great caution. This is not to argue against cross-national studies. It simply suggests that a degree of modesty and caution is required, for it is both utopian and dangerous to believe that all human competencies and qualities can be defined, measured, and compared.

The antecedents of the DeSeCo Project reinforce this caution. Inevitably, research projects entail compromises, all the more so when they are based on cooperation among nations and resources are limited. But caveats in the reporting of research results are easily overlooked in political pronouncements and press reports. The value of this project lies in the acknowledgment that the evaluation of educational outcomes cannot be limited to instrumental competencies. Moreover, it states at the outset that the development of competencies is to be considered among the outcomes of education, but, especially in the case of generic competencies, such development cannot be accounted for only by the performance of formal education. To the extent that the project succeeds in promoting serious study of the links between education and generic competencies, it will make a worthwhile contribution to our general understanding.

Teaching is an activity requiring the exercise of professional judgments based on training and experience, and often on intuition. An OECD project that encourages researchers and policymakers to reflect more broadly on general competencies and their relationship to educational outcomes is likely to be applauded by the practitioners, provided it leads to a better understanding of professional responsibility in the classroom.

The orientation of the project is laudable, insofar as it includes goals such as understanding the development of individual autonomy (Perrenoud, Chapter 6). The development of a balanced set of competencies – both generic and instrumental – enables individuals to become actors in their own futures, rather than victims or mere onlookers. In the context of lifelong learning, a continuum of learning throughout life, generic competencies, starting with learning how to learn, take on greater importance for all – not just for members of elites, as in the past.

This commentator therefore recommends that the DeSeCo Project pursue its valuable interdisciplinary approach, but eschew the notion that the essence of competence can be captured and compared only by using statistical indicators. Qualitative and descriptive studies across the OECD membership may well reveal more, and come closer to reality, than artificially constructed, compromise-bound quantitative research.

At the end of the day, policy-making in education cannot avoid being like democracy – imperfect and even a bit messy. But informed democracy is infinitely preferable to some kind of brave new world based on measurement and comparison of every element of our capacities, our motivations and our emotions.

References

Organisation for Economic Co-operation and Development. (2000). *Education at a glance.* Paris: OECD.

U.S. Department of Education. National Center for Education Statistics. (1998). *Adult literacy in OECD countries: Technical report of the first international adult literacy survey* (NCES Publication No. 98-053). Washington, DC: Government Printing Office.

The Knowledge Economy: A Business Perspective

Carlo Callieri

Changes in Work and the Crucial Importance of Human Resources

There has been a silent revolution in industry in recent decades. Technological progress driven by the extensive use of digital technology has gradually brought a shift from a predominant demand for manual labor to a widespread need for people working in modern production organizations to be highly qualified. This marks a transition from the traditional concept of "manpower" to the more modern one of "mindpower," describing the features of development along modern lines.

The new approach to production consists of a different balance between the technological and the human dimensions, calling into question the hierarchy of values which had been virtually elevated to the status of dogma in the classic industrial culture.

Nowadays, intellectual work is not just the work of intellectuals; workers in all types of industry are involved in a growing number of activities which are related to the new technologies but, above all, to new tasks, new responsibilities, and new resources.

In today's labor market, the creative and interpretative capabilities of individuals will increasingly tend to gain the upper hand. Managers, executive staff, professionals, and other workers and employees are changing roles, acquiring different competencies, and adapting work methods, resulting in a blurring of the traditional distinctions between the main occupational categories.

Competencies, skills, and the commitment required by the service performed have all been enriched, particularly in terms of complexity, knowledge, and attitudes towards change. In other words, we are witnessing a genuine anthropological mutation through which it appears clear that "brains that know how to move the hands" will replace the "hands that execute." In this process, human resources are the most significant dimension.

Knowledge Workers

Within this framework, the level of employee qualification is regarded by companies as the first strategic factor that can be used to boost productivity and market competitiveness, and by administrations as a key to survival.

The competitive system which requires the ability to focus and to constantly improve will increase the level of knowledge necessary and sufficient to satisfy corporate requirements; the number of *knowledge workers* is growing and will continue to grow. Consequently, increasing their numbers in the workforce and improving their level of knowledge is an essential commitment in order to allow national systems to develop the capacity to compete in a global market.

Important international research coordinated by the Research Institute on Organizational Systems (IRSO, which conducts research into organizational systems and is headed by Professor Federico Butera) has shown that knowledge workers are becoming the main workforce category in large- and medium-sized companies in major Western industrialized economies. These research findings point to how our future will be shaped. In a world dominated by global competition, the strongest will come out on top and the strongest will be, above all, those with a "knowledge resource" and the ability to organize it competently.

This is an area which could be described as belonging to an elite because, as often happens in innovative processes, it is the elites who owe it to themselves to be the driving forces behind such changes. In actual fact, while this is still partly true, it must be recognized that this situation will not remain for long: in the long term, all workers will be knowledge workers. Hence, the growing attention in public affairs to human resource development. In this sense, the need to support and facilitate these changes is already obvious. One only has to think of those countries – like Clinton's United States and Blair's Britain – which have stolen a march on the others and addressed these issues as genuine trail-blazers.

The Learning Society

Economic value is created through the manufacture, design, transmission, and sale of intellectual products based on a high degree of commitment to knowledge, even when they take on a physical dimension.

In a scenario like today's, which is characterized by economic globalization and worldwide competition, reinforcing the ability to compete is largely founded on the quality of knowledge workers.

While our socio-economic environment has made scientific knowledge and qualified human resources the strategic factor in growth and competitiveness, industry for its part has committed to an ongoing, broad-based effort to improve quality through far-reaching changes, including organizational ones, which are founded to an appropriate extent on upgrading individuals and their capabilities. Thus, it seems clear that the education/training system has to be involved in a wider and more comprehensive way. In this connection, the European Union's White Paper, "Teaching and learning: Towards the learning society" (1996), explicitly mentions the need to regard training as an investment. National industrial systems seem to have grasped this need to a large extent, as is shown by the spread in Western companies of programs and investments in lifelong education, although in this sense differences among the various national systems are still considerable, and delays, inadequacies, and unfocused efforts persist. Hence also the particular importance of the national survey conducted last year by Confindustria and the trade unions on corporate requirements, centered on the development of an archive of professional profiles and their respective competencies for 17 sectors of industry and services.

The Strategic Role of Training in the "Knowledge Economy"

For the individual worker (called to deal with scenarios in which work and knowledge are becoming increasingly integrated), the level of training is a fundamental factor in his or her future prospects, not only as regards citizenship but also as regards work and income. Seen in this way, training represents a factor in equality and social advancement. It provides access to opportunities enabling people to make better use of their talents and to have a greater freedom of choice on the labor market and in society.

The stock of knowledge and experience which individuals have managed to accumulate, systematize, and renew will increasingly explain many fundamental differences between them; in other words, people will be assessed and given recognition on the basis of the personal knowledge capital they have accumulated in the course of their education, training, and work experience.

While it is true that knowledge workers are becoming the key class in the working world, the advantages for workers in countries with strong training systems will be particularly great. On the other hand, workers in countries with weak training will continue to be penalized. It is worth recalling that training plays a fundamental role, not only in so-called "innovative occupations" (i.e., concerning knowledge workers) but also in traditional ones. Indeed, though demand for innovative staff is high, the demand for more traditional staff of the type found in small and medium-sized enterprises also frequently remains unsatisfied. And it is precisely in the latter field that the problems relating to human resource management center on reviewing and updating traditional profiles, in terms of complementary skills and flexibility, but above all in terms of the whole professional and organizational structure. Nor should we forget that traditional staff need to be kept up-to-date with respect to organizational and technological development in businesses, with a view to encouraging them to make major contributions to the permanent improvement of products and processes.

Concluding Ideas: Management of Complexity as a Future Challenge

The question of competencies is a central topic of the future. An epoch-making leap forward – the technological progress derived from using information and communication technologies – has taken place before our very eyes and its impact is not going unnoticed. In addition, another factor which we should not underestimate is the effects of globalization, first financial, and then economic, linked to the collapse of a conservative and conserving balance of power in the world, where three opposing blocs faced each other and held each other in a stalemate position. Indeed, the problem is a world in which uncertainty is growing as situations become increasingly complex. Uncertainty is what predominates in complex situations – those in which the knowledge worker manages to build up a store of potential responses to the individual problems that crop up. With this increasingly complex scenario, it is necessary to avoid the risk of answering complexity with further complexity. In other words, Western societies must equip themselves with tools that enable them to tackle complexity in a manageable way that conquers uncertainty. In this new perspective, the individual takes on an absolutely crucial function, creating the tools with which to manage uncertainty and turn it to his or her own advantage.

In this sense, we should do everything possible to give all individuals the competencies to address the continually changing needs of companies and to be able to achieve their ambitions and labor-market potential. Only in this way can uncertainty be perceived as a "salutary" element rather than a source of anxiety, as in the case of someone with no sound cultural and professional baggage, who is therefore defenseless in the face of complexity. By investing in knowledge and encouraging all workers, through a new and more efficient system of initial education, training, and lifelong education in order to have a sound stock of skills, we will succeed in turning uncertainty to our advantage.

In today's world, where extensive interdependence is constantly gathering momentum, it becomes a priority to establish rules through which management of uncertainty can generate progress for all: this is a supremely sensitive issue which Western democracies have to tackle in addressing the scenarios of the new millennium.

Editors' Note

This comment was translated into English from the original Italian.

Competency Management as an Investment: A Business Perspective

Jean-Patrick Farrugia

The topic of competencies is of growing importance for firms in all sectors, which should not come as much of a surprise, given the current state of the economy. As firms are faced with fierce competition within the global context and as population growth declines, workers' competencies are becoming an increasingly rare and valuable commodity, the key to a firm's edge over others. The recruitment of not only skilled workers but of highly competent ones will be a strategic initiative for all firms. In fact, to maintain their competitiveness, they will have to consistently invest in their principal asset: their employees' competencies.

MEDEF (*Mouvement des Entreprises de France*), representing employers in France, is mandated to explore new social relationships between employers and employees within firms, based on the development of skills and competencies. Several changes in industry are having a serious impact on the effectiveness and the competitiveness of firms and in turn, on their activities, their organization, their working environment, and the international mobility of their employees. Now more than ever it is necessary to produce varied goods and services and to meet clients' requirements in terms of proximity, quality, lead times, safety, and environmental compliance. As the economic environment is less and less predictable, firms will have to be flexible, open-minded, reactive, and prepared to face the unexpected.

It is evident that to meet these multiple challenges, it is the competencies of employees, individually and collectively, that will determine a firm's survival and success. Competency management is at the heart of these new conditions for productivity and MEDEF, as part of its mandate to explore new forms of social relationships, has focused its attention on competency management, within theoretical and practical frameworks.

MEDEF defines competency as a combination of knowledge, know-how, experience, and behavior used in a specific context in order to achieve specific objectives. The process by which employees acquire and make use of these competencies is a dynamic one, requiring them to assemble the various combinations of capabilities, skills, and competencies called upon to reach a given goal. The combinations are infinitely variable and dependent on the task at hand and the individual(s) involved. The worker's personal resources, including theoretical knowledge (primarily learned within formal educational institutions), know-how (learned in training situations, for example), and finally, the mastery of these tools through experience in the workplace, are some of the factors which will affect the worker's ability to combine competencies appropriately and effectively in order to achieve his or her goals.

The Role of the Employee

A model based on competencies must introduce the active and continuous development of employees' competencies as well as the links between the evolution of these competencies and the strategic aims of the firm. Employees must actively seek to develop their own competencies and take greater responsibility in the role they play within the firm. Valuable workers will not only be the ones who have vast knowledge and the most specialized skills, but also the ones with the ability to combine various competencies in order to deal effectively with the different types of projects or assignments with which they are presented. In essence, the strictly defined job description is a thing of the past, as it will only infringe upon the improvement of a firm's economic performance and the professional development of its employees.

Competency management will not only help firms improve their productivity, it will also have an effect on employees' employability and increase their value within the firm. The ability to perform multiple tasks and fulfil many functions will facilitate horizontal and/or upward mobility as specific work situations will no longer be quite so specialized and will require competencies which overlap between various sectors and/or levels within a firm. Thus, greater empowerment will lead to a reduction of hierarchical lines. Mobility will also be increased on an international scale, which is particularly relevant to the European market, as it is being re-structured and continually expanded.

As such, the hierarchy in most European firms will need to be readjusted. It will have to be more flexible and somewhat simplified with fewer rungs on the corporate ladder. An annual evaluation meeting between levels will be very important and the top level of management will have to involve itself in this process.

MEDEF Workshops

In its focus on competency management, MEDEF has been working for over three years with more than a thousand firms, conducting workshops on the following topics:

- competencies: a vested interest
- international practices related to professional competencies
- the conditions for implementing professional competencies
- identifying and describing professional competencies
- acquiring and developing professional competencies
- evaluation, validation, and certification of professional competencies
- the effects of developing professional competencies on vocational training
- the effects of using professional competencies
- professional competencies and social dialogue
- new communication technologies and new competencies

Through such workshops and its increased attention on competency management, MEDEF has set three targets: setting up new bases of social relationships in firms in France, encouraging and developing better performance in firms, and maintaining employees' employability. MEDEF has also met with social partners to discuss its research. Another important aspect of our work consists of dialogue with firms in other EU countries who are also using various forms of competency management. In fact, this has motivated MEDEF to create an international network to observe and diffuse the practices of competency management put in place by firms around the world. A major conference was also organized in Deauville, France, in 1998 to present and discuss MEDEF's findings. Finally, a network of firms who are explicitly committed to competency management has been set up in France, and a "charter" giving firms guidelines to develop and sustain competency management has been drawn up. Of course, we are continuing our search for pragmatic solutions which can be used by firms of different types and sizes.

A New Social Agreement

It is also very important for MEDEF to pursue the dialogue with social partners. It is necessary to have the same reference points, and to achieve this, we must talk about our common experiences. It is equally essential that theoretical concepts be elaborated, as they will become useful tools for firms to further develop competency management. If they have access to this research, they will make good use of it. This research is needed now, as firms are moving ahead, and it would be unfortunate for them not to benefit from the findings of theoretical research. Nonetheless, it is important for theory to take into account the actual practices of firms. It is important to communicate with them directly in order to make the theory relevant and useful.

If firms are being judged and appreciated by their capacity to analyze jobs and organize themselves for more efficient production as well as for the client's satisfaction, then it is even more important for them to take into consideration the importance of developing their employees' competencies. A new social agreement is being reached, based on a "win-win" situation. The employee is responsible for developing his or her own skills and competencies, and maintaining his or her position in the employment circle, this being the best protection against unemployment. The employer's responsibility is two-fold: first, the firm must make available to its employees the resources needed to allow them to stay in the employment circle, including the necessary recognition of their value in different ways (including remuneration); second, firms must know how to organize production in order to make the best possible use of employees' competencies.

self-employment, both delivered by a private trainer paid by the government and the firm as part of a "skills set" in an accredited adjustment program.

Despite their acknowledgment of the importance of context, none of the authors, however, challenge the justification for testing individuals. What if we turned this on its head and assessed the "competency" of OECD member states for:

- flexibility: require employers to be flexible in their accommodation of workers' learning with a legislated right to paid annual educational leave;

- tolerance towards minorities: provide substantive rights and services for newcomers, including language training for all family members;

- ability to apply appropriate strategies: institute public supports for neglected basic skills, literacy, numeracy, school upgrading;

- ability to manage both innovation and the continuity of supports: ensure a strong safety net of social supports;

- trustworthiness: require employers to justify workplace closures, and to observe "neutrality" during union organizing campaigns;

- teamwork building: provide labor with an equal vote in the introduction of new technologies and work methods;

- problem-solving ability: ensure that the overall pool of good jobs is growing.

Unemployment and underemployment remain the significant labor market problems of the day.

Concerns About Testing

There is no acknowledgment that the testing of individual workers for competencies can be problematic. In their chapter, Canto-Sperber and Dupuy seem to emphasize tests particularly, and this is a real concern. There needs to be more reflection on the principles of good adult education pertaining to tests and assessments. Most people fear tests, usually for good reason. There can be consequences if you do not measure up to the standards set by others and indeed, your pay, position, and job security may be jeopardized. (In the city of Toronto, a company wanted to test the basic literacy and numeracy skills of striking workers before they could return to work, though most had been employed for a decade or more). As Canto-Sperber and Dupuy suggest, there is a need for "meaningful context" when it comes to testing. I would argue, however, that people not only test better if given a "meaningful context," but in fact, learn better also. Those who observe good adult education principles try to avoid testing and, if necessary, then involve the adults in designing the assessment tool. Also, the language of the testing and the format of the testing is not addressed, except in passing (e.g., Canto-Sperber and Dupuy critique the "selection task" testing for the IALS and propose a "meaningful context" model instead). In a country like Canada, many of those who are most in need of support in upgrading basic skills have a first language other than French or English. And the literacy level of the test or survey instrument may be too high, skewing the results, even assuming it is read by the interviewer. If, as Canto-Sperber and Dupuy suggest, a favorable environment is key to learning, then perhaps it is this environment (material, institutional, symbolic) which should be tested.

I appreciate Haste's emphasis on a metacompetence that recognizes the skill of handling innovation and change as well as the continuity of that which is familiar and supportive (Chapter 5). Most workers cope daily with changes and uncertainty in their work assignments and schedules, job security and income, child and elder care arrangements, family relationships, transportation, housing, finances, etc., and for those who have immigrated, there are further changes involving adapting to a new community and culture, and in some cases, learning a new language. Ironically, some of these people might "test" as resistant to change, only because they already manage so much of it. Again, great care must be taken in framing assessment methods.

Indeed, are we looking for measurements that are intended to stir the development of the commitments necessary to improve the skills, knowledge, and learning opportunities of individuals, particularly those whose education has been neglected for a variety of reasons (economic policies, class, gender, race, etc.)? Or will these measurements merely give us a common measuring stick, a harmonized assessment "tool," for accrediting organizations providing training or education in "competencies" across borders, by direct delivery or "distant learning," the quality, affordability, and accessibility of which is left to the contracting local agencies?

Globalization

At times, there is an other-worldly quality to some of the chapters. Canto-Sperber and Dupuy's description of the "good life" is more controversial than they tend to assume for some living in OECD countries and for many outside the OECD. Furthermore, we are not just mulling over the character of the "good life," we are dealing with a set of measurements that may be used, for good or for ill, in the real world of education and labor markets. Some critical issues need to be addressed. For example, what is the significance of standardizing "competencies" in a liberalized trade regime? What strikes Goody as puzzling – the narrow focus on educational policy and its measurement restricted to OECD countries – may have its own internal logic, one which does not necessarily preclude a later play-out beyond OECD countries. The infamous ministerial meetings of the World Trade Organization (WTO) in Seattle in November 1999 would have been an occasion for OECD powers to move forward with greater trade liberalization in services, including education services – a battle which has now shifted terrain to the General Agreement on Trade in Services (GATS) negotiations. If the WTO is successful with its new GATS agenda, it will expand its already alarming authority to the point that commercial competition and privatization will make the education field unrecognizable within a few short years. Worldwide, education is a $1 trillion industry. The United States alone had education and training exports of $8.2 billion in 1996. Standardization of credits and competencies may be seen by some as key to expanding their trade in educational services. Indeed many industries argue that what is not standard and transferable poses a non-tariff barrier to trade.

There is a powerful drive towards standardization (and even "harmonization") in a deregulated, free-trade environment. Goody warns about the risk of the cultivation of a monoculture, which could be problematic (as I would argue is the case with the current corporate culture). But the lack of variation presents us with a different kind of danger. We risk losing particularities of geography, language, economics, culture, and politics, and the healthy cross-fertilization between them. Obviously, a single set of standardized indicators cannot be held responsible. It must be recognized however that they are an easy fit with the larger trend. Together with the increased commercialization of education, long-distance "virtual" education and accelerating international trade in educational services and products (e.g. CD-ROMs), a common set of context-free competencies could help deliver on the promise of the worldwide Holiday Inn chain: "no surprises."

Implications for Education, Training, and Business

It is not that I am skeptical of the ability to frame transnational measurements. The International Organization for Standardization does it all the time (e.g., ISO-9000 and 14000 series standardize practices and procedures for quality and for environment, health, and safety). There has been talk of a series for training but in the meantime some schools have already adopted the 9000 series and related Total Quality Management (TQM) programs in search of improved productivity and quality in an increasingly competitive environment between public and commercial education and training "providers." ISO sells itself as a uniform "results-based" approach which allows apples to be compared with apples so that the "consumer" can decide where they'll spend their savings or loans (or vouchers in some areas of the United States) and presumably get the best quality for the lowest price.

Who, you might argue, could be opposed to "quality" education? Well, when the Southern Alberta Institute of Technology in Calgary, Canada boasts about TQM quality improvements and gives as an example its regular surveys of companies "so that education is more closely matched with the skills they require," some of us worry. As one consequence, workers are paying for expensive college courses that have been adjusted to meet the needs of a local company, checking off the "competencies," and trying to buy themselves a job or a promotion. The courses are sometimes the same as the new-hire training programs the companies used to provide themselves. In still other cases, workers' pay raises may be contingent on completing these competencies.

While Perrenoud quickly dismisses the concept of competence as a new trend in the business world (Chapter 6), I would argue that this "fashion" has become the driving force in defining competencies in the workplace, and in schools. We need the support of thinkers, such as Perrenoud, who appreciate problems related to demands of greater flexibility on the job and rising job insecurity caused by the erosion of workers' protection negotiated in collective agreements. Our problem will soon become the problem of teachers and academics, as educational institutions are confronted by competition and judged on their "employability" outcomes. Education-business partnerships are already injecting some of these "competencies" into school curriculum. In fact, the Conservative government in the province of Ontario in Canada is already sanctioning such programs, going beyond co-op work placements to allow for industries' direct influence in a school's curriculum development. Curriculum that used to provide students with a basic understanding of micro-processing and micro-computing, for example, has been "dumbed down" to train them on specific equipment used in a specific company in a specific sub-sector. Who picks up the tab when that company goes bankrupt or moves? Will the new ideologies leave us with schools that are nothing more than pre-hiring training facilities, with the public paying for what used to be training provided by the company? This makes me feel that a certain word of caution must be expressed when Goody suggests that allowances be made for children to learn outside of the classroom and the school. Though he probably did not have in mind the bleak picture I am thinking of – and I would agree with him to a certain extent – modern capitalism is very powerful in rewriting the educational agenda to teach competencies that are job-specific, with less and less learning that can be considered generic and portable between jobs, and across life's many paths.

I was disappointed that Levy and Murnane (Chapter 7) did not provide a critique of mainstream neo-liberal economics and human capital theories that view training and education simply as "economic outputs" and not as democratic goals in their own right. At a minimum, there should have been a caution about economists who suggest that human capital theories dictate that it is the individual who should be investing in retraining. This is a transparently self-serving interpretation on the part of those defending the corporate dumping of training costs.

In short, the chapters defining and selecting key competencies raise important points about conceptions of society, but my principal concern is that insufficient consideration given to how this will affect workers in their everyday lives. If we are to measure, eventually, the acquisition and mastery of key competencies in the general population, it is essential to take into account how this might have an impact on the protections and rights of workers achieved in collective agreements, and furthermore, how this could result in education becoming nothing more than yet another lucrative business sector.

Defining Educational Goals: A Window on the Future

Uri Peter Trier

Education systems must adapt to the needs of future generations. Thus, defining educational goals – the discussion of key competencies being a part of this process – is unthinkable without a vision for the future. Recognizing that the specifics are unpredictable, I am proposing scenarios for the future from six perspectives, each of which I believe has important implications for education.

The Well-Being of State and Community

Two major issues will be key for the survival of societies in the 21st century. In addition to protecting the natural environment (which is already receiving much attention), societies need to be politically responsible in order to live in peace.

The issues at stake are crucial: providing a minimal threshold of welfare for all, promoting an equity-oriented distribution of wealth, safeguarding human rights, fighting violence everywhere and on all levels, assuring the implementation of judicial norms, and securing peace. The questions which future citizens will contemplate will be even more complex and opaque than those we are asking today, and the consequences, irreversible. Decision makers at all levels – from the community, to the state, to the world – will have to plan on developing interdependence between and within each level.

Organizations and institutions that were the traditional seats of political opinion making – such as churches, political parties, unions, and associations – are consistently losing their influence. At the same time, the influence of new forms of organizations developing within civil society – such as national and international nongovernmental organizations – is increasing, and the growing predominance of media-centered political discourse has heightened the risk of overdramatization of issues and subsequent polarization of opinion. In the future, the availability of information over many possible networks will increase radically, and it is uncertain how that information will be integrated into the political thinking of citizens.

The success of political action is always greatest within a decentralized system of partial autonomy. The basic dynamics of decision making should progress from the bottom up (rather than from top-to-bottom). Small-sized contexts can be overseen directly by citizens facilitating orientation and decision making. However, sometimes the top-to-bottom process is necessary for the sake of efficiency, and to set limits and constraints (though preferably with as much built-in flexibility as possible).

Perhaps the most important lesson we can learn from experiences of the 20th century is that political responsibility through democratic processes has priority above all other dimensions of social life. That is to say, it should be more than a goal for education; it should be a principle of social, and even economic, organization. Democracy exists only where it is lived.

Flexibility and Mobility: Independence of Production, Employment, and Workplace

The traditional integration of labor within a constant and stable institutional and work-oriented framework, with the accompanying predictable career paths, is in the process of breaking up (Sennett, 1998). This de-stabilization occurs with the convergence of two trends, and brings with it both new opportunities and new risks. The first is economic pressure for innovation, which demands constant restructuring of enterprises. Multinational networks, and the decentralization of production and services, make it easier for firms to adjust to changing markets. Flexibility in the specialization of production increases the degree of freedom that economic organizations have in their strategic decision making regarding the comparative advantages of certain locations for production and services.

The second, without which a development of this kind would be impossible, comes from the high-tech world. Production and services can become deprogrammed and, as such, directed with greater flexibility. Electronic communications networks facilitate the relocation of work from the traditional office to a setting chosen by the worker, which is independent of the place of business. Predictably, this development will lead to a completely new organization of work and new working conditions in this century. Employment opportunities will increasingly consist of contract work: clearly defined, specific, and time-limited projects completed by individuals or groups. The capitalization of such units of work (internally or externally) will replace the temporal physical presence of employees with which we are familiar today. The "classical" career and professionally determined career paths that constituted the goals of educational planning and life will disappear. Such changes bring insecurity and risks that are difficult for individuals to calculate. Although these risks may be moderated to some degree by social security systems in welfare states, strong market forces are imposing more and more deregulation.

Human Genetics and Genetic Engineering: The Extension of the Human Lifespan

Our generation in the developed world currently expects to live, on average, about 80 years. Yet the division of the lifespan into three segments – growth and education, work and reproduction, and finally, retirement – is no longer a viable model for the future because of the progress being made in medicine and genetics.

The consequences of completely exploiting the human genome for life expectancy purposes have not yet been fully comprehended, probably because the possibilities seem so far removed from reality at this stage. However, these consequences are far-reaching, spanning from disease prevention through gene manipulation, to therapies based on genetic technology, to control of the aging process itself. The point is, and this is not science fiction but scientific potentiality, that the newly born generation in OECD countries, with life expectancies of 100 years or more, can also expect a quantum leap in the improvement of the quality of their health.

This means that people we now call "old" will eventually be physically capable of fully participating in the social, economic, and cultural life of their society.

But this is only the beginning. According to recent forecasts by biologists, the 100-year life expectancy is conservative, and ages of 200 to 300 years are conceivable for upcoming generations (Mittelstrass, 1998). Furthermore, individuals will have access to their own genetic determinants, making it possible to deliberately change their own genetic constitution, as well as that of their progeny. The "*conditio humana*" will change in the sense that even its biological foundations will be alterable. What is emerging is a completely new area where ethical standards and political and juristic controls will be crucial.

Non-Salaried Work

As previously suggested, if lifespans become longer, and general good health is also maintained, then there are further consequences for the workforce to be considered. If more and more people are able to work longer in life, the nature of that work will probably have to change.

A paradigmatic change will be required in our attitudes towards the highly valued employed sector, and conversely, the devalued unemployed sector. Considering that retirees will be more numerous and healthier in the future, we will have to reconsider traditional labels such as "free time" and "retirement" in light of the human need for meaningful activity. I believe that in the future a new culture of work will come into being. Non-salaried work will thus have to be valued as equal to salaried work in the economic sector. In this scenario, non-salaried work will have little in common with what we call hobbies in today's leisure society. On the contrary, creative pursuits, recreational activities, social and environmental services, etc., will be fully recognized by society and organized through a barter or cooperative type of system.

Knowledge and the Learning Society

The three interrelated dimensions I have sketched out above, namely, the extension of the human life-span, increased flexibility and mobility in the workforce, and the higher valuation of non-salaried employment, have dramatic consequences for our understanding of education and learning:

- People will no longer have one career or profession, but rather several acquired skills or specializations that can be used for employment as well as non-salaried work. The primacy of a single career path throughout a person's life will be increasingly unusual. What people do during the non-salaried portions of life will require the same level of professionalism as during the employed segment.

- The increased flexibility and mobility of the labor market offers opportunities and risks that require a higher level of competence in managing one's own skills. This means that people will require (a) a broad palette of specialized, viable, and varied achievements, (b) the ability to conform to the labor market by adapting or adding qualifications, and (c) "safety-nets" allowing shifts or changes in our sense of identity and security. This is to be perceived as a positive challenge rather than a threat.

- The temporal division of life into phases of education and training, and employment and post-employment (or non-salaried), will become increasingly vague as applied to distinct portions of our lifespans. Perhaps even the distinction between schooling and adult education will no longer be clear. We could institute completely new models, such as shortening the first phase of education, and adding fully accredited second and third phases of education, or creating a formal training for new professional skills to be followed concurrently with part-time employment, either in the same field or in a new one.

In an effort to find an appropriate description for this radical change in our social and economic conditions, we have tried out the terms "post-industrial society," "information-society," "learning society" (Keating, 1998), and most recently, "knowledge society" (Bereiter & Scardamalia, 1998). The operating belief behind all of these terms is that added value occurs through the acquisition and application of knowledge.

One thing is certain: knowledge has always been invested in the production of goods and services. What is different now is that knowledge, increasingly taken for granted, is becoming a traded good independent of any process of production or service.

In the knowledge society, it is the educated individual who naturally remains the carrier of knowledge. But alone, the individual is hardly in a position to administer and develop the knowledge that is in demand. Research requires cooperation. When the creation of knowledge becomes the cardinal point for economic and social development in the knowledge society, then the concept that knowledge can only be produced through collective effort will become more concrete for many people.

In the knowledge society, cooperation will become the decisive production factor. Modern societies will come to a fork in the road in the 21st century: either society will be able to organize itself so that the masses participate in knowledge acquisition, development, and acquisition (i.e., it will become a learning society as the majority participate in the building of knowledge) or, it will split into a "knowledgeable" elite and marginalized masses, thereby endangering social cohesion. Thus, societies that develop and use collaborative and social learning will be able to secure their economic and social progress.

Computers and Learning

Knowledge is now inextricably linked to computers. The convergence of psychology, neurophysiology, and computer science is already in process (Frawl, 1997). Computers are becoming popular learning partners in many areas of cognitive learning, even in areas of "intelligent" learning. This interaction between humans and computers, which includes a high level of complexity in data entry, processing, and retrieval, has grown relatively slowly so far, but is now advancing at breathtaking speed. Coherent, cognitive human/computer interface systems are already being developed. For instance, in highly specialized fields, computers master the data procurement and operational problem solving, while humans take responsibility for the criteria-based decisions.

Concluding View

In conclusion, I have imagined *"homo seculi XXI"* with a very long lifespan. He or she will be healthy and active for a much longer period of life. During this long life, he or she will engage in a variety of activities which are at some times salaried and at others, not. With this change, work that is not connected to monetary compensation will increase in value. The traditional curriculum vitae will be replaced by a personal profile of multiple professions and competencies. Salaried employment often will not require a fixed place of work, nor will it be bound by fixed contracts.

Even more than today, this future generation will live in a globally connected world. This world will need to anchor itself to its local environment as a balance; it will bring together people of different languages and cultures; and it will be flooded by the media bringing messages and information. In this world, virtual experience will hardly be distinguishable from direct experience.

Society in the 21st century will become increasingly complex. The growth in technology and knowledge will continue to expand exponentially. So will the risks. On the one hand, we will be able to manipulate nature and human life increasingly; on the other, the direct and secondary effects of high technology will become less transparent and only conditionally controlled. The growth of individual and collective knowledge in the knowledge society will not only be necessary for further innovation but for the responsible control of the technological impulse we have created.

The potential for a high standard of living for all depends on continuing economic productivity. However, it is uncertain whether current social models that provide a safety net for the less fortunate, or for difficult times, can be sustained. For that reason, citizen participation in political discussions and decisions (from the city to the supra-state organization) will be a critical factor in further development.

The relative importance of learning in childhood and youth, compared to our adult years, spills far into what we understand as lifelong learning today, and in the approaching century. Professional training and education will increasingly be seen as a process that continues throughout life.

References

Bereiter, C., & Scardamalia, M. (1998). Beyond Bloom's taxonomy: Rethinking knowledge for the knowledge age. In A. Hargreaves (Ed.), *International handbook of educational change* (pp. 675ff). Dordrecht, the Netherlands: Kluwer Academic Publishers.

Frawl, W. (1997). *Vygotsky and cognitive science, language and the unification of the social and computational mind.* Cambridge, MA: Harvard University Press.

Keating, D. P. (1998). Human development in the learning society. In A. Hargreaves (Ed.), *International handbook of educational change* (pp. 693ff). Dordrecht, the Netherlands: Kluwer Academic Publishers.

Mittelstrass J. (1998). The impact of the New Biology on ethics. *European Review, 2,* 277–283.

Sennett, R. (1998). *The corrosion of character.* New York: W.W. Norton.

Concluding Remarks

Heinz Gilomen
Dominique Simone Rychen
Laura Hersh Salganik

We were conscious at the start of the DeSeCo Project that we were embarking on a challenging journey, and our initial expectations were more than confirmed. Obviously, the issues at stake in identifying key competencies are complex, multi-faceted, and far-reaching. Yet many valuable lessons can be learned from the heterogeneity of the approaches resulting from varied, and not necessarily compatible, premises and methodologies, as well as from the many convergences that transcend the differences among the reflections in this volume. However, consolidating a common understanding and an overarching frame of reference for defining, selecting, and assessing key competencies relevant for OECD member countries and possibly beyond, entails further efforts, actions, and debates. To conclude, let us contemplate DeSeCo's original objectives and ambitions in light of the results presented in this volume, and highlight several challenges and questions to cope with as work on key competencies continues.

The initial idea to view key competencies through the lenses of different scholarly disciplines proved to be an indispensable move for *gaining interdisciplinary insight* on the nature of key competencies. For the most part, the academics did not come to this task with preexisting, systematic foundations of knowledge from which they could draw in a straightforward manner, a theoretically grounded set of key competencies indispensable for an overall successful life. They needed to be *creative and innovative* in using their expertise in their respective fields in order to tackle these questions. Each of the scholars contributes crucial elements to the discussion about theoretical and conceptual foundations of key competencies. Yet the applicability and usefulness of the various proposed analytical tools and models still need to be further explored in light of concrete social practices, societal specificities, and important demands facing individuals and groups.

Through the working process, the various contributions, and discussions, it became clear that the level of *mental complexity* constitutes a crucial criterion for defining what key competencies are. Thinking abstractly and internalizing social norms and values are necessary abilities, but they are not sufficient. There is a convergence among many of the authors that coping with the demands and challenges of contemporary life requires an *active and reflective posture*. In fact, key competencies are often associated with self-initiating, self-correcting, self-evaluating, self-directed learning – abilities that imply stepping back from one's surroundings to make judgments and to act autonomously. At this point, it is important to emphasize that an active and reflective approach to life is not first and foremost a cognitive/intellectual question, but one that concerns complex action systems encompassing appropriate motivational, ethical, social, and behavioral components. However, whether the adequate level of mental complexity to cope with important everyday demands can be reached by everyone or to what extent its lack can be compensated for by other appropriate strategies, for instance, are questions for further exploration and consideration.

Although all of the OECD member countries are generally committed to expanding opportunities for individuals in various spheres of life, to improving overall living conditions in society, and to investing in the development of competencies for all as a means to these ends, inequalities still remain in all societies, and for the most part, individuals are prepared to function and participate in highly differentiated and segmented economic and social systems. Reducing the gap between the goals of equity and equal opportunity that are so prominently voiced at the discourse level and the social practices of a highly differentiated and segmented economic and social system remains a societal challenge. Consequently, the *distribution of key competencies* constitutes a core issue when educational reforms and lifelong learning strategies are discussed, formulated, and realized. Throughout the discussion, it became clear that the acquisition and maintenance of competencies imply lifelong learning and that the development of competencies is not only a matter of personal efforts, but to a large extent contingent upon the existence of *a favorable material, institutional, and symbolic environment*. Therefore, the debate about fostering competencies and, in particular, key competencies has to take into account a broad formal and informal learning context.

In discussions of competencies, the *sociological dimension* has often been neglected, and priority given to cognitive aspects and other psychological factors. Many authors in this volume emphasize the social embeddedness of individuals and of required competencies. It is important for the conceptualization, development, enactment, and assessment of competencies to understand the relationship between the individual and society as dialectic and dynamic: the actions of individuals are shaped by society and, in turn, affect society. Many of the proposed key competencies only make sense if the social component is taken into account. Thus, when conceptualizing competencies, as well as when considering their development, the structure of the environment in which the individuals or groups operate should be taken explicitly into account. The concept of *social field* proposed and discussed in this volume provides not only the means to consider the social environment as structured and to better understand the power relations and issues at stake in given fields, but also to construct key competencies as *transversal* in a meaningful way.

There is a consensus that normative ideas and questions of values are an integral part of defining and selecting key competencies. It is impossible to construct key competencies without making *ethical and political choices*. Once we come to a more or less scientifically grounded agreement of what components constitute the concept of competence, determining which competencies are relevant and key to a successful life and a well-functioning society is no longer an exclusively academic matter, but is dependent on what, in a given context and time, is considered to be a successful life and a good society. For instance, what does success involve? What makes a democratic society a just one? What social and economic development is seen as necessary and/or desirable? How does a society deal with challenges such as environmental threats or global inequality of opportunities? To answer such questions requires ethical choices that entail a delicate balancing of different freedoms, rights, and obligations. In terms of *accepting some common features*, contributors to this volume have pointed out several characteristics of a successful and responsible life and referred to the United Nations Declaration of Human Rights as a starting point for a description of a decent society.

The *conceptual link between key competencies and desired outcomes* (e.g., a successful life, a well-functioning society) is another central aspect of the topic. Compared to other social sciences, economics has thus far made more headway in developing theories and models of these linkages, both at the micro and macro level. The relationship between education and training in its various forms on the one hand, and economic performance on the other, is clearly and systematically described in human capital theory. However, the scope of DeSeCo has been to consider the topic not only from the perspective of productivity, economic growth, labor force participation, and earnings (economic well-being), but from the totality of life situations. Since, in our understanding, competencies are considered as key only if they are transversal, i.e., contribute to a successful life in all relevant social fields, broader measures of well-being will need to be considered. Promising areas that combine tools from economics and philosophy include normative economics, social choice theories, and theories of distributive justice.

A related issue for further consideration is how to recognize in the discussion and conceptualization of key competencies that there are multiple aspects of personal, social, and economic well-being. It seems worthwhile to learn from current *quality of life research*, which conceptualizes and measures quality of life along several continuous dimensions. This approach allows many of the dimensions relevant for an overall successful life, such as access to economic resources, formation of close relationships, and access to intellectual resources, to be recognized as contributing to quality of life. Further, it allows success/quality of life to be conceptualized as falling on a continuous scale ranging from low to average to high, rather than as dichotomous, such as embodied in the concept of a "survival kit." Using this approach, the notion of successful life could be defined as a multidimensional access and availability concept in terms of resources such as power and capital in its various forms.

To date, most discussions about key competencies have focused on their contribution to the success of individual lives. Analogous to the quality of life concept, the notion of the *quality of society* provides a complementary perspective. Peace and security, economic performance, social cohesion, equity, absence of discrimination, scientific excellence, environmental quality, etc., could constitute some of the many features that contribute to a society's quality. Various social fields (e.g., the economic, political, or cultural) could represent the dimensions based on which the societal quality of democracies could be assessed. With this shift of perspective, the issue of key competencies is taken from the purely individual level to the societal level. In this sense, successful life means not only occupying a position or making choices that are rewarding strictly on the personal level (e.g., a good income or material comforts) but also from the societal stance, i.e., contributing to the overall quality of society (e.g., ecology-minded behavior). Key competencies can be studied with respect to both the individual and societal perspective of a successful life. In some of the fields, the individual and societal perspectives are compatible, and in others, contradictory. As a result, conceiving key competencies relevant or necessary to achieve some of these desired outcomes inevitably raises questions related to trade-offs involved in balancing a commitment to the betterment of society and to individual success and happiness (or satisfaction). This approach also places cultural and individual characteristics at the forefront. The individual and societal goals and actions as well as the trade-offs between them are, of course, subject to cultural and individual factors and contingent upon power relations, and thus, will manifest in various ways according to personal, social, and/or political priorities. Herein the question of cultural, contextual, and biographical variability takes a clearer form for further consideration.

DeSeCo aims to provide an overarching framework for defining and selecting key competencies as well as to put forward guidelines for future development work for the assessment of key competencies in an international context. One of the major challenges remains the delineation of a *plausible set of key competencies* that is general enough to be used throughout the OECD and beyond while not losing the texture of the local and specific. So far, the discussion about key competencies has primarily been conducted in a relatively general way. Various analytical tools have been proposed to construct, at a rather high level of abstraction, key competencies partly independent of culture, context, and personal characteristics. It is clear, however, that a *concretization and contextualization* of key competencies is only possible through a combination of theoretical and empirical work. And it seems timely, within the ongoing project, to link the key competencies to important demands, issues at stake, and social practices specific to the various spheres of life, i.e., to study relevant and necessary competencies with regard to societal specificities (e.g., socio-economic context; political, institutional, and legal conditions; and cultural particularities) and individual characteristics (e.g., age or stage of life) and to identify empirically which competencies are key competencies, i.e., transversal across fields and implying a reflective and active posture. Thus, further quantitative, qualitative, and descriptive studies across the OECD need to be envisaged as the defining, selecting, and assessing of key competencies proceed.

Approaching key competencies from the perspective of academic disciplines has undeniable strengths, but also has its limitations. It has to be recognized that the result of this multidisciplinary approach cannot lead directly to a *coherent, overarching, conceptual framework*. In fact, it would be naïve to expect that the different proposals could be pieced together the way a puzzle is. Researchers can frame the question in theory- and concept-oriented terms, provide appropriate methodologies, and scientifically grounded criteria for defining and selecting key competencies. Yet, throughout the volume, all the authors acknowledge that the topic of defining and selecting key competencies is only to some extent contingent upon such scientific bases. First, the answers are also dependent on underlying normative premises about the individual and the society, and these assumptions are at times controversial and debatable, and second, defining and selecting a valuable and legitimate set of key competencies that warrant testing requires a continuous exchange of ideas between scholars and representatives from policy and practice. Therefore, to do justice to the complexity of the concept of key competence and to the far-reaching implications, it is imperative to understand the work as an ongoing effort, which implies both the *conceptualization of key competence* and the *development of definitional parameters*. A concretization of the concept of key competence therefore is only possible in the explicit presentation of the different interconnections. Thus, for instance, an indicator development and assessment strategy must not focus on competencies and their components only, but must also take into account the various factors behind the definition of key competencies: the concepts of successful life and the quality of society, socio-economic and cultural factors, the demands, etc. Yet in all these efforts it has to be recognized that many of the key factors are intangible, neither measurable nor easily comparable, at least with the approaches available today and in the foreseeable future. The framework we propose to further develop is to be designed in such a way as to incorporate the dynamic and dialectic interrelations at the individual and societal levels and to elucidate the many-layered and multidimensional reference points of key competencies.